Twelve Steps to Holiness

D1598824

Twelve Steps to Holiness

The Testaments of the Twelve Patriarchs

Translated and introduced

by

Jerome Bertram, Cong. Orat.

GRACEWING

First published in England in 2018
by
Gracewing
2 Southern Avenue
Leominster
Herefordshire HR6 0QF
United Kingdom
www.gracewing.co.uk

ISBN 978 085244 908 0

Typeset by Word and Page, Chester, UK

Cover design by Bernardita Peña Hurtado

CONTENTS

Preface

TWELVE STEPS TO HOLINESS

Early Christian Writers on the Virtues and Vices

Many writers on the spiritual life have used the analogy of climbing a ladder, as we progress towards that degree of perfection which Our Lord demands of us, 'Be ye perfect, as your heavenly Father is perfect' (Matthew 5:48). It must originate in the story of Jacob's Ladder, on which he saw the angels ascending and descending—and since humility is the key to all virtue, who is to say whether we should be trying to go up, or to go down?

St Benedict is the most familiar of those writers who speaks of the Ladder of Humility, in chapter 7 of his Rule. There are twelve steps, and that at once makes us look out for other things that go in sets of twelve. There are twelve Apostles, of course, and they respond to the twelve Tribes of Israel. There are twelve Minor Prophets. In the received text of St Paul's Letter to the Galatians (5:19–23), there are twelve Fruits of the Holy Spirit (although many early texts only have nine, and some Church Fathers confine themselves to that). Then if we look at the earliest Christian writings after the New Testament itself, we find the *Shepherd of Hermas*, which speaks of twelve virgins, who are virtues, opposed to twelve women who are vices (*Shepherd of Hermas*, Similitudo IV, xv). And a very important document, which has been strangely neglected, is the *Testaments of the Twelve Patriarchs*, which again looks at twelve virtues and their opposites. So it becomes a commonplace to list virtues and vices, to play one off against another. The poet Prudentius talks of the struggle between virtues and the attendant vices. St John Cassian also gives us twelve steps in the spiritual life (*Monastic Institutes* IV, 39), and we recognise that this is the primary source for St Benedict. Eventually

St Thomas Aquinas gives us the definitive analysis of the Fruits of the Spirit (*Summa Theologiae* I–II, 70, 3). He follows the twelvefold list, and reminds us that it is necessary there be twelve because they are mentioned in the Apocalypse (22:2). He imitates St Jerome in showing how each follows from the previous one, but in a different manner; and quotes St Augustine on the contraries of each fruit.

Christian art delights in portraying these opposing pairs, nowhere more dramatically than on the twelfth-century fonts at Stanton Fitzwarren, Wiltshire, and Southrop nearby in Gloucestershire, where the virtues, dressed as modest maidens, and all appropriately labelled, trample on the vices, dressed as men, which at Southrop are labelled in mirror writing.

Now the *Testaments of the Twelve Patriarchs* are worth reading, as it is seems to be the very first systematic Christian treatise on moral theology, for the twelve Patriarchs each discourse about some aspect of virtue or vice. It is written in the form of 'Testaments' or last speeches by the twelve sons of Jacob, addressed to their families gathered around them, each on his deathbed, on the model of the Biblical testament of Jacob. (Genesis 49) It was written in Greek, and published in 1765 by the great Oratorian scholar, Andrea Gallando, who dated it to the very end of the first century. He considered it was a Christian work, using the literary form of a *pseudepigraphon*, or what we might call a 'historical novel'. Later Protestant editors thought it was Jewish, and much earlier, as far back as the second century BC, but with a few Christian interpolations. This is probably why it has been neglected, though if it really is a pre-Christian work, we would have to put it among St Paul's favourite books, for he seems to quote it many times. More recent scholarship seems to have decided Gallando was right after all, and place it at the end of the first or beginning of the second century, contemporary with St Ignatius. In this case the author, whoever he was, counted St Paul's epistles among *his* favourite books, and frequently quoted them. When I say 'quoted', the texts in question are not expressed in exactly the same words, but they say exactly the same thing. If it were St Paul quoting an existing book, there could be no reason why he should carefully change every word to one of the same meaning; but if we have here an author who is trying to keep up the literary fiction that the book was written thousands of years ago, he has every reason not to quote St Paul, a recent author, word for word.

In fact, whether it is a late Jewish book which only survives in an early Christian edition, or a new composition by an early Christian drawing on Jewish predecessors, matters not a jot. The fact that early Christians edited it or wrote it, and certainly read it, is very significant: it is strange that it has been so neglected. It is an important witness to the Early Church, it shows what the second or third generation of Christians thought and believed about the path to virtue. I have therefore translated the whole text, and present it here not as a scholarly edition of an obscure work, but setting it in the context of our daily struggle towards holiness. Each of the twelve chapters corresponds to a step on the Ladder, and the Prophets and Apostles, with St Paul, join in to provide spiritual commentary. Using St Benedict as our warp, and the Patriarchs as our woof, let us weave together these themes of virtue and vice.

There is a more recent scholarly edition of the Testaments than Gallando: *The Greek Versions of the Testaments of the Twelve Patriarchs*, edited by Robert Henry Charles (Oxford University Press and Wissenschaftliche Buchgesellschaft, Darmstadt, 1908, reprinted 1960). This compares nine manuscripts, and provides a number of variant readings. Since my translation is not pretending to be 'scholarly', I have made my own selection from these variants, without feeling the need to mark the text.

References are also made to the following:

Benedict, St, *The Rule in Latin and English*, ed. Abbot Justin McCann (London: Burns & Oates, Orchard Books, 1952), cited as *RB* by chapter number.

Bernard, St, *Sermons for the Seasons and Principal Festivals of the Year* (Dublin: Mount Melleray edition, 1921).

Cassian, St John, *The Collations, Being a Collection of Twenty-Four Conferences Divided into Three Parts* (Leominster: Gracewing, 2015).

Cassian, St John, *The Monastic Institutes, On the Training of a Monk and the Eight Deadly Sins* (London: St Austin Press, 1999).

Catechism of the Catholic Church (London: Geoffrey Chapman, 1994). Cited as *CCC* by paragraph number.

Charlesworth, James H. (ed.), *The Old Testament Pseudepigrapha*, 2 volumes (London: Darton, Longman and Todd, 1983).

Code of Canon Law, Latin-English Edition (Rome: Typis Polyglottis Vaticanis, and Washington, DC, Canon Law Society of America, 1983), cited as *CIC* by canon number.

Francis of Assisi, St, *Little Flowers* (many editions, e.g. London: Orchard Books, 1953).

Francis de Sales, St, *Letters to Persons in the World* (London: Burns & Oates, *c.* 1900).

Gallonio, Antonio, *The Life of Saint Philip Neri* (Oxford and San Francisco: Family Publications and Ignatius Press, 2005).

Jerome, St, *Commentary on Galatians* (Verona: Benedictine edition, 1734–42, volume VII).

Mansi, Johannes Dominicus, *Sacrorum Conciliorum Nova et Amplissima Collectio*, 31 volumes (Florence and Venice: Antonio Zatti, 1759–98).

Newman, John Henry, *Certain Difficulties Felt by Anglicans in Catholic Teaching Considered* (London: Burns & Oates, 1976, often reprinted).

Newman, John Henry, *Letters and Diaries*, 32 volumes, various editors (London and Oxford: Nelson and Oxford University Press, 1961–2008).

Philip Neri, St, *Il primo processo per San Filippo Neri*, 4 volumes (Vatican: Studi e Testi, 1957–60).

Sibylline Oracles, in A. Gallandus, *Bibliotheca Veterum Patrum*, vol. I (Venice, 1765).

Tauler, John, *The Sermons and Conferences of John Tauler*, trans. Walter Elliott (Washington, DC, 1910).

Teresa of Avila, St, *Letters*, 4 volumes (London: Stanbrook edition, 1919–24).

Teresa of Avila, St, *The Way of Perfection* (many editions, e.g. London: Thomas Baker, 1925). Cited by chapter and paragraph.

Teresa of Calcutta, St, *Come be my Light*, ed. Brian Kolodiejchuk, MC (New York: Doubleday, 2007).

Thomas Aquinas, St, *Summa Theologiae* (many editions). Cited by part, question and article.

Citations from Scripture are mostly taken from the Revised Standard Version, except where ancient authors quote from the Septuagint version, marked as LXX.

Step One

CHASTITY

The Patriarch Reuben, Prophet Malachi and Apostle Jude

The Fear of the Lord is the First Stage of Wisdom (Proverbs 1:7)

St Benedict begins his chapter on the steps of the Ladder of Humility by talking about fear. 'The first degree of humility, then, is that a man keep the fear of God before his eyes, altogether shunning forgetfulness. Let him ever remember all the commandments of God, and how hell will burn for their sins those that despise him; and let him constantly turn over in his heart the eternal life which is prepared for those that fear him' (*RB* 7). St John Cassian, for his part, puts the Fear of the Lord as the pre-requisite needed before we even begin to climb the Ladder of Humility. 'The Fear of the Lord is the beginning of our salvation and its safeguard. Through this it is that we may achieve our first conversion, the reform of our life, the protection of our virtue, as we set out on the way of perfection' (*Monastic Institutes*, IV, 39).

The Fear of the Lord is not a popular subject these days—people shy away from the word, and try to gloss over references to it. Even those who translate the Scriptures or the liturgy like to substitute more soothing words. In the previous translation of the rite of Confirmation, for example, we find 'wonder and awe in your presence' substituted for 'the Fear of the Lord' (thus incidentally making eight gifts of the Holy Spirit). But the Scriptures do speak frequently of the Fear of the Lord, and all the great spiritual writers of the past have been able to cope, so who are we to decide we are too shy or too sensitive to name that Fear, or to think about it?

The prophet Malachi shows us how it is through the Fear of the Lord that we may find forgiveness. 'Then those who feared the LORD spoke with one another; the LORD heeded and heard them, and a book of remembrance was written before him of those who feared the LORD and thought on his name. "They shall be mine, says the LORD of hosts, my special possession on the day when I act, and I will spare them as a man spares his son who serves him"' (Malachi 3:16–17).

It is the remembrance of sin that generates fear. When we look back over our lives, unless we are remarkably obtuse and unbelievably forgetful, we cannot fail to remember occasions of sin, things said or done, or merely considered, which bring at once a blush to the cheek and a tremour of fear to the heart. Could it really have been me that behaved like that? Oh yes; and did I not know perfectly well what the commandments of God are? And is not the Gospel abundantly clear about the consequences of rebellion against God, and the deliberate hardening of my heart against the prompting of grace? And the more I think about it, the less I can claim to be innocently and invincibly ignorant, or shielded from guilt by 'inadvertence, duress, fear, habit, inordinate attachments and other psychological or social factors', as the Catechism reassures us (*CCC*, 1735). No, we have really no excuses, and when we remember our sins, how can we fail to feel fear?

Is fear then a good thing? In itself, no—neither fear nor guilt nor shame are good in themselves. But they are useful, right, and therefore good, if they provide occasions which make us turn back to God, and set us on the first step of the Ladder of Humility. We cannot rest on that step, or settle on it for a lifetime. Fear is only the *first* stage of wisdom: we must hurry on to the next as soon as we can. But it is fear, more often than not, which first brings us to that process of reflection on our own life that we may call examination of conscience, that regret for the past which we call remorse, that resolution to change our lives which we call contrition, that realisation that only God can change our lives which we call absolution.

St Benedict points out that the most common specific cause of fear is our consciousness of evil desires, 'for death lies close by the gate of delight; whence Scripture gives this command: Go not after thy lusts.' Evil desires of every kind—and there are as many different temptations as there are devils—are the inevitable accompaniment of our life-long struggle towards perfection. It is necessary that this should be so, for the Lord says, 'My power is made perfect in weakness' (II Corinthians 12:9). Awareness of temptation, particularly the more embarrassing or disreputable temptations, leads at once to the awareness of our need for grace, our utter dependence on the love of God. Very few of us are so refined that we can afford to do without temptations, for if we are not tempted by evil desires we run the terrible risk of imagining that we are already perfect. How can we be—we are only on the first step of the Ladder of Humility!

St Bernard put it very aptly—if we cannot imitate the purity of the humble Virgin, at least we can imitate the humility of the pure Virgin (*Sermons for the Seasons*, vol. I, p. 61). The virtue of chastity, the last and least of the fruits of the Holy Spirit, is defined by St Thomas as that which 'restrains a man from what is unlawful' (*Summa Theologiae*, I-II, lxx, 3). We have an obligation to refrain from what is unlawful—it is no credit to ourselves if we succeed, for 'we have only done what was our duty' (Luke 17:10). Whether we are successful or not in the struggle against temptation, we will always find plenty of ground for humility.

At the same we must admit that all virtue is impossible without grace. Left to ourselves, there is no sin or depravity which we would not commit. God always gives us grace sufficient to resist sin. At times He also gives us the grace even of being spared temptation, at least in some areas. Very often He protects us in ways we fail to appreciate. The fact that we have not actually committed whatever sins might have enticed us may be due entirely to lack of opportunity, ill-health, the ordinary decency of others around us, the embarrassment we might feel in front of friends or family—and all these are the work of God's grace. He is perfectly capable of removing every sort of temptation from our minds, but that would not always be good for us. We may pray frequently for our temptations to be taken away—but as St Paul discovered, God leaves us with the temptations, the 'thorn in the flesh, to keep me from being too elated ... My grace is sufficient for you, for my power is made perfect in weakness' (II Corinthians 12:7–9). If we were not aware of temptations and evil desires, how easy it would be to fall into the terrible sins of vainglory and pride!

The association which St Benedict makes between Fear of the Lord and evil desires is illustrated well in the *Testament of the Patriarch Reuben*, with which he may have been familiar.

Reuben, the eldest son of Jacob, introduces his Testament by recalling his great sin, which was only briefly mentioned in Genesis: 'While Israel dwelt in the land Reuben went and lay with Bilhah his father's concubine, and Israel heard of it' (Genesis 35:22).

1. A transcript of the Testament of Reuben, and all that he said to his sons, before he died in the one hundred and twenty-fifth year of his age. Two years after the death of his brother Joseph, his sons and his grandsons gathered to visit Reuben in his sickness. And he said to them, See, my children, I am dying, and going the way of my fathers. And observing that his brothers Judah, Gad, and Asher were there, he said to them, Lift me up, so that I may speak to my brethren and my children about all the things I have hidden in my heart. For now I am beginning to decline. They raised him up, and he embraced them, and spoke to them:

Listen to me, my brothers; and you, my sons, pay attention to everything your father Reuben is saying to you. Look, I call the God of heaven to witness what I am telling you today, walk not in the ignorance of youth and in fornication, into which I myself fell, and defiled the bed of my father Jacob. I have to tell you that the Lord struck me with a grievous pain in my loins, which lasted seven months. Had not Jacob our father prayed for me to the Lord, the Lord would have been willing to destroy me. I was thirty years old when I committed that sin before the Lord, and for seven months I was ill to the point of death. Then I did penance before the Lord for seven years, of my own decision. Wine and strong drink I did not take, and meat never entered my mouth, nor did I taste any pleasant food, but I lamented over my guilt, for it was great. Such a thing has never happened in Israel!

Reuben has told us that he was thirty years old when this happened—and he is now one hundred and twenty-five, so he has been worrying about it for nearly a century. The main theme of the entire Testament is his repentance for this sin, and his anxiety that his sons and descendants should not fall in a similar way, 'Walk not in the ignorance of youth and in fornication.' And he did penance before the Lord for seven years of fasting and abstinence, modelled on that of the prophet Daniel (Daniel 10:2–3). Incidentally, the Greek word Reuben uses is *meta-noiein*, and the context makes it abundantly clear that he means 'do penance', with fasting and abstinence. Many Protestant commentators, from William Tyndale onwards, have tried to eliminate doing penance from the Christian life by claiming that the Greek word *meta-noiein*, and its cognates, which are frequently used in the Gospels, only means 'change your mind' rather than 'do penance' (*paenitentiam agere*) as Catholics traditionally translate it. The use of the word in this first-century text to mean 'do penance' is thus an important witness to the validity of the Catholic tradition, whatever the etymology of the word!

Reuben continues:

2. And now listen to me, my children, what I saw during my penance concerning the seven spirits of deception. For seven spirits have been sent against mankind by the devil, and these are the causes of the actions of youth. And seven spirits were given to mankind at the Creation, so that all man's works should be done in them. The first spirit is Life in which all things are brought together. The second spirit is Sight, from which desire arises. The third spirit is Hearing, from which arises learning. The fourth spirit is Smell, with which is given the taste to savour the air and the breath. The fifth spirit is Speech, with which knowledge comes to be. The sixth spirit is Taste, from which arises the consumption of food and drink, and strength is gained by it, for it is by nourishment that strength comes into being. The seventh spirit is of Seed and intercourse, with which arise sins, through the desire of pleasure. That is why it is the last thing to be created, and the first stage of adolescence, for it is full of ignorance, and it leads a youth like a blind man into a pit, and like a beast over the precipice.

3. As well as all these, there is an eighth spirit, that of Sleep, with which is formed ecstacy of nature, and the image of death.

The spirits of deceit are mingled with these spirits. Firstly the spirit of Fornication lurks both in nature and in the senses. Secondly the spirit of Insatiability of the stomach. The third is the spirit of Conflict, seated in the liver and bile. The fourth spirit is that of Flattery and trickery, to make one appear attractive through elaboration. Fifth is the spirit of Arrogance, to move a man to boast and think much of himself. Sixth is the spirit of Falsehood, with destruction and guile, weaving words and concealing thought from family and household. The seventh spirit is that of Injustice, accompanied by theft and crooked dealing, for the sake of gladness of heart. For injustice conspires with the other spirits to take hold of guile. Besides all these, is the spirit of Sleep, the eighth spirit, which works with deceit and phantasy.

In this way all young men fall, their eyes self-blinded to the truth, with no thought for the law of God. Neither do they listen to the instructions of their fathers, any more than I did when I was a young man. So now, my children, be in love with the truth, guard it for yourselves. Listen to Reuben your father. Do not run after the face of a woman, do not be alone with a married woman, do not be concerned with woman's affairs. Had I not observed Bilhah bathing in a covered place, I would not have fallen into my great sin. My thoughts were excited by seeing a naked woman, and they would let me sleep until I had achieved my disgrace. Jacob my father was away, visiting Isaac his father. We were in Gader, near Ephratha, in Bethlehem. Bilhah was drunk, and fell asleep, lying uncovered on her bed. I came in, and seeing her uncovered, did what was unholy, without her being aware of it, and so I went out, leaving her still asleep. And immediately an angel of God informed my father about my wickedness; he came home and lamented over me, but her he never touched again.

4. And so, my sons, do not run after the beauty of women, nor think about anything to do with them. Walk in simplicity of heart, in the Fear of the Lord, labouring at useful work, and occupying yourselves with the scriptures, as well as your flocks, until the Lord give you a helpmate of his choice, lest you suffer as I did.

Until the day of my father's death I was ashamed to look him in the face, or to speak to any of my brothers, because of their reproaches. Even now my conscience reproaches me about my impiety. Yet my father greatly comforted me, for he prayed about me to the Lord, so that the wrath of the Lord might depart from me, as the Lord has revealed to me. Ever since then I kept myself under control and did not sin again. That is why, my children, I say to you that you should remember everything I tell you, and never fall into sin. For the sin of fornication is the bane of the soul, cutting it off from God, and bringing it close to idolatry, for it deceives the mind and the understanding, and leads young men down to hell before their time.

Fornication has been the destruction of many. Even if a man be old and of great status, be he rich or poor, it will shame him before the sons of men and the devil will laugh at him. You have heard of Joseph that he found favour before God and men because he kept himself clear of any woman, and preserved his imagination free of thoughts of fornication. That Egyptian woman made great efforts against him, employing magicians and plying him with philtres, but he would not agree to what she intended and her evil desires. That is why the God of my fathers delivered him from all evil and from an obscure death. If fornication does not gain control over your thoughts, the devil can have no power over you.

Reuben never attempts to excuse his sin, or to justify himself. He knows perfectly well that he has sinned, but we cannot fail to note that his repentance is motivated more by fear than by the love of God. Reuben fasted seven years for one sin, but still his conscience reproached him, all those years later. So fasting and penance alone are not enough, do not avail to wipe out the feeling of guilt. Fear remains, the fear of God's anger, and yet it is clear that the effect of sin is not an arbitrary punishment sent by God, but the inevitable consequence of the sin itself. Sin of any kind 'deceives the mind and the understanding', for if we refuse to admit that sin is evil, we are deliberately closing our minds to the truth, and turning away from God. Hence the references to 'idols', and the fate of those who surrender themselves to sin.

Reuben's awareness of forgiveness comes through knowing that his father Jacob has been interceding for him. He owes his life to the intercession of the very father he had wronged, otherwise the Lord would have allowed him to die. 'My father comforted me, for he prayed about me to the Lord, so that the wrath of the Lord might depart from me, as the Lord has revealed to me.' There is even a suggestion that this intercession has continued after Jacob's death, 'as the Lord has revealed to me.'

Reuben's practical advice to his family is the perfect remedy for sin: it is work and prayer, 'labouring at your work, and occupying yourselves with the scriptures, as well as your flocks'. St Benedict was perfectly familiar with the remedy, even if he was not acquainted with the text of the *Testaments* themselves. 'Idleness is the enemy of the soul. The brethren, therefore, must be occupied at stated hours in manual labour, and again at other hours in sacred reading' (*RB* 48). We are not meant to wonder which Scriptures Reuben is recommending, since Moses was not born until centuries after his time, and no part of the Old Testament had yet been written—after all, the author of the *Testaments* must have expected his readers to be aware this is a recent book, and to apply themselves to the existing Scriptures without quibbling. If the allusions to St Paul's Epistles in the *Testaments* are anything to go by, our author and his readers might already be treasuring them as 'scriptures'. Prayer and work are an important part of continuing penance, the most effective way of avoiding occasions of sin and opening ourselves to the grace of God that preserves us from future falls.

To conclude Reuben's speech:

5. Women are dangerous, my children, for since they do not have authority or power over a man, they resort to using their appearance as a crafty means of attracting him to themselves. And if they are not able to charm him by their appearance, they gain domination over him by guile. It was an angel of God who informed me about them and taught me that women are more subject to the spirit of fornication than men, and that they plot schemes against people in their heart. They begin by leading their thoughts astray through their beauty; with a glance they

instil their poison into them, and then they take them captive in reality. For a woman cannot overcome a man face to face, but has to work her wiles on him by impure designs. 'Flee fornication' (I Corinthians 6:18), therefore, my children, and instruct your wives and daughters not to adorn their heads and faces to delude men's thoughts (cf. I Timothy 2:8–9). Any woman who uses her appearance deceitfully like that is liable to eternal punishment. That is how they seduced the Watchers before the Flood, who stared at them continually until they began to desire them. They devised a way in which to act, taking on the form of men, so that they could appear to them in the appearance of their husbands. The women lusted after these appearances in their thoughts, and so brought forth the Giants, for the Watchers had seemed to them to be tall as the heavens.

6. Be on your guard, therefore, against fornication, and your thoughts will be pure. Guard your emotions away from all that is feminine. Warn your womenfolk not to keep company with men, so as to purify their own minds. Continuous association with each other, even if they do not do anything unclean, will cause an incurable weakness in them, the devil's destruction and an eternal reproach for us. Fornication has neither sense nor devotion in itself, and every sort of desire lurks in its attraction.

For this reason, I warn you, you will be jealous of the sons of Levi, and you will seek to be exalted above them, but you will not be able to. For God will bring about their justification, but you will die an evil death. For God has given authority first to Levi, then to Judah, and after him to me, Dan and Joseph, so that we should be princes. I tell you therefore, listen to Levi, for he will know the law of God, and give commandments about judgment, and he will sacrifice on behalf of all Israel, until the consummation of the times of Christ the high priest, of whom the Lord has spoken. I adjure you by the God of heaven, that each one of you should behave justly to his neighbour, and each of you should love his brother. Come close to Levi in humility of heart, that you may receive a blessing from his mouth. For he will bless Israel, and Judah, and it is in him that the Lord has chosen to set up kingship over all the people. You will worship his descendant, for he will die for you, in a conflict that is both seen and unseen, and he will be among you the King of the ages.

7.   And Reuben died after he had given these instructions to his sons. And they placed him in a coffin until they were able to carry him out of Egypt and bury him in Hebron, in the cave where his father lies.

Forgiveness is available to all those who repent, particularly if a righteous man prays for them. No sin is too heinous for forgiveness—the fact that in this case the man most wronged offers prayers of intercession and thereby demonstrates his forgiveness makes it all the more credible that God forgives.

As a matter of common observation, many young people fall away from virtue through evil desires. Not because such sins are in themselves more serious than any others, but because people refuse to admit that they are sins. Reuben tells us, indeed, that even the angels fell because of this sort of sin, in a cryptic allusion to the Watchers who fell before the Flood. This seems to have been a common theme among the later Jewish and early Christian writers, elaborating on the obscure reference to the 'Sons of God' and the origin of the Giants (Genesis 6:1–4). The Apostle Jude, in his rather neglected Epistle, refers to the same story, when he introduces a passage describing the decadent morals of the pagan society of his own time (Jude 6). There is also here an allusion to the rebellion of Reuben's descendants, Dathan and Abiram, against the Levites in the desert (Numbers 16).

We are perhaps rather too conscious of the falling away from Christian morality which has characterised modern society in the last two generations. It is indisputable that since Vatican II many even in the Church have failed to uphold the teaching of Our Lord and the Apostles on so many matters of intimate concern. The result has been exactly as St Jude foretold: 'these men revile what they do not understand, and by these things that they know by instinct, as irrational animals do, they are destroyed. Woe to them!' and, 'In the last time there will be scoffers, following their own ungodly passions. It is these who set up divisions, worldly people, devoid of the Spirit' (Jude 10–11, 18–19). Those outside the faith have some excuse, in their blessed state of Invincible Ignorance, although as St Paul reminds us, they still have the witness of their own conscience (Romans 2:14–16). There can be no excuses for us who have the gift of faith, who have heard the Scriptures and possess the Catechism of the Catholic Church!

And so the result is the Fear of the Lord. 'Conscience doth make cowards of us all.' A salutary Fear reminds us that we can claim no virtue in God's eyes, we have no rights against Him, we cannot pull ourselves together, nor bring about our own salvation, no matter what efforts we make. But fear is a negative virtue, even though the wrong sort of fear, 'servile fear', may successfully frighten us into trying to be good. Certainly in the past, when civil society was ordered in a more Christian manner, many did avoid actual sin for fear of punishment in this world, let alone in the next. But as St Thomas points out, 'human laws leave many sins unpunished, because of the condition of imperfect human beings, who would be prevented from gaining many benefits if every sin were specifically prohibited with an attached penalty' (*Summa Theologiae*, II-II, lxxviii, art. i, ad iii). If we only avoid sin out of fear of consequences in this world, we have left ourselves no room for love of God or neighbour. Neither Reuben nor St Benedict recommend servile fear, for that leaves us still slaves to sin, still yearning after evil desires, restrained only from carrying our desires into effect. If our regret for sin, and our efforts to reform, are motivated only by servile fear, they will be of little use. Servile fear can include the fear of losing the esteem of our family and friends, the fear of disease, expense, and publicity, even if there is no longer any civil penalty to fear. For those who believe, servile fear means the dread of purgatory, the terror of hell.

This sort of fear leads to what we call 'attrition', a regret for sin that is only external to the heart, retaining perhaps the lingering feeling that if only God would change His mind, or some clever theologian could convince us that the traditional teaching of the Church had been mistaken on this point or that point, then how much happier we could be! Attrition, we are taught, is sufficient for forgiveness, if combined with sacramental absolution, but it is still a pretty half-hearted and cold sort of thing. Attrition keeps us from sin grudgingly: it does not lead us to the burning love of God that makes us want to avoid sin for His sake and that of His Church.

The Fear of the Lord which sets us on the ladder of humility is what we call 'filial fear'. That is not at all incompatible with love. Above all, it makes us strive to be free from sin out of the fear of breaking the union of love between us and God. St Teresa writes about this fear which is closely united to the love of God, 'It is delightful to talk about the love of God ..., now let us think about the fear of God ... When such souls as those above mentioned are raised to contemplation, both their love and their fear of God are very evident even in their outward conduct' (*Way of Perfection*, XLI). This fear makes us feel the very worst aspect of hell would be the loss of the sight of God. It guides us in the avoidance of sin, because we fear the loss of grace, we fear to offend those we love, we are afraid to seem ungrateful or unresponsive to the many benefits God has poured out upon us.

Returning to the book of Genesis, the main thing we all remember about Reuben is that he was the one who tried to restrain his brothers when they had decided to kill Joseph. 'When Reuben heard it, he delivered him out of their hands, saying, "let us not take his life." And Reuben said to them, "shed no blood; cast him into this pit here in the wilderness, but lay no hand upon him"—that he might rescue him out of their hand, to restore him to his father.' And then, after Judah had sold the boy behind Reuben's back, 'when Reuben returned to the pit and saw that Joseph was not in the pit, he rent his clothes and returned to his brothers, and said, "the lad is gone; and I, where shall I go?"' (Genesis 37:21–2, 29–30) The implication is that Judah and the others never let on to Reuben that they had actually sold Joseph (though the Testament of Zabulon, later on, suggests that he did know, *T.Zab.* 4). Later on, in Egypt, while Joseph is teasing his brothers by pretending not to recognise them, Reuben remarks, rather insufferably, 'Did I not tell you not to sin against the lad? But you would not listen. So now there comes a reckoning for his blood' (Genesis 42:22). It seems the others have still not dared tell Reuben that they had sold Joseph, and have let him believe the story that he was eaten by wild beasts. When Jacob is reluctant to let Benjamin go down to Egypt, it is Reuben who first offers his own sons as hostages, although Jacob rather ungraciously refuses (Genesis 42:37).

Jacob, it seems, never does find out how Reuben tried to save Joseph, and is not totally appeased for the business about Bilhah. When it comes to the final blessings, although he acknowledges that Reuben is his first-born, he deprives him of his rights, 'Unstable as water, you shall not have pre-eminence because you went up to your father's bed' (Genesis 49:4). Again, when Moses prophecies over the twelve tribes, Reuben gets very little attention: 'Let Reuben live, and not die, nor let his men be few' (Deuteronomy 33:6). So it happens that the tribe of Reuben never takes any important part in further history, they settle on the wrong side of the Jordan, and are viewed with some suspicion by the tribes living on the West Bank (Joshua 22).

The author of the *Testaments of the Twelve* has obviously been influenced more by the blessing of Jacob than by any other Old Testament reference to Reuben. We hear much about the sin, and Reuben's repentance, but nothing of his good behaviour over Joseph. But we can take it into account, for surely it is precisely because Reuben had learnt the Fear of the Lord that he tried to save Joseph. He sinned, he repented, and he changed his way of life. From now on he tried to live in accordance with God's will, following his conscience (for the written Law had not yet been given). The later life of Reuben, nearly a hundred years, seems to have been exemplary, if uneventful. Sin can be forgiven, but the memory of it does not pass away. A salutary Fear of the Lord remains, long after we are conscious of having received absolution.

To return to St Benedict. 'In regard to the desires of the flesh, let us believe that God is always present to us, since the prophet says to the Lord: *All my desire is before thee.*' Whatever temptations we experience, whatever distracting thoughts plague us in times of prayer, God is aware of them. We may successfully deceive other people, we can never deceive God. The best of us needs to be continually aware of our potential for sin. We are usually conscious of the particular temptations that trouble us most, but we should never think smugly that there are sins that we could never possibly commit. However unlikely we may think it, the devil can always surprise us with new and unexpected temptations, or reappear with desires that we thought we had tamed long ago. That is why we can never cease to be sober and vigilant, for 'your adversary the devil prowls round like a roaring lion, seeking some one to devour. Resist him, firm in your faith' (I Peter 5:8–9). At this particular moment, today, we might be able to say that we are in a state of grace, and that if the angels were to come and call us home now this instant we would be more or less ready, but we can never tell how we would deal with the storm of temptation that may come upon us tomorrow. St Paul warns us, 'let anyone who thinks that he stands take heed lest he fall' (I Corinthians 10:12). He admits that he cannot be sure about himself, he has no 'assurance of salvation', but like the rest of us lives in hope. 'Not that I have already obtained this [the resurrection], or am already perfect; but I press on to make it my own, because Christ Jesus has made me his own' (Philippians 3:12). 'I pommel my body and subdue it, lest after preaching to others I myself should be disqualified' (I Corinthians 9:27). For this reason we are to be understanding and ready to forgive when we see anyone else fall. 'If a man is overtaken in any trespass, you who are spiritual should restore him in a spirit of gentleness. Look to yourselves, lest you too be tempted' (Galatians 6:1).

This reminds us of the story told by Cassian about the harsh confessor. Abba Moyses is speaking:

> I will briefly tell you of something that happened which can give you the warning you need. One of the young men, and not the least worthy of them, went to an elder (who is well known to us) for the sake of improvement, and confessed to him in all simplicity that he was troubled by lustful thoughts and the temptation to sexual sin. He trusted that the old man's prayers would bring him consolation, and that he would find a remedy for the weakness he suffered, but the other reviled him in bitter language, calling him a miserable wretch and unfit to be called a monk if he was tempted by such base lusts. By his reproaches he wounded him all the deeper, until he drove him out of his cell, depressed, discouraged and plunged into gloom. He was so dejected that he no longer looked for a remedy against temptation but was pondering instead on how he could fulfil his

desires, when Abba Apollo happened by, one of the finest of the elders. He deduced from his gloomy countenance that he was silently reflecting on some distressing and powerful temptations, and asked him why he was so depressed. Thus urged, he admitted that he was heading for the village, because the other elder had deemed him unable to be a monk, and that he was incapable of controlling the urges of the flesh and finding any cure for them, so he was going to look for a wife, abandon the monastic life and return to the world. The elder Apollo consoled him gently, admitting that he himself was troubled with the same sort of temptations and emotions every day, so that there was no need for him to give up, nor to be surprised at these passionate urges, which are overcome simply by the mercy and grace of God, not by sheer effort. He persuaded him to defer his departure for one day, and to return to his cell, while he went at once to the monastery of the aforesaid elder.

When he reached him he flung out his arms and burst into tears as he prayed, 'O Lord, who alone art the loving judge and the secret doctor of the hidden things of men and of all human weakness, transfer the temptations of that youth to this old man, so that he may learn in his old age how to be compassionate to the weakness of the labourer, and to understand the frailty of youth.' He had hardly finished this heartfelt prayer when he saw a loathly savage standing outside his cell and hurling fiery darts towards the old man. The man was deeply wounded by these, and dashed out of his cell, running hither and thither like a drunkard or a fool, rushing in and out. Eventually, unable to remain still within, he began to set out on the same path that the young man had taken. Abba Apollo realised that he had been driven mad by the assaults of the furies, and understood that his heart had been penetrated by the devil's fiery dart, which he had watched being hurled towards him; this was causing his mental confusion and the disturbance of his senses by its intolerable burning. He approached him and said, 'Where

are you heading for? For what reason have you forgotten
your age and dignity? Why are you running around like a
disturbed adolescent?' The other was so confused by his
guilty conscience and base passions, that he imagined that
the thoughts of his heart were revealed, but he concealed his
inner thoughts from Apollo, not daring to give any reply to
his urgent enquiry.

'Go back to your cell,' said Apollo, 'and be aware in future
that up to now the devil has either failed to notice you or
considered you beneath his contempt, not worth reckoning
among those whom he is daily provoked to tempt and torment
because of their progress in learning. Only one of his darts
has reached you, and after wasting so many years in your
profession you were unable even for a single day to endure
it, let alone repel it! The reason why Our Lord allowed you
to be wounded like that is so that at last in old age you might
learn to sympathise with the weakness of others, and your
own experience might teach you to understand the frailty of
youth. In dealing with a young monk suffering from the devil's
attentions, you not only failed to console him and care for
him, but you so depressed him that he despaired altogether.
All you did was surrender him into the enemy's hands, for
him to be tragically destroyed.

'So now learn to be sympathetic to those in difficulties,
after this experience; never drive the weak to despair nor
rebuke them with rough words, but build them up with mild
and gentle consolation. For no one can endure the assaults of
the enemy, no one can extinguish or repress the fires of the
flesh which burn with a natural heat, unless the grace of God
come to the aid of our weakness, protect us and strengthen
us. Now let us all pray together that the Lord will order the
removal of that scourge which he had allowed to be laid upon
you for your benefit.'

And so, at the prayer of that old man, the Lord took away
again the temptation which he had allowed to be so suddenly
inflicted. That story clearly shows us that we should never

rebuke someone for the sins he has confessed, nor easily despise the grief of one who suffers.

Conferences, II, 13

So far Abba Moyses. Each of us must 'work out our own salvation with fear and trembling', but we can take comfort that 'God is at work in us, both to will and to work for his good pleasure' (Philippians 2:12–13). We have to be constantly mindful of our own past sins, our past and present temptations, not to mention the sins and evil desires which do not trouble us at present only because God has been shielding us from them. That remembrance generates the Fear of the Lord, not the servile fear that deters us from sin only because we dread punishment, but the filial fear that makes us dread the loss of the love of God. Fear, then, leads us to repentance, and indeed to penance. Both St Paul, and the first-century author of the Testament of Reuben, consider penance involves mortification: 'I subdue my body', says Paul; 'I fasted for seven years' says Reuben. Manual labour and *lectio divina* enable us to grow in the knowledge of God, and in the strength needed to respond to His grace. By that grace alone can we resist sin. Penance leads to absolution, and the assurance that, for this moment, we are in a state of grace. But as long as this life lasts we cannot trust ourselves not to fall again, which is why confession and absolution is a regular repeated feature of the Christian life.

The Fear of the Lord is the first stage of wisdom—but there are many stages or steps to take yet.

Step Two

CONTINENCE

The Patriarch Judah, Prophet Zechariah and Apostle Judas

I pommel my body and subdue it (I Corinthians 9:27)

The second step on our Ladder of Humility is self-denial: 'that a man love not his own will, nor delight in fulfilling his own desires, but carry out in deed the saying of the Lord: *I came not to do my own will, but the will of him who sent me*. It is written also: *Self-will hath its punishment, but necessity wins a crown*' (*RB* 7). Cassian puts it more succinctly, 'if we have mortified all our desires' (*Monastic Institutes*, IV, 39).

The concept of mortifying our desires is probably almost as unfashionable as the Fear of the Lord. We live in a world of commerce, where most peoples' lives are totally dedicated to supplying and demanding goods. A world where everyone is encouraged to demand whatever they want immediately, with no delay—consequently a world dependent on credit and debt. In some ways that is nothing new, though we are always inclined to think our own age the most decadent in the history of the Church. Perhaps what is new is that Christians no longer consider themselves different from the surrounding population, but drift along in the same commercial whirlpool, demanding instant access to whatever takes their fancy.

At the same time, our modern world can be paradoxically puritanical. We are continually being urged not to eat this, not to drink that, and especially not to smoke the other. The same forces that frantically try to sell us things we do not need, are continually trying to shame us into self-restraint, trying to frighten us into denying ourselves things that we really do need, such as bread and milk. It is not surprising people are confused! It takes discernment to distinguish true mortification from fashionable austerity.

It may seem more surprising that the saints put this step so early on the ladder—we might think that once as we have succeeded in totally subduing the will, we have reached perfection. That is, if we ever do succeed. Perhaps the reason why it comes so early on our journey towards humility is that without the *intention* of mortifying the will we shall never get anywhere at all. It is the intention to obey that counts. We may fail again and again, but as long as we persevere in trying, we are climbing our ladder in the right direction. Perfect submission does indeed come later, much later, but our very perseverance in trying to mortify our desires is what counts.

And this reminds us that the twelve steps on the ladder of humility do not necessarily come neatly one after the other. Indeed, Cassian and St Benedict do not even place them in the same order. We cannot keep a diary of our spiritual life and record that on such a day I advanced from grade five to grade six as if we were learning the piano. All twelve steps need to be before our eyes all the time. Nor is it immediately obvious whether we should be going up this ladder or down it. Maybe the perfection of humility lies in being happy at the bottom, in the lowest place of all. Nevertheless St Benedict does say that 'we descend by self-exaltation, and ascend by humility', so it is a ladder of contradiction. Like the angels, we may go up and down endlessly, but as long as we keep turning back and trying to climb again, we shall eventually reach the top. But it will take the whole of our life in this world, and purgatory to finish off.

The words of Our Lord that St Benedict quotes come, of course, from that glorious chapter six of St John's Gospel. When Our Lord addresses the crowd at Caphernaum, He begins to introduce them to the idea of His relationship to the Father. 'All that the Father gives me will come to me; and him who comes to me I will not cast out. For I have come down from heaven, not to do my own will, but the will of him who sent me; and this is the will of him who sent me, that I should lose nothing of all that he has given me, but raise it up at the last day. For this is the will of the Father, that everyone who sees the Son and believes in him should have eternal life; and I will raise him up at the last day' (John 6:37–40).

This reminds us of the rather difficult passage in Hebrews where the author (surely St Barnabas) is commenting on Psalm 39 (Hebrews 10:5–10; cf. Psalm 39/40:6–8, LXX), 'Then I said, Lo, I have come to do thy will, O God.' (It is made unnecessarily obscure by the curious translation we still have to read in the liturgy.) The apostle interprets this Psalm in the person of Our Lord, beginning the great Christian tradition of exegesis which sees Christ anticipated by every word of the Old Testament. The words, 'I have come to do thy will' are placed on the lips of the Incarnate Word. He takes upon himself the requirements of the law, and carries them away, in order that the obligation of the Gospel might be firmly established (Hebrews 10:9). The entire psalm is about trust in the Lord and total confidence in His mercy. The extract quoted here speaks of how God is more pleased with obedience and trust than with the complicated sacrificial ritual of the Old Law. It makes the same point that Samuel had to make rather forcefully to Saul after the affair of the war against Amalek (I Samuel 15), and several of the Psalms and Prophets repeat the theme.

The patriarch Judah made his Testament at the age of one hundred and nineteen, and begins by telling them his own story as a warning to his sons about self-restraint.

1.   A transcript of the words of Judah, which he spoke to his sons before he died. They gathered and came to him, and he said to them, Listen, my children, to your father Judah. I was the fourth son to be born to my father Jacob, and my mother Leah called me Judah, saying 'I acknowledge before the Lord that he has given me a fourth son.' I was an astute youth, and I obeyed my father in every matter. I respected my mother, and my mother's sister. Thus it happened that when I had become a man my father Jacob prayed for me, saying 'You shall be a king, and shall be prosperous in all you do.'

2.   The Lord gave me joy in all my works, in the field and in the house. When I found that I could outrun the hart, and catch it, I made a supper for my father, and he ate of it. I excelled the gazelle in speed, and I could catch any beast on the plains. I captured a wild mare and tamed her in captivity; I slew a lion and rescued a kid from its jaws. I seized a bear by its paw and hurled it over a cliff to its destruction; any beast that attacked me I tore apart

like a dog. I ran alongside the wild boar, and as I overtook it in the race I tore it to pieces. A panther attacked my dog at Hebron, and I grasped it by the tail and dashed it against the rocks until it was rent in two. I found a wild bull grazing in the region of Gaza, and I seized it by the horns and whirled it around and confused it until I could throw it down and destroy it.

3. The two kings of the Canaanites came up in armour against our flocks, and a great army with them; I charged on my own against the king of Asour, I kicked him on the shins and knocked him over, and so I destroyed him. The other, the king of Tappuah, was seated on a horse, but I killed him, and so I scattered all his army. I also met King Achor on his horse, he was one of the Giants and shot his arrows both in front of him and behind; I hurled a stone which weighed sixty pounds at him, I hit his horse and killed it. I fought with Achor for two hours, and slew him. When I clove his shield in two I cut his feet off with the same stroke. While I was stripping off his armour, suddenly eight of his companions began to attack me. I wrapped my cloak around my arm, and used it as a sling to throw stones at them, with which I killed four, and the others fled. My father Jacob killed Baalishah, the king above other kings, a giant in his strength, twelve cubits tall. So fear came over our enemies and they ceased to attack us, our father could live without fear of war, since I and my brothers were with him. And he had a dream about me, seeing an angel of power who followed me at all times, so that I could not be touched.

4. Then a war came upon us from the South, more dangerous than the one against Shechem. I drew up a battle line with my brothers, and charged against a thousand men, of which I killed two hundred. I drove through them as far as the walls, and killed their king. Thus we liberated Hebron, and took everyone that those kings had captured.

5. On the next day we moved on to Aretas, a strong walled city, very difficult for us to approach, and threatening us with death.

Gad and I approached the city from the east, while Reuben and Levi came from the west and south. The men on the walls thought we were alone, and came out towards us. Then my brothers secretly climbed up the walls on both sides, using pegs, and so entered the city without their perceiving it. Thus we took the city with the edge of the sword, and when some of them fled into the citadel we set fire to it, and so took the citadel along with them. But while we were away, the men of Thaphue had attacked our collection of prisoners and captured them as well as our children. We pursued them as far as Thaphue and killed them, we burnt their city, and took possession of everything in it.

6.   While I was taking the waters at Chouzeba, the men of Jobel came against us and attacked. We engaged them, and routed them, and we slaughtered the men of Selon who were their allies. We left them no way clear to attack us again. On the fifth day the men of Mechor came against us, to plunder our train of captives. We fought them with the strong sword, and overcame them; it was a mighty conflict, for there were many strong men among them. We slew them before they could begin to climb the hills. When we came up to their city, the women hurled stones upon us from the summit of the mountain their city was built on. Simeon and I sneaked around the back of the hill and captured the high ground, and so we destroyed that city as well.

7.   On the next day we heard that Gaash, the king of that city, was coming against us with a great force. Dan and I disguised ourselves as Amorites, and entered their city as allies. At dead of night we opened the gates for our brothers to enter, and so destroyed them all, plundered all their goods and demolished their triple wall. We went on to Thamna, in which all their supplies were. They insulted me, and I lost my temper and assaulted their mountain stronghold. They hurled stones and shot arrows at me, and they might even have killed me, except that my brother Dan was fighting beside me. We rushed them furiously, and they all fell back before us. They escaped by another route, and made entreaty of my father

to conclude peace with them. So we did them no harm, but once we had made them pay us a tribute, we returned to them all our captives. I rebuilt Thamna, and my father built Rambahel. I was twenty years old when that war happened; the Canaanites learnt to fear me and my brothers.

8. I acquired great wealth, and my chief shepherd was Jeram the Odolamite. When I visited him I met Barsabah the king of Odolam, and he greeted us and prepared for us a drinking bout. Then he called me over and gave me his daughter Bathshuah for my wife. It was she who bore me Er, and Onan and Shelah. The Lord took two of them who would not have children, but Shelah lived on, and you are his descendants.

9. For eighteen years our father remained at peace with his brother Esau, and his sons kept peace with us, after we returned from Mesopotamia and the house of Laban. But after eighteen years had passed, when I was in my fortieth year, Esau attacked us, Esau, my father's brother, with a great and strong force. Jacob hit Esau with an arrow, and his body was carried into the mountains of Seir; for he had died on the heights of Eirramna. We went in pursuit of the sons of Esau; they had a strong city with a wall of iron and gates of bronze. We were unable to enter it, so we settled down around it to besiege it. They would not open to us, so after twenty days I brought up a ladder, while they watched, and held my shield over my head. I advanced on them, enduring stones up to three talents weight, and I slew four of their strong men. On the next day Reuben and Gad climbed up and killed six more. Then they begged us to make peace, and since our father wished it, we accepted them as tributaries. They paid us 500 kors of wheat, 500 baths of oil, and 500 litres of wine, up to the time of the famine when we went into Egypt.

10. After that my son Er married Tamar, from Mesopotamia, a daughter of Aram. Er was wicked, and perplexed about Tamar, because she was not from the land of Canaan. The angel of the

Lord destroyed him three days later, at night, but he had never slept with her, through the scheming of his mother, who did not want him to have children by her, and so he died in his sins. While the wedding celebrations continued, I married Onan to her, but he also, in his wickedness, did not sleep with her, but remained with her for a year. Then I was severe with him, and he did go to her, but he spilt his seed on the ground, as his mother had taught him. So he too died in his sins. I wanted to give her Shelah as well, but his mother would not permit it, for she detested Tamar because she was not a daughter of Canaan like herself.

11. I was well aware that the race of Canaan was wicked, but the desires of youth had blinded my perception. I had seen her pouring out wine, and I was deluded while drunk on her wine, and so I had fallen into her arms, without consulting my father. Now while I was absent, she went and took a wife from the land of Canaan for Shelah. When I realised what she had done, I cursed her, in the bitterness of my heart, and so she too died in the sins, along with her sons.

12. After all this had happened, the widow Tamar heard two years later that I was going to shear the sheep, and she dressed herself up like a bride and sat down outside the city of Enan, near the gate of the han. Now the Amorite custom is that a newly married woman must sit down near the gate for seven days, like a prostitute. I was drunk on the wine of Chouzeba, and did not recognise her. Her beauty, and the way she was dressed, deluded me, and I approached her and said, 'I will go with you.' She replied, 'What will you give me?' So I gave her my staff, my Ring and my royal crown as pledges. After I had been with her, she conceived, and I, being unaware of what had happened, intended to kill her. So she sent back my pledges in secret and put me to shame. I summoned her, and heard the secret words which I had spoken to her while I was lying with her, and drunk. Thus I was unable to kill her, for the Lord had made all this happen. I had thought she was perhaps deceiving me, and had been given the pledges by another woman. I never went near her again until the day of her death, because I out of all Israel had done this wicked thing. The people in the city told me that there was no such paid woman in the city, for she had come from another place, and only sat at the gate for a short time. So I thought no one would know that I had slept with her. After that we went into Egypt to Joseph, because of the famine; I was forty-six years old, and I have passed seventy-three years here in Egypt.

13. And now I tell you, my sons, listen to me, your father Judah; remember all my words, do all that the Lord's righteousness demands, and obey the commandments of God. Go not astray after your own desires, in the pride of your hearts, and do not boast of what you achieved in the strength of your youth, for this too is evil in the sight of the Lord. I boasted that during all my wars no woman's beauty had seduced me, and I blamed my brother Reuben over Bilhah our father's woman. But the spirits of jealousy and fornication were drawn up within me, until I was brought down by Bathshua the Canaanite woman, and for Tamar my daughter in law. I told my father in law, 'I will persuade my father, and so be able to accept your daughter.' He did not agree, but he showed me an uncounted quantity of gold on behalf of his daughter, for he was a King. He dressed her up in pearls and gold, and made her serve us with the wine during a banquet, such a beautiful woman! The wine confused my sight, and desire obscured my understanding. I fell in love with her, and sinned; I disobeyed the law of the Lord and the commands of my father, and so I took her as my wife. The Lord repaid me for the decision I had made, for I found no joy in her sons.

Both the patriarchal blessings in the canonical Old Testament emphasise Judah's military exploits, which he has taken such delight in recalling, even though they were not described in Genesis. Jacob says, 'Your hand shall be in the neck of your enemies; your father's sons shall bow down before you. Judah is a lion's whelp; from the prey, my son, you have gone up' (Genesis 49:8–9). And Moses answers, 'Hear, O Lord, the voice of

Judah, and bring him in to his people. With thy hands contend for him, and be a help against his adversaries' (Deuteronomy 33:7). The superficial reason for this is of course the later importance of the tribe of Judah, the real reason the coming of Christ in that tribe, for 'the sceptre shall not depart from Judah, nor the ruler's staff from between his feet, until Shiloh comes (until he comes to whom it belongs); and to him shall be the obedience of the peoples' (Genesis 49:10). This prophecy is picked up and made very explicit later on in the Testament of Judah (24).

So Judah devotes the bulk of his Testament to reminiscences of his military exploits, until he comes to understand that it was because of this pride that he was ensnared by his pagan wife Bathshua (or Bessue in another reading). His family life became terribly entangled (as we read in Genesis 38), for which he can blame his wife's father, who plied him with too much wine. This leads him to warn his sons against the demon drink:

14. So I tell you now, my children, be not drunk with wine, for wine confuses the mind away from the truth, and fills it with the passion of desire. It leads the eyes to stray, for the spirit of fornication employs wine like a minister [*diakonos*] to the pleasures of the imagination, and those two together take away a man's resistance. If you drink wine and become drunk, it will stir up sordid fantasies in your mind, and enflame your body for fornication and pleasure. It will commit sin, and be not ashamed. For such is the power of wine, my children, that a drunken man has no shame. See how it deceived even me, so that I was not ashamed in front of the city crowd, since I went aside to Tamar in the sight of everyone, and so committed a great sin, uncovering the secrets of the uncleanness of my own sons. Through drinking wine, I lost respect for the commandments of God, and took a Canaanite woman as my wife. One who drinks wine needs great discernment, my children, and the discernment proper to one who drinks wine is to let him drink as long as he has a sense of shame. If he passes that limit, he is letting the spirit of deceit into his mind, which makes the drunkard use foul language and break the commandments without shame; rather he glories in his disgrace and imagines it is something fine.

15. The fornicator does not realise what harm he has done to himself, he does not perceive his disgrace. If it is a king who commits fornication, he will be stripped of his kingship, and go out grieving over his sin, as happened to me. For I had given over in pledge my staff, which is the prop and stay of my tribe, and my belt, which is my strength, and my crown, which is the glory of my kingship. Since I repented of all this, I have not taken wine or meat unto my old age, and I have not shared in any celebration. The angel of the Lord showed me that as long as the world lasts, women will have power over king and beggar alike, and there is no hope of improvement in their lives. They take away the glory of a king, the strength of the bold, and the very last prop of the poverty of the poor.

16. Keep within the limits of wine, my children. There are four evil spirits in wine: desire, inflammation, dissoluteness and disgrace. If you drink wine with joy, and preserve your dignity in the fear of God, you shall live. But if you drink without dignity, and the fear of God is absent, then drunkenness intervenes and shamelessness enters in. But if you wish to live a sober life, do not touch wine at all, so that you will not sin in haughty words, in quarrels, calumnies and transgression of the law of God, and thus die before your time. Wine betrays the secrets of God and man to foreigners, to those to whom God said they should not be revealed, as I betrayed the commandments of God and the secrets of my father Jacob to my Canaanite wife Bathshua. Wine is the cause of war and disturbance.

17. Now I command you, my sons, not to love money, nor to look upon the face of women, for it was both through money and beauty that I was deluded to take Bathshua the Canaanite. I know that it is through these two things that my tribe will fall into wickedness, for they will lead astray even the wisest of my descendants, and will reduce to nothing the kingdom of Judah, which the Lord gave me because of my obedience to my father. I never caused any grief to my father Jacob, for I carried out whatever he bade me.

Abraham, my father's father, blessed me with the kingship over Israel, and Isaac blessed me in like manner. I knew full well that the Kingdom will depend on me.

18. I have learnt from the books of Enoch the righteous how much evil you will do in the last days. Keep away, my children, from fornication and from the love of money. Listen to your father Judah, for those things take you away from God's law, they make the deliberations of your hearts blind, and teach you pride. They do not allow a man to have compassion on his neighbour, and harden his heart against all good deeds. They entangle him in sorrow and pain, and deprive him of sleep. They eat away at his flesh, they hinder his sacrifices to God; he becomes forgetful of God's blessings, does not listen to the teaching of the prophets, and takes offence at the message of holiness. A man who is enslaved by these two vices, which are opposed to the commandments of God, becomes unable to obey God, for they will have blinded his soul, so that he walks in the daylight as if it were night.

19. My children, 'the love of money leads to idolatry' (Colossians 3:5), for those who are deceived by money call non-existent beings 'gods'—avarice makes those who possess her fall into ecstacy. It was through money that I lost my sons, and were it not for the combination of the penance to which I subjected my flesh, the humiliation of my soul, and the prayers of Jacob my father, I would have had to die childless. But the God of my Fathers had mercy on me, and recognised that I acted out of ignorance. The prince of deceit had blinded me, and I did not know what I was doing, as a man, as flesh, so corrupted I was by sin. Thus I came to learn how weak I was, I who thought I was invincible.

20. You should be aware, my children, that there are two spirits that devote themselves to mankind, the spirit of truth and that of deceit. Between them is the spirit of understanding which can incline to whichever one it chooses. Whatever truth dictates, whatever error, is 'engraved on the heart of man', and the Lord knows each and every thought. (Romans 2:14–15) There is no moment in which a man's actions can be kept secret, for they are engraved on his bones as if on a monument before the Lord. The spirit of truth bears witness to everything, and brings every accusation, so that the heart of the sinner burns within him, and he is unable to lift up his head before the Judge.

21. Now, my children, I urge you, love Levi that you may endure, be not roused against him, lest you be destroyed. To me God has given the kingship, to him the priesthood, and he has subjected the kingship to the priesthood. To me he has given the things of earth, to him the things of heaven. As the heavens are high above the earth, so the priesthood of God is high above all earthly kingship, unless it happen that he fall away from the Lord through sin, and allow himself to be ruled by the earthly power. The angel of the Lord has told me that the Lord has chosen him above you, to draw close to him, to eat from his table, and to bring to him the first-fruits of all in which the children of Israel delight; but it is you who shall be King over Jacob. You shall be to them like the sea. For just as on the sea both the just and unjust are driven by the storm, prisoners and merchants alike, so in you are all the race of men, some taken prisoner in peril, some growing rich through plundering the goods of others. Those who bear rule are like whales, swallowing men up like fishes. They reduce the sons and daughters of freemen into slavery, they seize houses and lands, flocks and all men's possessions. They feed the crows and kites with the flesh of many, unjustly, and they increase in wickedness through their extravagance and pride. They will prophesy falsely like squalls, they will persecute every righteous man.

22. The Lord will rouse up divisions among them, one against another, so that there will be war continuously in Israel. My kingdom will be dispersed among the pagans, until the Salvation of Israel comes, until the Appearing of the God of righteousness. He will bring peace and tranquillity to Jacob, and to all the nations. He will preserve the strength of my kingdom to all ages, for the

Lord has sworn me an oath, that my kingdom will never depart from my race at any time, for ever.

23. I shall have much grief, my children, over the dissolute way in which you will practise divination and idolatry in my kingdom, running after fortune-tellers, omens and lying spirits. You will turn your daughters into singers and harlots, imitating the abominations of the pagans. Because of this the Lord will bring upon you famine, plague, death and the sword (Apocalypse 6:8), you will be besieged for your punishment, dogs shall tear your flesh, foes shall plot against you, and friends shall revile you, your eyes shall be plucked out and decay, your children stolen away, your wives ravished, your goods plundered, your land devastated, the Temple of God burnt down, and you yourselves shall be slaves to the pagans. They shall cut off your sons to be eunuchs for their wives, until you turn back to the Lord with all your hearts, until you repent and walk again in all the commandments of God. Then the Lord will look upon you with mercy, and lead you back from captivity among your enemies.

The reference to the Books of Enoch in paragraph 18 may refer to the prophecy of the future history of God's People, and how those who were supposed to be their rulers were responsible for so much suffering, 'every excess and destruction will be wrought through the shepherds' (I Enoch 89, in Charlesworth, *Pseudepigrapha*). The original Hebrew or Aramaic text of Enoch does not survive, and only the Ethiopian version is available; yet there must have been a Greek version which is quoted by early Christian writers. It was written towards the end of the Fifth Age, thousands of years later than the named author, Enoch, the seventh descendant of Adam in the First Age, and belongs in that class of pseudepigrapha, writings in the name of long-dead heroes, like the *Testaments* themselves.

Every author on the spiritual life, whether saint or not, emphasises the necessity of mortification, self-denial, doing penance. To refrain from doing anything evil is the natural duty of us all—to refrain from doing something good, or at least neutral, out of a sense of obedience is the challenge. This is how St Thomas distinguishes the virtue of continence from chastity—'chastity restrains a man from what is unlawful, but continence from what is lawful.' (*Summa Theologiae* I-II, lxx, iii in corp. art.) The Testaments of Judah and Reuben have both spoken of *metanoia*, 'penance', clearly meaning the regime of fasting they set themselves. This was not only to express their regret for former sin, but more importantly to enable them to avoid sin for the future. If we can restrain ourselves from excessive desire of what is in itself lawful, it becomes easier to restrain ourselves from what is unlawful. Specifically they copied the prophet Daniel, who began his career by refusing meat and wine, and went through periods of fasting with sackcloth and ashes.

Self-restraint may well begin with food and wine. In fact it is the universal tradition of the Church that fasting and abstinence are the best preparation for spiritual advancement. That is not because any type of food or drink is evil in itself—on the contrary, it was revealed to St Peter, 'What God has cleansed you must not call common' (Acts 11:9), and St Paul is stern against those who 'enjoin abstinence from foods which God created to be received with thanksgiving by those who believe and know the truth' (I Timothy 4:3). He does not mean that abstinence for a limited period is not beneficial, for he practised that himself, taking the Nazirite vow as we have already observed: he is condemning those who forbid certain types of food or drink absolutely. In the same passage St Paul condemns those 'who forbid marriage', as if all marriage were sinful; on the contrary, as he tells the Corinthians, 'each man should have his own wife and each woman her own husband' (I Corinthians 7:2). Yet continence for a limited period may be beneficial (I Corinthians 7:5), and in a dramatic break with both Jewish and pagan expectations, he proclaims that there can be a praiseworthy vocation to the unmarried state (I Corinthians 7:7–8).

With regard to drink, St Paul bids St Timothy, 'no longer drink only water, but use a little wine for the sake of your stomach and your frequent ailments' (I Timothy 5:23). The blessing of Judah by Jacob includes the blessing of wine, 'His eyes shall be red with wine and his teeth white with milk' (Genesis 49:12). Wine is good, all nourishing foods are good, marriage is holy: it is wrong to say otherwise, indeed a most serious heresy constantly condemned by the Church. The virtue of mortification or continence is that by which we refrain from what is in itself good for the sake of what is better—the Gospel, the Kingdom of Heaven. In other words, fasting and abstinence is not by *precept*, not something obligatory on all Christians because the opposite is sinful, but by *counsel*, something strongly recommended as a means of advancing in the pursuit of perfection. (Except, of course, when fasting or abstinence are imposed on us by *precept* of the Church.)

If we fail to notice the difference between precept and counsel in the Gospels, we will be unable to make sense of much of Our Lord's teaching. When he reminds the rich young man of the commandments, 'You shall not kill, You shall not commit adultery, You shall not steal,' and so on, these are precepts binding on everyone. His specific invitation is to that specific young man, made clearer if we use the old English singular forms, 'if thou wouldst be perfect, go, sell what thou possessest, and give to the poor, and thou wilt have treasure in heaven; and come, follow me' (Matthew 19:18, 21). That is a counsel, for one person, not binding on everyone. (After all if everyone tried to sell what they owned, there would be no one to buy!) There is a long catalogue of saints who have heard these words and understood them to apply to themselves, but they have never dared to disparage those who did not hear that specific call. There have been a few deviant groups who did try to make these counsels obligatory on all Christians—the Church was quick to clarify the truth. Perhaps there have been more who fail to see the value of the evangelical counsels in anyone's life, and thereby close their ears to a large portion of the Gospel.

Christian fasting, like all means of mortification, is a response to the call 'If you would be perfect'. It means in the first instance reducing the quantity or refinement of our food, exercising self-restraint in order to tame our natural appetites. Abstinence means refraining from eating meat, or drinking wine, not because we consider them wrong in themselves, but because we have a greater good in view. Both fasting and abstinence are for certain times and seasons only, for the tradition of the Church has ever been to follow a fast with a feast. After forty days of Lent follows fifty days of Easter, after four weeks of Advent come forty days of Christmas. An early Church council went so far as to say that 'He who fasts on a Sunday is not a Catholic' (Carthage IV, AD 398, canon 64; Mansi III, col. 956).

St John Cassian, as always, has sensible practical advice to give on fasting:

> When it comes to fasting, it is not easy to observe a common discipline, since our physical strength varies, and such strength cannot be produced by sheer will-power, as in the case of other virtues. It is because it does not depend on mental effort alone but requires the cooperation of the body, that we have come to agree on the following rule which was handed down to us: the time, manner and quantity of food should be varied according to physical strength, age and sex, whereas all alike can observe a common rule of self-denial to strengthen the mind and steel the soul. Not everyone is able to prolong the fast all week, but they can put off eating for three days or perhaps two. Many, enfeebled through sickness, or particularly through old age, cannot even endure to fast one day until sundown without great discomfort. Not for all is it enough to eat steeped vegetables, nor can everyone endure to live on nothing but leeks, and it is not universally acceptable to eat dry bread. One man may find that he can eat two pounds of bread without feeling full, whereas another may be glutted with one pound or even six ounces. Nevertheless there is one goal in mind, that no one should be sated and burdened with having eaten his fill. It is not just the quality of food but also its quantity which can blunten the point of the soul, and when the mind is fattened with the flesh it kindles a dangerously fiery spark of vice.
>
> *Monastic Institutes*, V, 5

Fasting, therefore, varies with the individual. That is why St Benedict recommends a choice of dishes in the refectory, 'on account of individual infirmities', and the abbot may permit more food for those who have heavier work, and the use of meat for those who are very weak (*RB* 39). Two things are to be observed: one is that we may fast by reducing the sheer quantity of what we eat and drink, the other is that we may reduce the quality, and be contented with plain ordinary fare.

Cassian continues:

> The opinion of the Fathers is very true and admirable, that the standard of fasting and self-denial depends on moderation in abstinence and penance. The common goal of perfect virtue for all is that in eating the food which we need to sustain our bodies, we check ourselves while still hungry. No matter how frail someone may be physically, he can acquire as much virtue as the sturdy and healthy, if he mortifies the mental desires which his weak body is incapable of fulfilling. St Paul says, 'do not worry about the body and its urgings' (Romans 13:14). He is not totally prohibiting care for the body, but prevents us from giving in to its passions. He prohibits luxurious pampering of the flesh, but does not exclude necessary care for life. The former, lest we tumble into vile and passionate practices through pandering to the flesh; the latter lest the body, weakened by our fault, be unable to carry out its necessary and religious work.
>
> *Monastic Institutes*, V, 8

The alternation of fast and feast has its own dangers. We are not to go to extremes in either direction, otherwise any benefit we might have gained will be lost at once. 'No matter how strict the fasting, if it is followed by over indulgence, it is useless, and much more likely to lead to the sin of gluttony. It is better to eat a sensible amount every day than to keep occasional severe prolonged fasts. Unreasonable fasting has been known not only to weaken the will, but even to make it impossible to pray, when the body is so enfeebled' (*Monastic Institutes*, V, 9).

A third point to notice is that self-denial can very usefully be practised simply by keeping strictly to set meal-times. 'Let no one venture to take any food or drink before the appointed hour or afterwards', says St Benedict (*RB* 43). Cassian expands on this: 'That is why a monk who aspires to the interior conflict must first of all take this precaution, that he be not enticed by the enjoyment of any food or drink to indulge himself in partaking alone, away from the table, before the proper procession at the time for the common meal. Nor, when the meal is over, should he allow himself to take the least morsel. In the same way he should observe the statutory hours and period of sleep' (*Monastic Institutes*, V, 20).

So in our practice of mortification we can fast in three ways. One is simply to take less food than our appetite suggests. That can easily be done, even when eating in company—as dishes are passed round, one simply dips in the spoon one time less. The second is to be less fussy about the quality and nature of our food. Again, even when dining in company it is perfectly easy to exercise self-restraint— taking the portion nearest to us on the dish instead of looking for the most interesting, or refraining from adding some sauce or condiment. And the third method of fasting is to be scrupulous about not eating between meals. Even in a closely regulated community, those who work in the kitchen or the garden have plenty of opportunity for exercising this sort of mortification.

Now all this about fasting and self-denial in matters of food and drink can look remarkably similar to the totally secular pursuit of health and beauty. In fact in the modern world, if people notice us being sparing in our diet, they will take it for granted that it is out of concern for our figure. In other words they will assume we fast out of vanity. And that misunderstanding is an excellent mortification in its own right! It is nothing new: many of the great spiritual writers of the past, beginning with St Paul, have drawn attention to the similarity between Christian mortification and sports training. Indeed the Greek for training, *askesis*, has become our word asceticism. The difference is, 'they do it to receive a perishable wreath, but we an imperishable' (I Corinthians 9:25).

Self-restraint must also be exercised in matters of ownership and property. Again, the pursuit of perfection may involve the voluntary acceptance of utter poverty, but that is a counsel, not a precept. And 'poverty' of course has two distinct meanings in the Christian tradition. One is community of possessions, 'no one said that any of the things which he possessed was his own, but they had everything in common.' As a result, 'there was not a needy person among them' (Acts 4:34). Community of possessions is not incompatible with a very comfortable life indeed, as some French convents demonstrated in the eighteenth century. But even there, the principle of mortification is not lost, for the use of anything depends not on the will of the individual but of the community, expressed through the superior. Poverty also, of course, can mean being content with very little in the way of material goods, living among 'the poorest of the poor', as was the ideal of such modern saints as Teresa of Calcutta. That sort of poverty can be practised without being a member of any community, without vows, as in the case of such originals as John Bradburne. St Philip Neri was very insistent on poverty in the latter sense, encouraging his followers to live simply, and to account for everything they spent because all they had really belonged to the poor, but the same saint was equally insistent that his followers should not take any vow of poverty, but should 'possess what they have'.

Of Our Lord's Apostles, it was Judas who was especially exercised in this virtue of poverty, and in this he failed. St John tells us that the Apostles had a common purse, in other words that they already practised some sort of community of possessions, but it was Judas who kept the purse, and 'used to take what was put in it' (John 12:6). From that it was but a small step to demanding thirty pieces of silver, 'the lordly price at which I was paid off by them'. Too late, Judas remembered the Scriptures, that passage from Zechariah, and tried to fulfil the prophecy, 'So I took the thirty shekels of silver and cast them into the treasury in the house of the LORD' (Zechariah 11:13). But it was too late, the treasury would not accept them, the money cannot be given back (Matthew 27:3–10).

An important part of our mortification must be restraining the desire of riches. Judah counselled his sons, 'I command you, my sons, not to love money ... My children, the love of money leads to idolatry, for those who are deceived by money call non-existent beings "gods"—avarice makes those who possess her fall into ecstacy through money—I lost my sons [i.e. Er and Onan], and were it not for the penance (*metanoia*) to which I subjected my flesh, and the prayers of Jacob my father, I would have had to die childless.' (*T.Jud* 19) Here the author is clearly quoting St Paul, 'covetousness, which is idolatry' (Colossians 3:5), although he is careful to choose slightly different words so as not to break the fiction that this is an ancient patriarch writing.

All the Church Fathers, and the early monastic authors, agree that the purpose of penance and mortification is to enable us to strengthen our will so that we can deny ourselves, take up the Cross and follow Jesus (Luke 9:23). By restraining our desires for what is lawful, we strengthen our will to avoid what is unlawful. In the great days of monasticism, this mortification was expressed chiefly through self-restraint in food, drink, and material possessions, to which we must add denying oneself sleep, in watching and vigils.

More direct means of mortification are viewed with suspicion by many of the saints, even though 'sackcloth and ashes' are so frequently mentioned in the Scriptures. Cassian, for instance, does not recommend the hair-shirt:

> A shirt of coarse hair, worn in an ostentatious manner for all to see, cannot bring any spiritual benefit, and in fact is a cause of pride; moreover it is a positive hindrance to the carrying out of necessary work (which a monk should always be ready and willing to do) and should never be allowed. Even if we do hear of some worthy men who wore hairshirts, it should not therefore be countenanced by us in a monastic rule, nor should the ancient decisions of the Fathers be set aside just because a few men, relying on the privilege of special virtues, can perform things which are different from the general custom without being blamed for it. For the common universal custom should not be set aside or condemned because of the opinion of a few. Our unwavering trust should be placed in, and our unhesitating obedience should always be given to, those customs and rules which derive from antiquity and the majority of the holy Fathers, handed on in an undisputed tradition, not those introduced by the whim of a minority.
>
> *Monastic Institutes*, I, 2

This brings us immediately to the important paradox that self-denial can often turn out to be a form of wilfulness. So far from subduing our will and desires, if we choose special penances for ourselves, and cling to them obstinately, we are not exercising obedience at all, but quite the opposite. For this reason a great many ascetic authors emphasise that no one should ever undertake any unusual form of penance without the express permission of their superior or confessor, and that they should be ready immediately to leave it off when commanded to do so. It is told of St Simeon Stylites that his bishop had heard of his extraordinary way of life perched on a column, and came in person to order him down. The saint immediately began to descend, whereupon the bishop called up that he was satisfied with this prompt obedience, and the stylite might continue to live on his pillar. Fasting and self-denial may be a sublimated form of self-will and selfishness. This was noticed by the prophet Zechariah: 'Then the word of the LORD of hosts came to me: Say to all the people of the land and the priests, When you fasted and mourned in the fifth month and in the seventh, for those seventy years, was it for me that you fasted? And when you eat and when you drink, do you not eat for yourselves and drink for yourselves?' (Zechariah 7:4–6)

St Philip Neri, who read Cassian diligently, constantly repeated to his followers that what was necessary above all was the mortification of the will, and of the understanding, *mortificazione del' razionale*. He would tap his forehead and say that all the perfection of man lay in the space of three inches, if you but mortify the understanding. Many stories are told about how he would give his penitents extraordinary and bizarre mortifications, designed to help them control their desires, rather than to boost their sense of self-importance by carrying out the traditional penances. In his time everyone expected religious people to 'take the discipline', to wear hair-shirts, and to fast ostentatiously. St Philip used such things only in strict moderation. He was much more likely to bid a fashionable young man carry his revolting dog, Capriccio, through the streets, or to help him move his household cooking equipment from his previous residence to the new Oratory church. One dignified scholar was sent on a fool's errand to buy a tiny quantity of wine in a huge flask, other pompous youths were led through the streets munching away on huge slices of cake which the saint thrust upon them. The result was that when he asked them to do serious works of charity, such as carrying a beggar to the hospital, they were prompt to do it.

Above all, St Philip, and his disciple St Francis de Sales, stress the value of embracing the mortifications which come upon us in the course of daily life. Acceptance of the will of God is most perfectly expressed by accepting those innumerable inconveniences, difficulties, obstacles and pains that are inflicted upon us every day. Rather than trying to construct comfortable crosses to fit our own requirements, we have to take up the cross which is laid on our shoulders by other people, by our health, by the weather, by the circumstances of daily life. Rather than inventing new and peculiar ways of mortifying ourselves, we should be careful to observe all the provisions of our state of life. We should not be so careful about our own health and welfare that we readily dispense ourselves from our common obligations.

Remember St Teresa's shrewd observation, 'directly we fancy our head aches, we stop away from choir which would not kill us either. One day we are absent because it aches, the next because it has ached, and three more lest it should ache again; but we love to invent penances for ourselves' (*Way of Perfection*, X, 5). She displays a great deal of common sense in her advice about mortification and penance. 'The body possesses this defect—the more you give it the more it requires. It is wonderful how fond it is of comfort, and what pretexts it will offer to obtain it, however little needed ... Believe me, my daughters, when once we begin to subdue our wretched bodies, they do not trouble us so much' (*Way of Perfection*, XI, 2,3).

If all this is true of bodily inconveniences, it is even more true of the mortification of the mind and understanding. St Teresa continues, 'Why do we draw back from interior mortification, which is the mainspring of all the rest? ... Be most watchful over your secret feelings, especially such as concern precedence ... When such thoughts arise in your minds, you must suppress them at once ... God deliver us from people who try to serve Him yet who care for their honour or fear disgrace' (*Way of Perfection*, XII, 1,3–4,7).

There is a wonderful agreement on these matters among the saints of every generation. All recommend mortification, particularly interior mortification, particularly in the shape of making a virtue of necessity. The end result must always be a greater degree of docility and self-denial;

any 'penance' which makes us wilful and disobedient is no more than sublimated selfishness.

That is why St Benedict included the obscure quotation, 'Self-will hath its punishment, but necessity wins a crown' (*RB* 7; D. Justin McCann tells us it is from the Acts of Saints Agape, Chionia and Irene, or from the fourth-century St Optatus of Milevis). If we submit to necessity, and mortify our self-will by willingly accepting what is necessary, then there is a crown awaiting us.

Judah concludes his long *Testament* with a directly Christian prophecy:

24. And after these things there shall arise for you a star from Jacob in peace, and there shall stand up a Man of my line, like the sun of righteousness. He shall walk in company with the sons of men in humility and righteousness, and no sort of sin shall be detected in Him. And the heavens shall be opened above Him, pouring out the Spirit, the blessing of the Father of holiness. And He Himself shall pour out the Spirit of charity upon you, and you shall be to Him as sons in truth, walking in His precepts both first and last. He is the child of God most high, He is the fountain of life for all flesh. Then the sceptre of my kingship shall shine forth, and from your root a scion shall grow. In Him shall arise a rod of righteousness for the Gentiles, to judge and to save all those who call on the name of the Lord.

25. After that Abraham, Isaac and Jacob will rise again to life, as will I and my brothers the princes, and we shall wield the sceptres in Israel. Levi first, then I, Joseph third, Benjamin fourth, Simeon fifth, Issachar sixth, and so all of us in order. And the Lord will bless Levi; the Angel of his presence will bless me, the powers of glory Simeon, the heavens Reuben, the earth Issachar, the sea Zabulun, the mountains Joseph, the Tabernacle Benjamin, the lights Dan, the food Naphtali, the sun Gad, the olive Asher. There will be a single people of the Lord, and a single language, and there will no longer be among you a spirit of deceit from the devil, for he shall be thrown into the fire for ever. Those who died in sorrow shall rise in joy, those who were poor for the Lord's sake will be enriched, those in want will be satisfied, those in weakness strengthened, and those who died for the sake of the Lord shall be awakened into life. The harts of Jacob shall course in gladness, the eagles of Israel soar for joy. But the impious will weep, and sinners lament, and all the nations will give glory to the Lord for ever.

There can be no doubt that this passage is full of clear references to the Gospel, as well as well-known Old Testament texts like the prophecy of Isaiah, that 'there shall come forth a shoot from the stump of Jesse, and a branch shall grow out of his roots' (Isaiah 11:1). We hear of Christ's baptism, when the 'heavens opened' (Matthew 3:16), and of His pouring out the Holy Spirit on his disciples (John 20:22); as well as the affirmation that Abraham, Isaac and Jacob, are alive (Matthew 22:32). We may observe that if the *Testaments of the Twelve Patriarchs* is really a pre-Christian book, these two whole paragraphs must be an addition, but it seems to fit better if we accept that the book is entirely early Christian in its present form, even if it does draw on a lost earlier composition.
   And so at last Judah ends:

26. Keep the whole of the law of the Lord, my children, for there is hope for everyone who walks straight in his way. And Judah said to them, Today I am dying in your presence, at the age of one hundred and nineteen. Let none of you bury me in precious garments, or cut open my body, for that is the manner in which they bury reigning kings. Take me with you to Hebron where my fathers lie. So saying, Judah died, and his sons did for him exactly as he had requested, and buried him in Hebron with his fathers.

Step Three

MODESTY

The Patriarch Levi, Prophet Obadiah and Apostle Matthew

Behold, to obey is better than sacrifice (I Samuel 15:22)

'The third degree of humility is that a man for the love of God subject himself to his superior in all obedience, imitating the Lord, of whom the apostle says: *He was made obedient even unto death*' (*RB* 7). Cassian also makes this his third step, 'if we act never at our own will but at our master's bidding, listening to his commands eagerly and willingly' (*Monastic Institutes*, IV, 39).

It has never been easy to submit our own will to the will of another, or even to the Will of God, and people have always found excuses to justify themselves in refusing obedience. From the very beginning the cry of revolt went up, 'I will not serve'. The primaeval sin of Adam was the refusal to obey God's word in one small matter, so very small, so trivial—but that refusal to obey led very swiftly to the murder of Abel, and the sevenfold vengeance for Cain, and the wickedness of the men of the First Age that provoked the Deluge. From small beginnings, how quickly great things grow.

In the time of Moses, too, the people were quick to rebel, to disobey God. Moses gave them innumerable little details of ritual, countless ways in which they could exercise the virtue of obedience, yet tested in these things they fell away quickly. They rebelled against the authority of Moses, as did even his own brother and sister (Numbers 12); they refused to accept that the priesthood was for God to dispose, in the time of Korah, Dathan and Abiram (Numbers 16); they rejected outright the liberation God had given them and attempted to return to slavery (Numbers 14); and it all led to serious idolatry, from the worship of the Golden Calf (Exodus 32) to the endless wandering away after the Baals and the Astartes throughout the history of the Judges and the Kings.

The model for our obedience is the obedience of Christ Himself, the subjection of the will of the Son of God to that of the Father. When Our Lord addresses the crowd at Capernaum, he begins to introduce them to the idea of his relationship to the Father. 'All that the Father gives me will come to me; and him who comes to me I will not cast out. For I have come down from heaven, not to do my own will, but the will of him who sent me; and this is the will of him who sent me, that I should lose nothing of all that he has given me, but raise it up at the last day. For this is the will of the Father, that everyone who sees the Son and believes in him should have eternal life; and I will raise him up at the last day' (John 6:37–40). At the end, we overhear Our Lord's prayer of submission to the will of his Father in the garden; 'not what I will, but what thou wilt' (Mark 14:36).

The Epistle to the Hebrews says, 'he offered up prayers and supplications, with loud cries and tears, to him who was able to save him from death, and he was heard for his godly fear' (Hebrews 5:7). We are amazed that it says that he was heard, for he was not delivered from suffering the pangs of death, but the point is that he was delivered from death itself. He 'became obedient unto death, even death on a cross. Therefore God has highly exalted him and bestowed on him the name which is above every name' (Philippians 2:9). It is through his obedience, his submission to the will of the Father, that he came to the Resurrection. The Epistle to the Hebrews goes so far as to say that, in his humanity, Christ actually had to learn obedience, although in his divinity He is equal with the Father: 'Although He was a Son, he learned obedience through what he suffered' (Hebrews 5:8).

The relationship between the Father and the Son, within the Holy Trinity, is impossible for us to comprehend, but it is clear from these passages that no opposition can be set up between the will of the Father and of the Son, as if the Father wished to destroy humanity and the Son undertook to save them, nor is there any conflict between the human will of Christ in his humanity, and the divine will of the Son of God in his divinity. Moreover we know what the will of the Father is: he 'desires all men to be saved' (I Timothy 2:4). Christ came 'not to judge the world but to save the world' (John 12:47).

Our salvation is given to us by God, if only we accept it. Our acceptance of that salvation must involve our own submission to the will of God. It is useless claiming that we have faith, if we refuse to obey. 'Why do you call me "Lord, Lord", and not do what I tell you?' (Luke 6:46) Our obedience is tested in little things, but these lead us straight on to the 'weightier matters of the Law', all 'summed up in this sentence, "You shall love your neighbour as yourself"' (Romans 13:9). Even the smallest acts of obedience can be important. In the Law of Moses the LORD says more than once that you must obey not only the laws and commandments but even the customs of God's people (eg. Deuteronomy 4–5). In every community, in every family and place of work, there are innumerable little unwritten customs; none of them are in themselves of any importance, but if people deliberately ignore them or oppose them it damages the entire community and demonstrates that the person in question is not really trying to be one with the others. But on the other hand, 'You have been faithful over a little, I will set you over much' (Matthew 25:21).

The *Testament of Levi* is largely dedicated to the virtue of obedience, and to warning against that pride which is the greatest enemy of obedience. The Levites were set apart in the Law of Moses as the tribe who were to be dedicated to the ritual of the Tabernacle, and later of the Temple. They were to have no lot or share in the distribution, for the LORD Himself was their lot; conversely they were the portion or lot assigned to the LORD out of the people of Israel. The choice was not theirs, but that of God alone. He singled out the tribe from among its brothers; he singled out the family of Aaron from among the Levite clans to hold the priesthood. No one takes the priesthood on himself, but it is given to him by God. When the Old Testament priesthood failed, ending with priests like Annas and Caiaphas, God raised up a new priesthood, 'according to the Order of Melchizedek'. The new priesthood also is conferred 'not by the will of the flesh nor of the will of man but of God' (John 1:13), upon those that God chooses. They too are to be marked by obedience to the rite, conformed to the image of Christ who was obedient unto death, serving the 'altar from which those who serve the tent have no right to eat' (Hebrews 13:10).

However the Testament of Levi begins with the disreputable story of how he and his brothers treacherously slaughtered the men of Shechem (Genesis 34). Levi tries to excuse himself by saying he was barely twenty at the time, but the blessing of Jacob on the two of them together is more like a curse: 'Simeon and Levi are brothers; weapons of violence are their swords. O my soul, come not into their council; O my spirit, be not joined to their company; for in their anger they slay men, and in their wantonness they hamstring oxen. Cursed be their anger, for it is fierce; and their wrath, for it is cruel! I will divide them in Jacob and scatter them in Israel' (Genesis 49:5–7). Nothing much here about obedience or service! But the fulfilment of the prophecy about scattering them in Israel is that the Levites are spread throughout the twelve tribes as priests and ministers of the ritual.

1. A transcript of the words of Levi, which he delivered to his sons concerning all that they were to do, and all that would happen to them until the Day of Judgment. He was still in good health when he called them to himself, for it had been revealed to him that he was about to die. When they had assembled, he said to them:

2. I, Levi, was conceived in Haran, and I was born there; after that I came with my father into Shechem. I was a young man, around twenty years old, when I and Simeon wrought vengeance for our sister Dinah, against Hamor. When we were pasturing our flock in Abel-Meholah, the spirit of understanding came upon me from the Lord, and I saw that all men conceal their ways and that wickedness is built up upon walls (cf. Psalm 54:11–12) and lawlessness sits upon towers. And I grieved over the race of mankind, and I besought the Lord that I might save them. Then a sleep came over me, and I saw a high mountain, which is the mountain of the Shield in Abel-Meholah. And behold, the heavens opened, and the angel of the Lord said to me, 'Levi, Levi, enter!' And so I entered, from the first heaven into the second, and I saw that there was water, suspended between the one and the other. And I saw a third heaven, shining much brighter than the other two, and its height was boundless. And I said to the angel,

'Why is it thus?' And the angel said to me, 'Be not astonished at these things, for you will see four heavens more, brighter still and without comparison, when you ascend thither. For you will stand near the Lord, and you will be his minister, and declare his mysteries to men, and announce the liberation that is to come upon Israel. The Lord will appear among men through you and through Judah, in whom he shall save the entire human race. Your livelihood shall be from the portion of the Lord, and he will be for you field and vineyard, harvest, gold and silver.

3. 'Now hear about the seven heavens. The lowest one is the most gloomy, for it observes all the unrighteousness of men. The second has fire, snow and ice, prepared for the day of the Lord's command and the just judgment of God. In this abide all the spirits that punish sins and set them right. In the third are the Powers of the array drawn up for the Day of Judgment, to do justice on the spirits of deceit and on the devil. In the fourth heaven above the others are the Holy Ones, since in the upper part of all things abides the great glory in the Holy of Holies, above all holiness. In the next heaven after that are the angels before the face of the Lord, ministering to him and making satisfaction for all the errors of the just ones. They offer to the Lord the sweet-smelling and reasonable sacrifice, and the Bloodless Offering. In the heaven above that, are the angels who carry the responses to those Angels who stand before the face of the Lord. And in the one above that are the Thrones and the Dominations, and here they offer hymns to God for ever. For when the Lord looks upon us, we are all shaken; the heavens and the earth and the depths tremble before the face of his mightiness. Yet the sons of men take no notice of all this, they commit sins, and provoke the anger of the Most High.

4. 'So now, learn that the Lord will give judgment on the sons of men, when the rocks are shattered and the sun refuses its light, the waters are dried up and the fire sinks into ashes, when all creation is thrown into confusion and the invisible spirits fade away, and

hell is despoiled by the Passion of the Most High (cf. Colossians
2:15). Those men who refuse to believe will remain in their sins,
and because of that they will be condemned to punishment. But
the Most High has heard your prayer, to deliver you from sin and
constitute you his son, his servant, the minister before his face.
As a shining light of wisdom you will shine upon Jacob, you will
be like the sun for all the seed of Israel. To you will be given the
blessing, as to all your sons, until the Lord shall look upon all the
nations in the compassion of his son, for ever (cf. Luke 1:78). But
it is your sons who will lay their hands on Him, and crucify Him.
That is why you are given counsel and understanding to instruct
your children about Him. For they who bless Him shall be blessed,
while they who curse Him shall be destroyed.'

5.   And with that the angel opened the gates of heaven for me.
And I saw the holy temple, and the Most High upon his throne
of glory. And he said to me, 'Levi, to you have I given the blessing
of the priesthood, until I come and dwell in the midst of Israel.'
Then the angel brought me to the earth, and gave me a shield
and sword, and said to me, 'Wreak justice in Shechem on behalf
of Dinah, and I will be with you, for the Lord has sent me.' And
I put an end to the sons of Hamor on that day, as it is written
in the tablets of the Fathers. And I said to him, 'I beg you Lord,
reveal to me your name, so that I may invoke you in the day of
distress.' He said, 'I am the Angel who intercedes for the race of
Israel (cf. Daniel 12:78), so that they may not be struck down for
ever, although every wicked spirit is arrayed against them.' And
after that I awoke, and I blessed the Most High and the Angel who
intercedes for the race of Israel and for all the just.

6.   When I went back to my father, I found a bronze shield, which
is why the name of that mountain is the Shield; it is near Gebal,
to the right of Abila. And I kept these words in my heart. After
that, I took counsel with my father and my brother Reuben,
to say to the sons of Hamor that they should be circumcised,
for I was zealous about the abomination which they had done

against Israel. I began by killing Shechem, and Simeon killed Hamor. Then our brothers came and destroyed their city with the edge of the sword. Our father heard of this and was angry, distressed because they were killed although they had accepted circumcision, though in his blessings he overlooked this. We were wrong to act without his knowledge, for he was ill on the day that it happened, but I knew that God had given sentence to punish Shechem, for they had desired to do to Sarah and to Rebecca what they had done to Dinah our sister, but it was the Lord who prevented them. They had pursued our father Abraham when he was a stranger, and they had exhausted his flocks which had multiplied. Also they had treated Jeblah outrageously, he who was born in Abraham's house. Indeed they treated all strangers like that, seizing their women by force, and making them apostatise. The wrath of God came upon them (cf. I Thessalonians 2:16) and endures for ever.

7. And I said to my father, 'Be not angry, sir, for in you the Lord will bring the Chanaanites to nothing, and he will give their land to you and to your descendants after you. From now on Shechem will be known as the city of the unwise, for we shall mock them as one mocks a fool, for they acted foolishly against Israel when they defiled our sister.' So we brought our sister Dinah away from there, and took her with us to Bethel.

8. After we had passed seventy days there, once again I saw a vision like the one before. I saw seven men in white garments, who said to me, 'Arise and put on the stole of your priesthood, the crown of righteousness and the rational of understanding, the tunicle of truth and the cap of faith, the mitre of the sign and the ephod of prophecy.' Then each one of them brought these things in turn, and placed them upon me, saying, 'From now onwards be a priest of the Lord, you and your descendants for ever.' And the first one anointed me with the sacred chrism, and gave me the sceptre of judgment. The second washed me with clean water and gave me a morsel of bread, with wine, that which is Holy. And he

placed the holy and glorious stole around me. The third placed a
linen garment like an ephod upon me. The fourth girded me with
a girdle, like one of purple. The fifth gave me a branch of olive,
the fruit of fatness. The sixth placed a crown upon my head. The
seventh placed the diadem of priesthood on my head and put
the sacrificial offering into my hands, to make me a priest for the
Lord. And they said to me, 'Levi, your descendants shall be divided
into three principalities, as a sign of the glory of the Lord who is
to come. The first, after he has come to believe, will be the great
Portion, and there shall be none above him. The second will be for
the priesthood. The third will be called by a new name, for a king
shall arise from Judah and he will set up a new priesthood, after
the style of the nations, and for all the nations. His appearing will
be unexpected, as a prophet of the Most High from the seed of
Abraham our father. All that is desirable in Israel shall be for you
and your seed; you shall eat all that is delightful to see, and your
descendants shall set in order the table of the Lord. From them
shall come high priests, judges and scribes, for that which is Holy
will be received at their words.' And I awoke and understood that
this vision was similar to the other. I hid all these things also in
my heart and did not reveal them to any man on earth.

9.   After two days Judah and I went to see Isaac our grandfather,
with our father Jacob, and my father's father blessed me using
the same words as in the vision which I had seen. But he was not
willing to return with us to Bethel. When we did come back to
Bethel, our father Jacob had a dream about me and saw that I was
to be a priest for them. Rising in the morning he made his whole
offering of tithes to the Lord through me.

Now we begin to hear about the choice of the Levites for the liturgy,
which is to be their destiny for the remainder of the Old Testament.
At the end of the book of Deuteronomy, Moses does mention their
liturgical role, 'Give to Levi thy Thummim, and thy Urim to the godly
one', but the reason is that 'he disowned his brothers, and ignored
his children', referring to the second time the Levites appear in brutal

and violent guise, when Moses let them loose among the rebellious children of Israel after the making of the Golden Calf, bidding them 'slay every man his brother, and every man his companion, and every man his neighbour' (Exodus 32:25–28). Nevertheless their obedience on that occasion is commended, 'For they observed thy word and kept thy covenant.' They have obeyed Moses even when his command was bloodthirsty and cruel; that then entitles them to teach obedience to others. 'They shall teach Jacob thy ordinances, and Israel thy law; they shall put incense before thee, and whole burnt offering upon thy altar' (Deuteronomy 33:9–10).

And so we came to Hebron, to live there, and Isaac called me at once so that he could instruct me in the Law of the Lord, as the angel had shown me. He taught me the law of holiness, of sacrifices, holocausts, first-fruits, sin offerings and peace offerings. He continued to instruct me every day, and he persisted in saying to me, 'Beware of the spirit of fornication, for it will long endure and will defile the holy things with your seed. Take yourself a wife while you are still young—one with no blemish, undefiled—not of foreign or pagan birth. Before you go into the Sanctuary, wash, and while sacrificing rinse your hands, do so again after you have completed the sacrifice. Bring to the Lord twelve trees which always have leaves, as Abraham taught me to do. Offer sacrifice to the Lord of all clean beasts and clean birds, and of all your first fruits and the first pressings of the vine; offer them to the Lord your God, and every sacrifice you shall salt with salt.'

10. Now therefore observe whatever I command you, my sons, for I have passed on to you as much as I heard from my fathers. I am guiltless of all your wickedness and the offence which you will work against the Christ, the Saviour of the World when the ages have run their course, when you will lead Israel astray, and stir up against him great woes before the Lord. You will sin, along with Israel, so that Jerusalem will not be able to endure the sight of your wickedness. But the veil of the Temple will be rent in two, so that it cannot conceal your abominations. You shall be scattered, taken captive among the nations, and you shall be a reproach, and a curse, and trampled underfoot among them. But every house which the Lord may choose shall be called Jerusalem, as is found in the book of the righteous man Enoch.

11. I was twenty-eight when I married a wife, whose name was Melchah. She conceived and bore a son, and I called him Gersam, for we were but sojourners in our own land. (Gersam means 'sojourn.') However I discerned that he was not of the first class. Kaath was born in my thirty-fifth year, at sunrise. In a dream I saw that he would stand in the midst of the highest ones of the assembly. That is why I called him Kaath, which means 'the beginning of greatness' and 'instruction.' And she bore me a third son, Merari, in the fortieth year of my life. Since his mother had a difficult birth of him, I called him Merari, which means 'pains.' And he himself has died. My daughter Jochabed was born in Egypt, when I was sixty-four, and at that time I was honoured in the midst of my brothers.

12. Gersam took a wife, and by her he had issue, Lomni and Semei. The sons of Kaath were Abram, Isachar, Chebron, and Oziel. The sons of Merari were Mooli and Moishe. When I was ninety-four, Abram took my daughter Jochabed as wife, for they were born on the same day, he and my daughter. I was eight years old when we entered Chanaan; I was eighteen when I killed Shechem. At the age of nineteen I became a priest, and at twenty-eight I married my wife. I was forty when we came into Egypt—now see, my children you are the third generation. Joseph died when I was an hundred and eighteen.

The genealogy of Levi is important for Old Testament worship, and is given in much greater detail in the first book of Chronicles (I Chronicles 6). (The three sons are now more normally spelt Gershom, Kohath and Merari.) From Levi alone are descended all the priests and their assistants who conduct the incredibly complicated ritual of temple sacrifice, ritual which had to be followed in complete obedience.

13. And now, my sons, I command you to fear the Lord your God from all your heart, and walk in simplicity of heart in all his law. Teach your children to read, that they may have understanding in all their life, reading ceaselessly the Law of God. For everyone who knows the Law of the Lord will be honoured, and will not be a stranger wherever he goes. Many friends he will find, as well as his family, and many men will be eager to serve him and to hear the Law from his lips. Do what is right, my children, while you are on earth, and you will find righteousness in heaven, you will have treasure in heaven. Plant good things during your mortal life, that you may reap them in eternity. But if you plant evil things, you will harvest total grief and distress. Acquire wisdom diligently, in the fear of God, for if there should come a time of captivity, when cities and countryside are destroyed, when gold and silver and all possessions are lost, no one can take away the wisdom of a wise man, unless he be blinded by impiety and maimed by sin. If a man guards himself from such evil things, wisdom shall be to him a light amidst his enemies, and a fatherland on foreign soil, and a friend in the midst of his foes. Whosoever teaches good things, and puts them into practice, will be enthroned beside kings, as happened to our brother Joseph.

14. But now, my children, I have discovered in the writings of Enoch that at the End of the Ages you will become sinners against the Lord, and will lay violent hands on him in utter wickedness; your brothers will be ashamed of you, and you will be an object of scorn for all the pagans. Our father Israel will be clean from all the impiety of the chief priests who will lay their hands on the Saviour of the world. For as the sun is pure in the sight of the Lord and above the earth, so you should be the lights of Israel, like the sun and the moon. If you are made dark by your wickedness, what is there for the Gentiles, who live in darkness? You will bring a curse upon our nation, on whose behalf was given the Light of the Law, to be the light of every man, you will attempt to destroy Him, and so will teach commandments that are contrary to the laws of God. You will plunder the sacrifices of the Lord and you will appropriate the best portions, and in his despite you will eat them together with whores. In avarice you will teach the commands of the Lord, you will defile married women and deflower the virgins of Jerusalem; you will consort with harlots and adulteresses, you will take the daughters of pagans to wife and purify them in unlawful rites; your commerce will be like that of Sodom and Gomorrah, in impiety, while you vaunt yourselves over your priesthood, not only setting yourselves above other men, but against the law of God as well. You will trample the holy things underfoot and mock at them in your arrogance.

15. That is why the Temple, which the Lord will choose, will be laid waste, through your defilement, and you will be taken captive into every nation. Despised by them, you will earn everlasting reproach and shame before the just judgment of God. All those who hate you will rejoice over your distress. Had it not been that you would find forgiveness through Abraham, Isaac and Jacob your fathers, not one of your descendants would survive upon the earth.

16. This too I have learnt from the book of Enoch, that it will be for seventy weeks that you will go astray, disgracing the priesthood and defiling the sacrifices. setting aside the law and ignoring the message of the prophets, persecuting righteous men in your perversity, hating those who are pious and despising the words of those who speak the truth. You will denounce as an imposter the Man who renews the law in the power of the Most High, and in the end you will destroy Him, as you imagine, knowing nothing of His resurrection. You will call down upon your heads that Blood which does no harm. Yet I tell you, because of Him your holy place will be made desolate, desecrated to its foundations, no place will remain clean for you but you will become a curse among the gentiles, and you will be scattered until once again He will look upon you and in his loving mercy He will welcome you through baptism into faith.

17. Now that you have heard about the seventy weeks, hear now about the priesthood. There is a priesthood at each Jubilee. In the first Jubilee, the first to be anointed to the priesthood will be great, and will speak to God as his Father. His priesthood will be full of the fear of the Lord, and in the day of his joy he will rise again as the world is saved. In the second Jubilee, the anointed one will be conceived in the grief of those whom he loves, his priesthood will be honourable, and he shall be glorified by all. The third priest will be taken up in grief. The fourth will be in sorrow, for sin will lie upon him in its fulness, and all Israel will be full of hatred, each for his neighbour. The fifth will be caught up in darkness, as will the sixth and the seventh. In the seventh priest there will be abomination such as I cannot speak, before the Lord and before men. For those who do such things will know what they are doing. That is why they will be captured and taken away. Their land and their possessions will be lost. Yet in the fifth week they will turn back to the land of their desolation, and they will renew the house of the Lord. In the seventieth week priests will appear who are idolators, fighters, seekers after money; proud, lawless and arrogant, they will be molesters of children and of beasts.

18. Then after judgment has been given against them by the Lord, the priesthood will fail, and the Lord will raise up a new Priest, in whom all the words of the Lord will be unveiled. He shall give a judgment of truth upon the earth, in the fulness of days. His star will rise in the heavens, like the Star of a King, shedding the light of knowledge as the sun illumines the day. He shall be exalted throughout the world until He is taken up. He shall shine like the sun upon the earth, and will banish all darkness from what is under heaven; He shall be peace in every land. The heavens will be glad to see his days, the earth will rejoice, the clouds exult, and the knowledge of the Lord will be poured over the earth as the waters cover the sea. The angels of glory before the face of the Lord will rejoice in Him (Matthew 17:5). Then shall the heavens be opened, and from the temple of glory sanctification will come upon Him with the voice of the Father, as came upon Isaac from his father Abraham. The glory of the Most High will be spoken over Him, the spirit of understanding and sanctification will hover over Him in the waters (Matthew 3:16–17, Luke 3:22). He shall give the greatness of the Lord to all his sons, in truth and for ever. He shall have no successor, from generation to generation for ever. Through His priesthood the Gentiles shall be filled with understanding all over the earth, and they shall be enlightened by the grace of the Lord. But Israel shall be laid low in its ignorance, and overwhelmed with darkness in grief. Through His priesthood all sin shall be wiped away; the wicked shall cease from their evil ways, and the righteous shall find rest in Him. He shall open the doors of paradise and put aside the sword that threatened Adam; He will allow the holy ones to eat of the Tree of Life, and the spirit of holiness will rest on them. The devil will be bound by him, and he will give his sons power to trample evil spirits underfoot. The Lord will rejoice in his children, and will be well pleased in those he loves, for all ages. Then Abraham, Isaac and Jacob will be glad, and I too shall rejoice and all the saints will be clothed with bliss.

19. So now, my children, you have heard it all. Choose among yourselves either darkness or light, the law of the Lord or the works of the devil! And his sons answered him, saying, We will walk before the Lord, according to his law. And their father said to them, The Lord is witness to this, and all his angels; you are witnesses, and I am a witness to the words you have spoken. And his sons said to him, We are witnesses. Thus Levi came to rest, giving these commands to his sons; he stretched out his feet upon the bed, and was gathered to his fathers after he had lived a hundred and thirty-seven years. They enclosed him in a coffin and afterwards buried him in Hebron, by the side of Abraham, Isaac and Jacob.

The book of Jubilees, like the books of Enoch already quoted, are among the many Old Testament pseudepigrapha (Charlesworth, 1983), curious writings which the Church rejected without hesitation, but which can still be interesting as background to early Christian writings.

The anger of Levi against the sons of Shechem, and the massacre after the Golden Calf, are typical of Old Testament passages which must be re-read in a spiritual sense, lest the letter kill (*cf.* II Corinthians 3:6). The Church Fathers were not slow to see this zeal as a zeal against sin, and against our own rebellious selves. 'If by the Spirit you put to death the deeds of the body, you will live', says St Paul (Romans 8:13). The practice of mortification, of submitting our will to the will of others, of crushing our pride, must be carried out ruthlessly, even though our pride and our self-will are as close to us as brother, companion and neighbour.

The Epistle to the Hebrews consistently follows this principle of looking for the spiritual meaning of an Old Testament text. Much of it is concerned with the interpretation of the old ritual law, the law of sacrifice described in Leviticus, and how it is transformed and fulfilled in Christ. Our Lord did say that 'not an iota, not a dot will pass from the law until all is accomplished' (Matthew 5:18). Every little detail of ritual has its place: in the first instance it has all been 'accomplished' once and for all in the one Sacrifice of Christ, which unites all the innumerable different sorts of sacrifice described by Moses. And then every detail has its spiritual or allegorical interpretation, so that nothing is wasted of the five books of Moses, like the five loaves in the wilderness.

That is not to say that literal sacrifice does not still have a place, for even St Paul still offered the sacrifices of the Nazirite Vow (Acts 18:18, 21:26). However what is made clear is that the ritual in itself did not take away sin or guilt—no one ever promised that it would—and those who relied on ritual alone were often blind to what Our Lord calls 'the weightier matters of the Law' (Matthew 23:23). The details of ritual come after that—important, yes, but they do not take precedence over charity. In the parable of the Good Samaritan, we remember that the Priest and Levite are being very careful to obey the ritual requirements of the Law by passing by on the other side, for if they came into contact with blood, or a dead body, they would be unable to perform their duties in the Temple, as is clearly laid down in the Law of Moses (Leviticus 21).

The reason why ritual and ceremonial are good and important is precisely because in obeying the rubrics we are practising the virtue of obedience, surrendering our own will. It is particularly tempting, in these days when the ritual has been so debased, to say that we know better, and can do things much more correctly than the liturgical books at present allow. In fact the future Pope Benedict XVI expressed the view that 'the crisis in the Church that we are experiencing today is to a large extent due to the disintegration of the liturgy' in the 1960s and 1970s (Joseph Ratzinger, *Milestones: Memoirs 1927–1977* (San Francisco), p. 148). That is because what happened then was a period of chaos and rapid transition, when carefully tended rituals were swept away without warning. Priests who had been perhaps too punctilious in observing every detail of the rite were suddenly told that these things do not matter any more. As a result they rather made a point of treating the new rules with careless disdain, lest they fall back into the old attitude of 'rubricism' which had just been condemned.

Liturgy and ceremonial became matters of the private taste of the priest (or of the nuns who ran his parish), and the instructions that came with the liturgy were treated as optional, irrelevant or oppressive. As more and more detailed instructions have appeared in the last fifteen years, they have been very largely ignored, and even denounced as attempts to stifle the freedom of the individual. Explicit instructions have not been applied, on the pretext that they do not apply in this country, or that they are not appropriate to the culture of the time.

Now once that attitude of disobedience took root with regard to liturgy, it was not long before the same principle was applied to the rest of Canon Law. Clearly stated laws were simply ignored, and overruled on the grounds that we now know better. 'Twas but a step from ignoring Canon Law to ignoring civil law, and the Law of God. The terrible revelations about the conduct of a few of the clergy during the chaotic years demonstrates that once you prove unfaithful in little things, you will very soon find yourself being unfaithful in greater. It is so easy to forget that the purpose of law is to protect the weak against the strong, and great injustices can be perpetrated in the name of liberty.

If we cultivate the virtue of obedience over little things we will have a much greater chance of being obedient in great. It we think we are too grand to obey trivial commands, we will find it very difficult to obey important ones. That is why traditional training in obedience has always begun with little things, as in Evelyn Waugh's famous example:

'My sister Cordelia's last report said that she was not only the worst girl in the school, but the worst there had ever been in the memory of the oldest nun.'

'That's because I refused to be an Enfant de Marie. Reverend Mother said that if I didn't keep my room tidier I couldn't be one, so I said, well, I won't be one, and I don't believe our Blessed Lady cares two hoots whether I put my gym shoes on the left or the right of my dancing shoes. Reverend Mother was livid.'

'Our Lady cares about obedience' (Evelyn Waugh, *Brideshead Revisited* (Harmondsworth: Penguin, 1951), p. 88).

Perhaps a more serious discussion of the virtue of obedience can be quoted from Cassian.

> Abba John, who lived near the city of Lycon in the Thebaid, through the virtue of obedience was even given the grace of prophecy, and was so universally famed that his merits became well known even to the rulers of this world. For although as we have said he lived in the most remote region of the Thebaid, the Emperor Theodosius never dared to proceed to war against his wicked enemies without taking advice of his foresight and hearing his answers. He would trust them as if he had heard them from heaven, and bring back trophies of victory from the most overwhelming foes.
>
> The same saint John served his novice-master from his youth until he was of full age, as long as the old man remained alive, and followed his commands with such humility that his obedience astounded even the superior himself. The latter wished to ascertain whether this virtue proceeded from true faith and a real simplicity of heart, or from affectation only, under duress, or for display before the superior, and so he often used to order him to do unnecessary, futile or even impossible things. I will give you three examples so you may have the opportunity of knowing how genuine was his heart and his obedience.

The old man took a stick from his woodbox, which had already been cut and got ready for the stove, and, since there had been no occasion to cook, it had not just become dry but was almost rotten through the passage of time. He stuck this into the ground before John, and ordered him to fetch water every day and irrigate it twice a day, so that through regular moistening it could take root and revive to its former growth, and its spreading branches would please the sight and provide shade in the summer's heat for those seated beneath it. The youth, with his usual devotion, took no consideration of the impossibility of the request, but carried it out daily, never failing to bring the water from about two miles away, and he never stopped watering the stick. For a whole year he allowed neither bodily illness, nor the celebration of a feastday, nor any other necessary task to give him a legitimate excuse from carrying out the command; not even the harshness of winter was able to prevent him from obeying his orders. The old man silently and secretly watched him, diligent at his daily task, and observed how he obeyed his orders in simplicity of heart, as if they had come to him from God, without so much as a grimace or a grumble. Glad at his genuine and humble obedience, he took pity on his long labour, which he had fulfulled with such devotion for a whole year. He approached the dry stick and said 'Oh, John, has this tree put out roots, or not?' When he said that he didn't know, the old man, as if investigating whether it was so, easily pulled out the stick in front of him as if testing whether the roots gave any resistance, and throwing it away ordered him to stop watering it henceforth.

So it was that, trained by this sort of exercise, the youth grew daily in this virtue of obedience, and the grace of humility was seen in him, so that the sweet savour of his docility perfumed the monastery, as it were.

Monastic Institutes, IV, 23–5

Thus far Cassian. The other two tests were of a similar nature, for Abba John was asked to throw away the only oil jar the community possessed, and afterwards to roll over an immense boulder, both of which he was prompt to attempt. Now when we first read this passage our instinct is to guess that obedience will be rewarded, that the stick will blossom and flourish, that the oil jar will be miraculously replenished, and that the boulder will obediently roll over. But none of these things happen: the exercises of obedience are as pointless as they appear to be. Not only the novice John, but the other brethren of the community must have been perfectly well aware that the novice-master was giving unreasonable commands, and at least in the case of the oil jar might have registered an indignant protest. That they do not, shows that they already understood the virtue of obedience which the novice was to learn.

That takes us immediately to the nub of what obedience means—it is obeying an authority even when we think we know better, even when we really do know better. Only then can obedience be a real virtue. If we are asked to do something which we can recognise is good and useful, we may have to grit our teeth to do it, and dislike it intensely, but there is little element of mortification or self-denial, since we know that the command is justified. When we are asked to do something which seems pointless, we can make ourselves obey cheerfully trusting that there is a good reason for it and that we shall discover that in due course. But when we are told to do something that really is pointless, futile or even destructive, then self-denial and mortification can begin to bite.

It is the same when we are asked to obey a lawful command even if it tells us to refrain from doing something good. We may have great ideas and plausible plans for the good of the Church and the world, but if our legitimate superiors forbid them, we must obey. Often enough the result will be a greater good that we can see and appreciate, but at times the result will be distressing, and the temptation to gloat irresistible. That is when we need the modesty and faith to accept that sincere and prompt submission to the will of a confessor or superior is worth far more than any good works we could do.

St Philip Neri himself had to exercise this prompt obedience when the Vicar General of Rome had been influenced by malicious gossip to forbid St Philip to lead the exercises of the Oratory.

The Vicar General was stirred to great anger in his zeal for the faith, and his concern for peace in the City (which was indeed his responsibility); he sent for Philip, received him with severe words, rebuked him, threatened him with prison, and ordered him to abstain from such works, not to take any companions around with him, to appear for judgment promptly whenever he was summoned, not to hear any confessions for the next fortnight, and not to preach to the people until he had received a new licence issued by himself. All this Philip received with a cheerful countenance and gave the only answer he could, with a submissive and modest manner, saying that he was equally prepared to continue the work he had begun or to leave it off at his superior's request, for he had no intention in mind other than the honour of God and the benefit of souls. This example of humility and this extraordinary constancy induced the authorities to kindly feelings towards him. Once they were convinced of his innocence and his moral integrity, the scheming of his malicious foes was brought to nothing, and he was granted full liberty to live in the manner he chose, and to use whatever means he liked to bring sinners back to God.

Antonio Gallonio, *Life of St Philip Neri*, §§62–3

Cardinal Newman struggled to express the same spirit of obedience and submission when his enemies were poisoning Pope Pius IX against him during the attempt to found the Oxford Oratory. 'It is my cross to have false stories circulated about me, and to be suspected in consequence. I could not have a lighter one. I would not change it for any other' (*Letters and Diaries*, XXIII, 191). The work he wanted to undertake in Oxford could have brought forth abundant fruit for the Church in this country, and there is no doubt that the Catholic community suffered greatly from the severe discouragement which Rome gave to Catholics from studying at a university. But when anxious and indignant Catholic parents complained to Newman about this, he counselled them to obey. He knew, as well as they, that Rome had been maliciously misinformed about the situation, but once Rome had spoken, he made no attempt to defend himself in public, or to allow his name to be included in the storm of public indignation. Obedience in the first instance means obeying the laws of the Church, and of our lawful superiors, even if we consider them inconvenient or misguided. Perhaps we should say, *especially* if we consider them inconvenient or misguided! Whatever might have been, had Catholics been allowed to study at University, and the Oratory allowed to give them pastoral care, what actually did happen was an occasion for growing in the grace of obedience, and therefore for sanctification unto eternal life.

Newman, of course, is quite clear on the difference between obeying a prohibition on doing something good, and obeying an order to do something bad. Writing a private letter to a parent who wanted to send his son to Oxford, despite the Pope, he says, 'We must recollect St Paul's strong words, "Obey those that have the rule over you" … The chance is it will turn out right' (*Letters and Diaries*, XXIII, 380–3, to Sir John Simeon, 9 Dec. 1867). In his very public Letter to the Duke of Norfolk, he imagines the possibility that the Pope might command a priest to run a lottery, and in this case, if the priest believed gambling was sinful, he ought to disobey the Pope (*Difficulties of Anglicans*, II, 260).

Different ages in the Church offer different challenges. There have been times like the tenth century when the Holy See has appeared to be asleep, and people crying out for reform have heard no answer. There have been times, like the thirteenth century, when the Holy See seemed to interfere too much, and made demands not only of a spiritual nature but even of a heavy financial nature. At times the Pope, at the helm of the Barque of Peter, seems to have steered too close to the rocks, at other times he appears to be searching out such calm waters that we lose patience and demand more excitement. Obedience is tested in different ways and at different times, but obedience is always necessary. St Thomas More gave his life for the papacy in the days of Clement VII, a time of such corruption and indifference on the part of the Holy See that the loss of half Europe hardly stirred the Curia at all. But at all times, it is the little things that test our obedience. If we are faithful in the small matters, the things of apparently no importance, then we shall find it in ourselves to be faithful in great.

One of Our Lord's apostles was surnamed Levi, the one who sat at the customs desk until the Lord called him. St Matthew alone tells us that his personal name was Matthew. If he was a tax-collector, he was someone who had betrayed his people, and abandoned his inheritance for the sake of gainful employment. He was one of the despised collaborators, someone that a good Pharisee would not speak to, let alone eat in his company. But the Lord called him, and he sprang up at once, and followed him (Matthew 9:10). That prompt obedience marks him out as truly a son of Levi after all. Whatever he did in later life, he had been brought up as a Levite, disciplined by obedience to the innumerable intricate details of the ritual Law, and the ceremonial of sacrifice.

And another characteristic of St Matthew we cannot fail to notice is that he tells us nothing more about himself. We know from the early second-century writer Papias that it was Matthew who collected the Lord's sayings in Aramaic, and the uncontradicted tradition of the Church is that it was also Matthew who arranged them, with narrative interludes, and the opening and closing stories, into the Gospel we now have. But we know much less of Matthew than we do of Mark, Luke or John. He obscures himself, conceals his own character, puts nothing in the way of the picture he is painting of his Lord. His early training in Levitical ritual, and his shameful period as a publican, combine to instil in him the great virtue of modesty. And we should not forget Our Lord's parable about an unnamed publican, whose prayer was no more than, 'God, be merciful to me a sinner!' (Luke 18:13)

Modesty is not a virtue we associate with the Old Testament at all. Few indeed are the passages in the prophets which instil it, and humility is more often seen as a punishment than a virtue. We hear, for instance, the rebuke of the prophet Obadiah: 'Behold, I will make you small among the nations, you shall be utterly despised. The pride of your heart has deceived you, you who live in the clefts of the rock, whose dwelling is high, who say in your heart, "Who will bring me down to the ground?"' (Obadiah 2–3) Humility here is a penalty, not a means of grace.

It is part of the revelation of the Gospel that humility is after all a good thing, and modesty is a virtue. Our Lady was startlingly original when she said, 'He has regarded the low estate of his handmaiden' (Luke 1:48). The ancient world never knew that humility is a virtue, just as the modern world has forgotten it. Yet modesty is essential if we are ever to be obedient, obedience essential if we are to become saints. The difference between the obedience of the Levite and that of the Christian is that the Levite is told to obey with the prospect of a reward in this world, 'that you may live and go in and take possession of the land' (Deuteronomy 4:1), whereas we are trying to cultivate obedience out of a real sense that others know better than us, and that God in His wisdom knows what is best far beyond anything we could think of for ourselves.

Modesty, continence and chastity are the three last of the Fruits of the Holy Spirit as we find them in the later editions of the Latin Vulgate (Galatians 5:22). St Thomas groups them together as the virtues by which we relate to matters beneath us. 'A man is well disposed towards that which is beneath him, firstly with regard to exterior actions through modesty, which observes moderation in all his words and deeds; with regard to interior desires through continence and chastity', making the distinction we have already noted between restraining lawful and unlawful desires (*Summa Theologiae*, I-II, lxx, iii).

We should note again here that the earlier Fathers knew only of nine or ten Fruits of the Spirit, not always giving the same list, and usually counting continence and chastity as one. It is St Jerome who makes the distinction between them, leading the way to inserting the inspired gloss into the text as we find it in the Clementine edition of the Latin 'Vulgate' Bible. (Not surprisingly, the Johanno-Pauline edition reduces the list to the nine found in the Greek.) Modesty is not in the Greek at all, yet it is one of the essential virtues, and is rightly interpolated into the text as an expansion of the list given by St Paul.

True obedience grows when we have the modesty to accept the will of God in every aspect of our life. Nothing can happen to us unless it is either directly willed by God, or else it is permitted by God's will because he knows that a greater good can come out of it. Therefore even if a lawful superior forbids us to do something which we are quite certain would be beneficial, our act of obedience is equally certain to result in something even better. Not that we can expect to see that straight away—often the good result comes very much later, and indeed not in this life. That too is part of our submission to the will of God. Just as the prayer of Christ in the garden was not 'heard' until after he had passed through death, so our prayerful submission to the will of God may not receive its reward until after our own death. For such is the prayer of martyrs. It is a commonplace that the blood of martyrs is the seed of the Church. Many martyrs just before their death prayed openly that the Church in their land would grow in the future, and that prayer was answered. They too were obedient even unto death.

Step Four

PATIENCE

The Patriarch Simeon, Prophet Haggai and Apostle Andrew

By your endurance you will gain your lives (Luke 21:19)

The fourth degree of humility is that, meeting in this obedience with difficulties and contradictions and even injustice, he should with a quiet mind hold to patience, and enduring neither tire nor run away; for the Scripture saith: *He that shall persevere to the end shall be saved*; and again: *Let thy heart take courage, and wait thou for the Lord.* And showing how the true disciple ought to endure all things, however contrary, for the Lord, it saith in the person of sufferers: *For thy sake we face death every moment. We are reckoned no better than sheep marked down for slaughter.* Then, confident in their hope of the divine reward, they go on with joy to declare: *But in all these things we overcome, through him that hath loved us.* And again in another place the Scripture saith: *Thou, O God, hast put us to the proof: thou hast tested us as men test silver in the fire. Thou hast led us into the snare: thou hast bowed our backs with trouble.* And to show that we ought to be under a superior, it goeth on to say: *Thou hast set men over our head.* Moreover, in adversities and injuries they patiently fulfil the Lord's commands: when struck on one cheek they offer the other, when robbed of their tunic they surrender also their cloak, when forced to go a mile they go two, with the apostle Paul they bear with false brethren, and they bless those that curse them.

RB 7

Cassian is more succinct: 'fourthly if we preserve at all times obedience, docility and endurance' (*Monastic Institutes*, IV, 39).

Endurance, or patience, is one of the virtues most emphasised by Our Lord, and by all his Apostles. Yet it does not appear in the Greek text of the Fruits of the Holy Spirit. Patience too is an example of inspired interpolation into the Clementine edition of the Vulgate. It is a virtue to which everyone pays lip-service, but in practice is one we resist to the best of our ability.

St Benedict gives us four aspects of the virtue of patience or endurance. In the first instance, it means persevering to the end in prayer and the spiritual life, without giving up. Secondly it involves accepting the suffering brought on us by the ordinary ills of this life. Thirdly it teaches us to submit to the will of a superior. And lastly, patience and endurance are exercised in putting up with the injustices and cruelties of the world, without trying to excuse or explain ourselves, or to claim what we imagine to be our rights.

Perseverance is the key to the spiritual life, and the easiest of all ways to heaven. Our Lord tells parables about the need to keep praying without giving up: the man who insists on borrowing three loaves of bread at midnight (Luke 11:5), and the woman demanding justice from the unjust judge (Luke 18:1–8). We remember also the blind men who repeat over and over again, 'Have mercy on us, Son of David', until they are heard and healed (Matthew 9:27–8, 20:29–32 and parallels), and the Canaanite woman who insists on the healing of her daughter (Matthew 15:21–8 and parallels). The parable of the unjust judge is introduced by St Luke as, 'a parable, to the effect that they ought always to pray and not lose heart.' The nagging woman, going on and on about her rights, is a familiar enough character: Our Lord is not commending either her behaviour or that of the judge, but making the one clear point that we should be equally persistent in our prayer. 'Will not God vindicate his elect, who cry to him day and night?'

It is a consoling doctrine, that sheer dogged perseverance will win us salvation. As long as we never give up, neither on ourselves nor on God, as long as we return over and over again to the confessional, the act of contrition, the aspiration 'Have mercy on us, Son of David', we can be certain that we are still on the road to salvation. We may fall over and over again, but as long as we get up again no harm is done. We may cry out to the Lord asking for grace to overcome sin, and fret with anxiety that still we are no better than we were before. We may even demand the gift of patience immediately, but we have no right to complain if our prayer is not answered, for the gift is granted precisely on the condition that we persevere in asking for it without seeing any results.

A holy parishioner of ours, not long before her death, remarked that the spiritual life is like a journey on the Trans-Siberian Railway. The train goes ever on and on, over the limitless and monotonous plains. Occasionally it comes into a station, and there is a brief moment of excitement, the bustle of people getting on and off, waving of flags and blowing of whistles, but then on it goes again. Occasionally the samovar boils and the babushka makes tea. Otherwise the train just goes on, steppe by steppe across the endless plain, the little villages of wooden houses glimpsed through the birch trees beside the line. The scenery looks exactly the same, day after day. But despite appearances we are moving, we are getting somewhere, and one day, perhaps unexpectedly and to our surprise, the train shall arrive in Moscow.

Our life of prayer consists most of the time in performing the same endless round, morning prayer and evening, midday and night, much the same day after day, week after week. There are occasional excitements—a moment of conversion, the reception of the Sacraments, our First Communion, Confirmation, Matrimony, Ordination, or Religious Profession. And from time to time we may be aware of the touch of the love of God that for a brief moment reassures us that we are on the right way. That has to sustain us through the weeks and months to come. We do not seem to be noticeably more holy, more kind, more patient even than we were a year ago or twenty years ago. That is when the virtue of plodding perseverance is most important, the endurance of days and years of routine prayer, routine repentance, routine attempts at charity. Until suddenly we arrive at the terminal and we find that, yes, after all, we have been travelling along the right road, and despite the dust and tedium of the journey, we have arrived.

The same parishioner likened Purgatory to arriving at our destination covered with dust and grime from the journey, and being glad to defer joining the company until after we have had a hot bath.

All we have to do is persevere in trying to love God, and trying to love our neighbour. The more we try, of course, the more dissatisfied with ourselves we shall be, and that is all to the good. There is nothing more dangerous than thinking we have made some progress. But as long as we can still say to ourselves, 'at least I am still trying', then we can be confident that we are still on the way to perfection.

The same patience and endurance are needed when we consider the state of the world around us, our nation, our city. Centuries pass and they seem to be no nearer conversion. It is the same with the Church Universal, the local church, our own parish and community. We should never be discouraged, even when the reforms we long for do not take place, and sin seems to reign everywhere. We are tempted to cry out with the Psalmist, 'How long, O Lord, how long?' (Psalm 93:3) But his answer is still that we should persevere and trust.

The prophet Haggai spoke to those who were impatient to see the restoration of Israel: 'Who is left among you that saw this house in its former glory? How do you see it now? Is it not in your sight as nothing? Yet now take courage ... all you people of the land, says the LORD; work, for I am with you, says the LORD of hosts, according to the promise that I made you when you came out of Egypt. My Spirit abides among you; fear not. For thus says the LORD of hosts: Once again, in a little while, I will shake the heavens and the earth and the sea and the dry land; and I will shake all nations, so that the treasures of all nations shall come in, and I will fill this house with splendour, says the LORD of hosts' (Haggai 2:4–8).

How long is this 'little while'? St Peter warns us not to be impatient: 'Do not ignore this one fact, beloved, that with the Lord one day is as a thousand years, and a thousand years as one day. The Lord is not slow about his promise as some count slowness, but is forbearing toward you, not wishing that any should perish, but that all should reach repentance' (II Peter 3:8–9). God acts slowly in the lives of those around us in order to give them an opportunity to repent. For that matter, he acts slowly in our own lives, giving us ample time to change our life, to do penance and to be healed. When we become impatient over our own faults, and eager to be rid of them, when we complain that God is slow to take us at our word and set us free from our sins, his answer is always the same, 'My grace is sufficient for you, for my power is made perfect in weakness' (II Corinthians 12:9).

Patience must be exercised also in accepting the pains, sorrows, and inconveniences of daily life. St Paul boasted of his endurance under extreme provocations, 'in danger from rivers, danger from robbers, danger from my own people, danger from Gentiles, danger in the city, danger in the wilderness, danger at sea, danger from false brethren' (II Corinthians 11:26). But endurance in those dramatic circumstances may feed pride: what is much more significant is patience under the ordinary little things, in danger from draughts, danger from flies, danger from rattling windows, danger from squeaking shoes, danger from snuffles, danger from headaches, danger from telephones, danger from computers, danger from late buses, danger from the irritating habits of those closest and most dear to us. There is no glamour in putting up with such things without grumbling, no heroism in enduring them with patience. But in a thousand ways our patience is tested every day. Heroic sanctity can in fact be lived in the ordinary circumstances of family or community life. As St Philip used to say, the greatest penance can be in community life, *vita communis mortificatio maxima*.

Abba Piamun, in Cassian's *Collations*, gives us an example of this sort of patience.

> There was a certain religious woman, who pursued the virtue of patience so eagerly that so far from avoiding trials, she went to the extent of devising for herself occasions of grief, although she never let herself be overcome by these frequent troubles. She lived in Alexandria, and came from a distinguished family, serving the Lord devoutly in the house her parents left her. She went to bishop Athanasius, of sainted memory, and asked him to provide her with a widow to care for, who was being looked after at church expense. To give the actual words of her request, she said, 'Give me a sister to care for.' The prelate was pleased with the woman's request, and saw that she really desired to do a work of mercy. He asked for a widow to be chosen who was distinguished above all the others for respectable conduct and sobriety, so that the

generosity of the donor would not be daunted by the greed
of the recipient, and in her desire to profit by meeting her
needs she might not suffer loss to her faith through offence at
the other's bad conduct. The holy woman brought the widow
to her home, and looked after her carefully, discovering how
gentle and modest she was, and finding herself continually
loaded with thanks for her kindness.

A few days later she came back to St Athanasius. 'I did
ask,' she said, 'for you to arrange for me to be given someone
to care for, and to serve in her difficulties.' He still did not
understand the woman's intention and desire, and thought
that her request had merely been neglected through his
provost's laziness. He asked, with some indignation, why
the delay had occurred, and soon found that a widow, more
respectable than most, had been sent to her. Accordingly
he gave secret orders that the most wicked of all of them
should be sent to her, who exceeded all the others in bad
temper, arguments, drunkenness and garrulity. It was much
easier to find this one—and she began to give her a home,
serving her with as much or more care as she had the previous
widow. All she received in the way of thanks for her attentions
was foul abuse, continual trouble from her complaints and
reproaches, slander and grumbling with muttered curses;
thus her request to the bishop had brought her not repose,
but a cross with dishonour, and her way of life was changed
not from labour to leisure, but from leisure to labour. When
these frequent arguments had reached the point that the vile
woman could not be restrained even by laying hands on her,
the other redoubled her attentive service, learning not so
much how to overcome the ranting widow by restraint, but
to overcome herself by humble subjection. Bruised by many
assaults, she smoothed the harridan's rage with meekness
and kindness. Being fully strengthened by these exercises,
and having acquired the perfect virtue of patience which
she had desired, she returned to bishop Athanasius, and
thanked him for his discerning choice and the benefit she had

received from the exercise. As she had hoped, he had finally given her a mistress to teach her patience, so that she was daily strengthened by those frequent complaints, as if by an athlete's ointment, till she had achieved a perfectly patient soul. 'At last', she said, 'you have given me someone to relieve, for that one you sent me before gave me more relief, by her honour and gratitude.'

Collations, XVIII, 14

A special trial of our patience is the one described so graphically in the published letters of St Teresa of Calcutta, *Come, be my Light*. For many years she felt herself cut off from God, trapped in darkness and depression with no consciousness of him, of grace, of any hope or faith. Eventually she came to realise that her vocation was precisely to embrace the darkness, to share in the pain and isolation of the 'poorest of the poor' for whom she had offered herself to God. Her experience was, of course, the familiar 'dark night' of St John of the Cross, but protracted for very much longer than usual. Many people, in their own way, have to embrace the darkness, and wait patiently for God to reveal himself, with nothing to sustain them but sheer perseverance. For most, in God's mercy, the period of darkness is shorter than it was for St Teresa.

There are more obvious tests too, of course, the tests of serious inconvenience, or of genuine sickness. Patience under the relentless attacks on our faith which have become a feature of modern Britain, or the severe persecutions which our fellow Catholics endure in an increasing number of countries of the world: that is a real test of our faith, and our charity. During times of persecution, the saints and martyrs prove their love for God by enduring all things, accepting misrepresentation and slander, fines, imprisonment, torment and death. At times when persecution slackens, many of the saints endure severe illnesses, and accept incapacity without grumbling or complaining. St Teresa of Avila was hardly ever free from severe pain, but continued to write those cheerful and humorous letters. St Philip Neri was frequently ill, the despair of doctors, whose attempt at remedies were worse than the disease. These and other sixteenth-century saints in Catholic countries suffered in patience, knowing that their contemporaries in

England were undergoing the most savage and prolonged persecution the world has known. All had a share in the Cross, in their different ways. 'In all these things we are more than conquerors, through him who loved us' (Romans 8:37).

A third field in which St Benedict invites us to exercise patience and endurance is in accepting that we ought to be under a superior. In the modern world more than ever before, people resent authority in any form. The idea that some should be preferred over us, that someone else should have the right to tell us what to do, clashes with our over-developed sense of 'rights'. Not that the problem is new: long ago, in the rebellion of Reuben's descendants Dathan and Abiram in the desert, the cry was that all should be equal, and that Moses and Aaron had no right to tell the others what to do. 'All the congregation are holy, every one of them, and the LORD is among them; why then do you exalt yourselves above the assembly of the LORD?' (Numbers 16:3) Whether in the Church or in the state, the voice of Dathan and Abiram is frequently heard. We are very reluctant to admit that we are not in charge, very slow to accept that someone else has been appointed over us.

Perhaps we can learn something here from the example of the Apostle Andrew. He was one of the first two disciples to follow Our Lord, after John the Baptist had pointed him out as the Lamb of God. The two of them spent the whole day with Our Lord, and after that Andrew went at once to find his brother Simon, to tell him, 'We have found the Messiah' (John 1:35–42). There can be no doubt that the other unnamed disciple was John, the brother of James. Some time later Our Lord came to the lakeside, where he found Simon and Andrew in one boat, James and John in the other, and he called them to leave everything and follow him (Mark 1:16–20). Andrew might therefore think, quite reasonably, that he should be one of the innermost group of four disciples. But after that he is passed over again and again: it is always Peter, James and John who are singled out, to witness the raising of the daughter of the ruler (Mark. 5:37), to be present at the Transfiguration (Mark 9:1), to watch with him in the Garden of Gethsemane (Mark 14:33). Even in the Acts of the Apostles, after James had been killed, it is not Andrew who takes his place but the other James, the son of Alphaeus, named together with Peter and John as one of the three pillars of the Church (Galatians 2:9).

Andrew has been passed over. But he does not complain or grumble: he continues quietly on his mission as an Apostle, introducing people to Our Lord. It is he who finds the small boy with five barley loaves and two fish (John 6:8–9); it is he who brings the Greeks to meet Our Lord (John 12:22). He lives out the saying of John the Baptist, 'he must increase, but I must decrease' (John 3:30), and has the humility to recognise without complaining that he will always be in the second rank of the disciples. In the same way, of the four sons of Alphaeus, James and Joset and Simon and Jude (Mark 6:3), three are called to be Apostles, but Joset is not, even though his mother is explicitly mentioned at the foot of the Cross (Mark 15:40). If he is the same person as Joseph surnamed Barsabbas, he is even passed over a second time (Acts 1:23–6). Patience means accepting the choices which God makes, whether for preferment in this world, or in the Church, or in heaven. Some of us are called to be great saints, others to be little saints. But the small glass can be just as full of water as the big one.

The most difficult of all the four exercises of patience is enduring unjust and wicked accusations and attacks. We can steel ourselves to accept someone else being preferred over us if we can convince ourselves that they are really more suitable than us. But often we have to accept a ruler, whether in church or state, who is quite genuinely unfit to preside and who will really do great damage to God's people. We can be rather proud of resisting those who attack our faith and who accuse us of teaching Christian doctrine. But how can we tolerate false accusations of serious wrong-doing, which make us despicable in the eyes of everyone? We can train ourselves to be patient in perseverance when the tedious and monotonous tenour of our lives can be seen to produce useful results. But how can we tolerate days and years wasted in doing nothing of any possible use to God and man?

Yet such has been the destiny of many of the saints. Such is the truest and most heroic test of patience. 'When struck on one cheek they offer the other, when robbed of their tunic they surrender also their cloak, when forced to go a mile they go two, with the apostle Paul they bear with false brethren, and they bless those that curse them' (*RB* 7).

The patriarch Simeon was very conscious that he deserved to suffer for his sins. He admits that he was the instigator in the plot against his brother Joseph, because he could not tolerate the fact that his brother had been preferred above him.

1. A transcript of the words of Simeon, which he spoke to his sons before his death at the age of one hundred and twenty years, at the time when his brother Joseph died. His sons came to visit him when Simeon was ill, and he gathered strength to sit up and embrace them, and this is what he said:

2. Listen, my children, listen to Simeon your father, and I will tell you all that I have in my heart. I was the second son to be born to Jacob my father, and my mother Leah named me Simeon, for the Lord had heard her prayer. I was very strong, and feared no work, nor was I afraid of any task. But my heart was hard, and my liver unmoved, and my bowels without compassion—for it is the Almighty who gives strength to mankind both in soul and body. In the days of my youth I conceived great jealousy against Joseph, because our father loved him more than all the others, and I steeled my feelings against him to determine his death, because the ruler of deceit, the spirit of jealousy, blinded my understanding. I did not treat him as a brother, and I had no pity on my father Jacob. But his God, the God of our fathers, sent forth his angel and delivered him from my hands. For it was when I had gone to Shechem to buy some ointment for the sheep, and Reuben had gone to Dothaim where we kept our necessities and all our stores, that Judah my brother sold Joseph to the Ishmaelites. Reuben was distressed when he heard of this, for he had intended to restore him to our father. I on the other hand, when I heard it, was furious with Judah for sending him away alive, and I kept up my resentment for five months. Then the Lord struck me with a paralysis, and deprived me of the use of my hands. My right hand shrivelled up for seven days, until I came to understand, my children, that it was because of Joseph that this had happened to me. I repented, in tears, and implored the Lord God that if he would restore my hand I would abstain from all defilement and from jealousy and from all sin. I realised

that I had been planning an evil deed before the Lord and my father Jacob, against Joseph who was my brother, because I was jealous of him.

3. And now, my sons, listen to me, and keep away from the spirit of deceit and envy. For envy dominates all the thoughts of man, and does not allow him to eat or drink or do anything good, but is ever urging on the destruction of the envied one. And the envied one ever flourishes, and the jealous one declines. For two days I afflicted my soul with fasting, in fear of the Lord, and I came to understand that it is through the fear of God that jealousy is dispelled. If anyone seeks refuge in the Lord the evil spirit flees away from him, and his mind is relieved. From then on, he has compassion on the one whom he had envied, and rejoices with those who love him; in this way he puts an end to his jealousy.

4. My father made enquiries about me, since he saw that I was depressed, and I said to him, 'I am grieved in my bowels.' Everyone was distressed over me because I had been guilty of the sale of Joseph. When we went down to Egypt, and Joseph imprisoned me as a spy, I knew that I was suffering justly, and I did not complain. But Joseph was a good man, and the spirit of God was in him. He was merciful and compassionate, and did not bear resentment against me; he loved me as he did my brothers. O my children, guard against any sort of jealousy and envy; live in simplicity of heart and in a generous heart. Remember your father's brother, so that God will grant you also the grace and the glory, and the same blessing on your heads that you see upon Joseph. For all his life long he did not reproach us about that matter, but loved us as his own soul, and gave us honour above his own sons. He enriched us all with a wealth of herds and crops. And so, my dear children, let each of you love his brother in a pure heart, and drive away from you the spirit of jealousy, for it makes the soul savage and destroys the body, turns counsel to wrath and war, and sharpens it for bloodshed.

Jealousy drives a man out of his mind and prevents the operation of the human understanding. It deprives a man of sleep, afflicts his soul with violence, and the body with trembling. If he does sleep, evil jealousy creates images that eat away at him, and disturbs his soul with spirits of wickedness. It makes his body shake, and awakens the mind to anxiety, appearing to men as a wicked spirit pouring out poison.

5.   The reason why Joseph was so good-looking and his face was so attractive is that there was nothing of evil within him, for the countenance betrays any disturbance of the spirit. So now, my children, make your hearts holy in the Lord's sight, and make your ways straight in the sight of men, so that you will find favour before God and man. Keep guard over yourselves against fornication, for fornication is the mother of evils, it takes us away from God and brings us nearer to the devil. I have discovered, in reading the writings of Enoch, that your descendants after you will be corrupted by fornication, and will wreak evil against the sons of Levi with the sword. They will not prevail against Levi, for he will fight the battle of the Lord and will overcome all your array. Your descendants will be few, divided between Levi and Judah, and there will not be one of you to take the lead, as our father Jacob prophesied when he gave his blessings.

6.   See, I have spoken all these things to you, so that I shall not share the guilt of your sins. But if you banish envy from you, and all hardness of heart, my bones will blossom like a rose in Israel, and my flesh like a lily in Jacob, my scent will be as the scent of Lebanon; holy ones will multiply from me like the sacred cedars for ever, and their branches will spread wide. Then shall the spawn of Chaanan be destroyed, and there shall be no survivor in Amalek, all the Cappadocians shall perish, and the Hittites shall all be swept away. Then shall the land of Ham be forsaken, and all its peoples destroyed. Then all the land shall have rest from disturbance, and all that is under heaven from war. Shem shall be glorified, for the Lord God, the mighty one of Israel, shall appear on earth as a

man, and in him he shall save Adam. All the spirits of deceit shall be given over for him to trample them underfoot, and mankind will have dominion over the evil spirits. Then I too will rise up in righteousness, and I will bless the Most High in his wonders, for God has taken a human body and has saved mankind by eating together with them.

7. So then, my children, listen to Levi, and to Judah. Do not rise against those two tribes, for out of them will the salvation of God arise for you. For the Lord will raise up one like a high priest from Levi, and like a king from Judah, who is both God and Man. He will save all nations, as well as the race of Israel. Therefore I tell you all these things so that you in turn may tell your children, so that they may ponder these things in all their generations.

8. And after Simeon completed his instructions to his sons, he fell asleep with his fathers at the age of an hundred and twenty. They enclosed him in a coffin of imperishable wood, so that his bones could be taken to Hebron. They carried them away secretly while the Egyptians were at war, for the Egyptians had secured the bones of Joseph in the Tombs of the Kings. This was because their seers had said that when the bones of Joseph went forth there would be darkness and obscurity throughout the whole land, and a great plague would come upon the Egyptians, so that no man would be able to recognise his brother even with a lamp.

9. And the sons of Simeon mourned for their father according to the customs of mourning, and they lived in Egypt until the days of their Exodus under the leadership of Moses.

So Simeon acknowledges that his 'heart was hard, and his liver unmoved, and his bowels without compassion'—out of jealousy against Joseph. Although Judah decided to sell Joseph instead of killing him, and Reuben was compassionate towards him, Simeon kept up his resentment until he had a stroke, when he came to his senses and repented. He was now able to accept suffering with patience.

The patriarch goes on to claim Enoch as his authority to predict that his sons will have difficulties in the future with the descendants of Judah and Levi, and they are not to resent the pre-eminence granted to those tribes, 'For the Lord will raise up a high priest from Levi, and a king from Judah, who is both God and Man. He will save all nations, as well as the race of Israel.' If Our Lady's father was descended from David, and her mother from Aaron, then both tribes are united in him, and Christ can be both King and Priest.

Now Simeon was not guilty of spying on the land of Egypt, and Joseph knew this perfectly well, when he 'took Simeon from them and bound him before their eyes.' He may have been aware that it was Simeon who had instigated the plot against himself, but he did not ill-treat him, and brought him out promptly when the brothers returned (Genesis 42:25, 43: 23). No more was said, and the blessing of Simeon in Genesis makes no mention of any of this—as we have already seen it couples Simeon with Levi and rebukes them both for their behaviour over the Shechemites (Genesis 49:5–7). Moses did not bless Simeon at all (Deuteronomy 33). In other words, Simeon had a bad reputation, and one that he thoroughly deserved, and it was for that reason that he did not protest at the unjust treatment he received at the hands of Joseph, knowing that, even though he might not have been a spy, he was a bully, a murderer, and an intended fratricide, and deserved all that he suffered.

It is for this sort of reason that many of the saints have cheerfully accepted grave injustice inflicted on them, because they knew that for completely different reasons they did deserve to suffer. Unmerited suffering, for them, was offered up in reparation for their own real past sins. This is the spirit of patient acceptance that St Benedict recommends to us, and that Our Lord himself commands, when he talks about turning the other cheek and offering the wicked man no resistance. He took upon himself the burden of our sins, and accepted suffering for them: we have genuine sins of our own, and therefore cannot grumble if suffering is inflicted upon us, even if those who inflict the suffering are doing so for quite the wrong reasons.

As usual, Cassian gives us an example of a saint who accepted wrongful accusation without trying to defend himself. Abba Piamun is speaking again:

The other example is that of Abba Paphnutius. He persevered constantly and diligently in the remote part of that desert of Skete, so famous and talked about, and he is a priest there now. The other anchorites there call him 'Wild Ox', because he always prefers to live alone as if it were his natural inclination. Even in youth he was so virtuous and graceful that the most distinguished men of the age admired him for his seriousness and unshaken constancy. They considered him the equal in merit and virtue of his superiors, despite being much younger than them, and decided he should be enrolled among the elders. Then that jealousy, which once aroused his brothers against the Patriarch Joseph, inflamed one of Paphnutius' brothers with a gnawing bitterness. He wanted to spoil his good reputation with some excrescence or stain, and thought up an evil plot, finding his opportunity when Paphnutius had gone to church on a Sunday and was thus absent from his cell. The other crept in quietly and hid his own book among the woven mats which Paphnutius used to weave out of palm fronds. Confident in his cunning scheme, he too went to church as if his conscience was clear and pure.

Once the usual ceremony was over, he raised a complaint in front of all the brethren before St Isidore, who was the priest in that part of the desert before our own Paphnutius, claiming that his book had been stolen out of his cell. This complaint disturbed everyone, particularly the priest, since they had no suspicion or policy on such matters, and everyone was amazed at such an unheard of crime. No one in that part of the desert could remember anything like this before, nor has such a thing happened since. The accuser who had reported the deed urged that everyone should be kept in the church until some were chosen and sent to examine the cells of each brother in turn. The priest laid this charge on three of the elders, and they searched all the cells until they finally found the book hidden in Paphnutius' cell among the palm-mats or *siras* as they call them, just where the schemer had hidden them. The searchers brought it straightaway to the church and showed it to everyone, and Paphnutius, despite being really clear in his own conscience, offered himself for punishment as if he were admitting his guilt. He humbly begged to take the place of a penitent, considering in his bashful modesty that if he tried to argue himself out of the accusation he would only incur the reputation of a liar as well, since no one suspected anything other than what appeared to have been discovered.

He left the church, not cast down in mind but confident in God's judgment, and prostrated himself humbly before everyone, with profuse tears and prayers, and triple fasting. For about two weeks he subjected himself in bodily and spiritual penance, and on Saturday and Sunday mornings came back to the church, not to receive Holy Communion, but to prostrate himself on the church threshold and beg pardon. He who witnesses and scrutinises all hidden things did not suffer him either to punish himself more, or to be despised by others, for he made use of the devil who had been the instigator of the crime to reveal what that wicked brother had done, that thief of his own property, that detractor of another's reputation, in front of no human witness. He was seized by a dire demon, and revealed every sin he had committed in secret: the culprit betrayed his own crimes and deceit. He was severely troubled by that unclean spirit for a long time, and was unable to find deliverance even through the prayers of the saints who lived around him, though they could give orders to the demons through the power of their God-given gifts. Not even the special grace granted to the priest Isidore could drive out that cruel tormentor, although the Lord had given him such virtue that any one who was possessed and brought to him was cured no sooner than he crossed his threshold. No, Christ reserved the honour for young Paphnutius, so that the villain would be healed at the prayers of the one he had injured, and so be compelled to declare the fame of the one whom he had hoped, in his enmity, to strip of his reputation; thus he received pardon for his sin, and relief from his present suffering.

So it was that Paphnutius, while still young, showed promise of his future distinction, and in his early years sketched the outline of the perfection he was to increase in his maturity. If we would arrive at the summit of his virtue, we too should lay such a first foundation.

Collations, XVIII, 15

In all this, Paphnutius followed the example of Christ, for 'when he was reviled he did not revile in return; when he suffered he did not threaten; but he trusted to him who judges justly' (I Peter 2:23). St Philip used to call those who defended themselves against unjust accusation 'Madonna Eve', remembering how Adam blamed Eve and Eve blamed the serpent, but neither was prepared to take responsibility for their own sin. It is so easy to react angrily against unjust accusation, and defend ourselves so vigorously that we leave people with the impression that we must have something to hide after all. Meek submission to slander and insult will not impress the children of this world either, but the meek shall inherit the earth. True patience is found when we are unconcerned about what others think of us, and have no regard for our own status. God alone is our judge: if we are innocent in his eyes, we need not fret over what the world thinks. Since we are, in reality, all guilty in his eyes, we need do no more than repent, confess, and accept his loving forgiveness. As penance for our real sins, we can accept with patience the punishment unjustly inflicted upon us for the few sins which we did not happen to commit.

Step Five

MEEKNESS

The Patriarch Zabulon, Prophet Zephaniah and Apostle Philip

Confess your sins to one another   (James 5:16)

The fifth degree of humility is that he humbly confess and conceal not from his abbot any evil thoughts that enter his heart, and any secret sins that he has committed. To this does Scripture exhort us, saying: *Make known thy way unto the Lord, and hope in him.* And again: *Confess to the Lord, for he is good, and his mercy endureth for ever.* And further: *I have made known my sin to thee, and my faults I have not concealed. I said: I will be my own accuser and confess my faults to the Lord, and with that thou didst remit the guilt of my sin.*

RB 7

Cassian makes this his second step: 'secondly if we conceal nothing from our master not only of our actions but even of our thoughts' (*Monastic Institutes*, IV, 39).

Liturgical experts often tell us that frequent confession was unknown in the Early Church, and was a mediaeval aberration which ought to be abolished. St Benedict and Cassian would beg to differ—as would St James: 'Confess your sins to one another, and pray for one another, that you may be healed' (James 5:16). Not only monks, but layfolk as well were encouraged to confess their sins regularly, of that there can be no doubt.

However there is an important distinction to be made (for the sake of the liturgical experts): confession in the Early Church was not necessarily made to a priest, and was not linked to the Sacrament of Penance.

The Power of the Keys was wielded by the bishop, and a sacramental Absolution conferred, only in the case of the greatest sinners who had cut themselves off from the church and truly needed reconciliation. For many centuries the sins concerned were no more these three, murder, adultery and apostasy—and the greatest of these is apostasy. For these sins, which cut one off completely from the life of the Church, serious public penance was required, and reconciliation was equally serious and public. It was, therefore, extremely rare, and quite reasonably might be expected to be conferred no more than once in a lifetime. Most Christians would never receive sacramental absolution, and indeed at some periods those who had once done so were debarred from ever being considered for ordination.

It seems it was the Irish monks who flooded Europe in the wake of St Columbanus who first began to put confession and penance together, and made it a regular feature of Christian life. This was partly because they were dealing with rough and semi-barbarous penitents, and partly because the threshold of 'grave matter' was being set lower and lower. The original list of only three grave sins was increased until it appeared to be impossible for anyone to pass a week without committing at least one such sin, so that weekly absolution became a necessity. There may well have been a need to correct the balance, which was done in the Catechisms of the Councils of Trent and the Vatican, which give a very clear definition of precisely what constitutes mortal sin. 'Mortal sin is sin whose object is grave matter and which is also committed with full knowledge and deliberate consent' (*CCC* 1857). Such full knowledge and deliberate consent is, mercifully, very difficult to achieve, which means that even now it is rare for a confessor to deal with genuine mortal sin. Grave matter, yes, we hear frequently, but remembering the same Catechism's list of modifying factors ('ignorance, inadvertence, duress, fear, habit, inordinate attachments and other psychological or social factors' *CCC* 1735), we know that in the majority of cases there has never been a real break with the love of God, never, therefore, a real need for reconciliation or the full exercise of the Power of the Keys. Which means that, in strict terms, it is very rare in any Christian's life for them to need the Sacrament of Reconciliation, and many never do.

Nearly all the confessions we hear are 'confessions of devotion', but they are none the less valuable for that. The wisdom of St Columbanus' monks in joining confession to absolution is abundantly vindicated, when we see the huge benefits which flow from regular confession. Once people are accustomed to approaching the confessional regularly, and it becomes a familiar routine, they will find it much easier to use the sacrament if by any chance they do fall into serious sin. Indeed it is the ease of forgiveness that they often find most difficult—like Naaman the Syrian (2 Kings (IV Kings) chapter 5) they expect to do something difficult in order to be cleansed, and have to be persuaded that the simple familiar formula of confession, contrition and absolution is all that is required.

In the early centuries, then, the frequent confession prescribed by St Benedict was always a 'confession of devotion' and not yet linked to the Sacrament of Penance. Therefore there was no reason why it needed to be made to a priest. St Benedict, in fact, expects his monks to confess to their abbot, who was not usually a priest. No doubt St Scholastica expected her nuns to confess to their abbess. (Modern Canon Law, of course, discourages religious superiors from hearing the confessions of their subjects, but this is an innovation, the decision of Leo XIII, and contradicts centuries of monastic experience, *CIC* 630 §4.) Confession to a lay person, man or woman, can have a real value, not as a sacrament, but as a sacramental. St Thomas teaches us, quoting St Bede, that 'Confession to a layman is a sort of sacramental, although it is not the full sacrament; as it proceeds from charity, venial sins are remitted in this way, just as they can be by beating the breast or sprinkling holy water' (*Summa Theologiae*, Suppl. 8, iii). Such was the routine confession to the abbot recommended by St Benedict and Cassian. In our own country priests are not yet so overburdened with hearing confession that it would be difficult to confess to a priest, but I can imagine in some countries, where priests really are scarce, confession to a suitable lay man or woman, nun or friar, might be a useful exercise.

Confession, and the examination of conscience which precedes it, must go deeper than the virtue of the Scribes and Pharisees. The requirements of the Old Law are entirely for external conformity. The young man in the Gospel boasts that he has kept all the commandments from his youth, and he is probably being quite truthful. It would not be difficult for someone in confession to be able to say in all honesty that he had not, that week, worshipped a false god, perjured himself in court in the name of the True God, failed to observe Sunday, been openly rude to his father or mother and so on. Even the last two commandments, which might be thought rather more interior, are observed to the letter if we do not dedicate ourselves consciously and eagerly to plotting means of extracting our neighbour's wife, ox or ass from his premises.

But the New Law goes deeper. 'You have heard that it was said to the men of old, "You shall not kill; and whoever kills shall be liable to judgment." But I say to you that everyone who is angry with his brother shall be liable to judgment' (Matthew 5:21–2). The Old Testament prophets knew full well that the Lord tries 'the heart and the mind' (Jeremiah 11:20), and the Psalmist goes so far as to invite his scrutiny: 'Prove me, O Lord, and try me; test my heart and my mind' (Psalm 25:2). It is not only our exterior actions, our spoken words, but our thoughts as well that we must account for, not only deliberate and long-hoarded thoughts and plans, but passing whims and fancies.

That is why Cassian devotes so much of his book on monastic training to an examination of the eight deadly sins. He does not in fact call them sins, but viruses: they are the germs of sin which exist in every bloodstream, the potentiality for every sort of wrong-doing which lurks in every heart. When we read the last eight books of the *Monastic Institutes* (or Abbot Jamison's book, *Finding Happiness*), we cannot fail to recognise in ourselves every one of the eight. Not all of them are equally virulent at the moment, certainly, and there are probably several which have never given us any particular trouble, but the potential is there in every one of us for any of them to break out and plunge us into actual sin in any direction.

That is why it is important to be aware of the little sins, the trivial complaints which can be the surface symptoms of a multiplying viral infection deeper down. Not that we need fear the wrath and condemnation of God for them, rather that we fear a diminution in our love for him and for our neighbour. Every sin, every tendency to sin, is an aspect of selfishness, and selfishness, if unchecked, will lead us further and further away from love. Cassian gives us an example of how valuable the confession of an apparently trivial sin may be. The Abba Sarapion is speaking:

> When I was very young, and living with Abba Theonas, I was habitually troubled by an assault of the enemy in this manner: after I had eaten my noon meal with the old man, I used to conceal one bun every day in my clothing, and eat it in the evening without his knowledge. Although I was continually committing this theft through sheer self-indulgence, and the lack of discipline which concealed desire brings, as soon as my deceitful greed had been satisfied, I would come to my senses and be more distressed with guilt than the pleasure of eating it had been worth. I found that I was being compelled, day after day, to perform that dismal deed, forced to do it as if by Pharoah's slave-drivers, to make a change from bricks (cf. Exodus 5); how it grieved my heart! I was quite unable to rid myself of this terrible obsession, and too ashamed to admit my secret pilfering to the old man.
>
> But God determined to free me from the yoke of slavery; one day some of the brethren came to Theonas's cell to seek for instruction, and after our meal was over a spiritual conversation began. In response to the questions they put, the old man spoke about the vice of greed and how hidden thoughts oppress us. He explained the nature of such thoughts, and how terribly powerful they are until they be revealed. I was struck with remorse at the truth of his teaching, and terrified by my accusing conscience, almost believing that Theonas spoke thus because the Lord had revealed my secret to him. At first I was roused to private grief, then as remorse grew in my heart I burst out into open sobs and tears, till I produced from my pocket, the witness and receiver of my theft, the bun which I had secreted to eat later as my naughty custom was, and placed it in the open. Lying on the ground, I confessed that I had been secretly eating every day and asked forgiveness. With freely flowing tears, I begged the Lord for

absolution for my terrible obsession. Then Theonas said, 'Courage, my boy, your confession has absolved you from your sin even without my saying anything. You have today triumphed over the foe which had defeated you, and your confession has frustrated him more than ever you suffered from him through your silence. Unless you or someone else had refuted him by speaking out, you would still be letting him dominate you. As Solomon said, "because sentence is not speedily pronounced against the evil, the heart of the children of man will be filled that they may commit evils" (Ecclesiasticus 8:11, LXX). That is why the foul fiend can no longer disturb you now you have made this admission, and the evil worm can no longer claim a lair within you, for your saving confession has pulled him out of the darkness of your heart into the open.'

Collations, II, 11

No one even among the monks of old would claim that secreting a bun was a serious sin, but it is certainly an offence against community life and discipline. Yet the mere act of confessing it, without any need for sacramental absolution, brought relief to the young Serapion. The greatest value of his confession, of course, was that it was public, in front of his fellow novices: it is not always advisable to confess in public, and in fact the Church actively discourages it, unless it is, as here, a matter of a breach of community trust. That is why in the traditional Chapter of Faults it is only offences against the customs of the community that are mentioned, unless the fault itself has been so public that a public admission is required.

St Benedict and Cassian do not only talk about the confession of actual sins, however trivial, but they urge one more urgently to confess 'any evil thoughts that enter his heart'. It is the regular confession of stray thoughts, temptations and fancies that is so useful in making spiritual progress. All are agreed that these thoughts are not sinful in themselves, but they are certainly occasions of sin, and if left to fester will bring forth fruits of sin. That is why they should be dashed against the rock of Calvary as the psalmist longed to dash the infants of Babylon.

'O daughter of Babylon, you devastator!... Happy shall he be who takes your little ones and dashes them against the rock' (Psalm 136:8–9). The Fathers made sense of this violent verse of the Psalm, as of all the others, by finding its spiritual meaning. Just as infant Babylonians could grow up to become dangerous enemies, so incipient evil thoughts can grow until they poison the heart and cause us to act in ways destructive of charity.

The confession of evil thoughts does not, of course, mean describing them in the confessional, for that would be to commit them all over again and bring danger on the confessor. It is sufficient to confess to 'thoughts of anger', 'feelings of jealousy', 'a long-standing resentment that I cannot shake off'. By naming these infant devils we deprive them of their power. And the more shameful the thoughts, the greater the benefit of confessing them. Perhaps the most insidious, and the most difficult to reject, are thoughts of resentment against those who have hurt, not us but the people we love. No matter how many times we resolve to want to try to forgive them, the thought reappears again and again. There is no other way of resolving this burden than by bringing it regularly and laying it at the foot of the Cross in the confessional.

We have already quoted Cassian's story of the unsympathetic elder who was so discouraging to the young monk when he confessed to evil thoughts. The reality is that there is no one on earth who is not troubled by thoughts and temptations towards sin in one form or another. Usually it is only towards one sin or two, hardly ever to all at once, but we may never consider ourselves exempt from any temptation, or pretend that there is any sin which we are incapable of committing. It is only the grace of God that preserves us from serious falls every day. If we ever forget that, he will withdraw that protection just long enough for us to learn the lesson.

These thoughts or temptations can do us no harm whatever if we are prompt to bring them to the confessional. Cassian, again, quotes Abba Moyses: 'An evil thought withers away as soon as it is made known, so that even before any discerning judgment can be pronounced, by the sheer virtue of confession, the evil worm is dragged out into the open, as if from a dark and secret lair, and once exposed and shamed, crawls away. For his vile suggestions remain within us only as long as they are concealed in our hearts' (*Collations*, II, x).

The reason why the very act of confession is so useful is, of course, that it results immediately in humiliation, which is the gateway to humility. It is only when we are meek enough to admit our own weakness that there is any chance the grace of God will make us strong. Meekness, *mansuetudo*, is one of the Fruits of the Holy Spirit, and it also, of course, carries a beatitude with it: 'Blessed are the meek, for they shall inherit the earth' (Matthew 5:5). As Pope Benedict XVI points out, the same Greek word *praus* is used by St Matthew in the Beatitude, in Our Lord's words, 'I am gentle and lowly in heart' (Matthew 11:29), and in the quotation from the prophet 'Behold your king is coming to you, humble and mounted on an ass' (Matthew 21:5, Zechariah 9:9), and its cognate *prautés* is used by St Paul. (Pope Benedict XVI, *Jesus of Nazareth*, Bloomsbury 2007, pp. 80–82). Different English words are used to translate *praus*, 'meek', 'lowly', 'humble' and 'gentle' (as indeed different Latin words are used by St Jerome in his translation of Scripture, *mansuetus*, *mitis* and *modestus*). The virtue we are talking about has no exact equivalent in English, for after all the very concept is foreign to our modern age, almost as foreign as it was to the people of Our Lord's time. The world encourages us to be assertive, aggressive, to stand up for our rights: but to be meek, to be like Our Lord, means quite the opposite. Meekness means allowing others to trample on our 'rights', letting others go first, refraining from putting ourselves forward. It is a very unfashionable virtue, and all the more valuable for that.

The means to acquire meekness is the awareness of our own frailty. That is why confession of secret sins and evil thoughts is so important. Once we have faced up to our own wayward tendencies, and admitted to ourselves that we are drawn to this sin or that sin, we are beginning to become aware of how weak our virtue is. Once we have taken the next step of expressing these temptations out loud to another person, we are driving home that awareness. Because we know how easily we could fall into real sins of deliberate design, we know that we have nothing to boast of before God. If we do not actually commit these sins, it is entirely due to the grace of God.

The next result of frequent confession should be compassion. Because we recognise the seeds of sin in our own souls, we must be aware that it is only grace that separates us from the worst of sinners. How much worse than they would we have been were it not for the grace of God? How much better would they have responded had they been given the graces we have received? The distribution of grace remains a mystery: it is God's privilege to distribute to this one so much, to that one so much more. But he demands of us in proportion to what we have received: that is why in the face of eternity we may have no advantage over those who have struggled against sin without the graces given to us.

This is made clear in many passages of the Gospels. 'To you has been given the secret of the kingdom of God, but for those outside everything is in parables' (Mark 4:11). 'To one he gave five talents, to another two, to another one, to each according to his ability' (Matthew 25:15). 'That servant who knew his master's will, but did not make ready or act according to his will, shall receive a severe beating. But he who did not know, and did what deserves a beating, shall receive a light beating. Every one to whom much is given, of him will much be required; and of him to whom men commit much they will demand the more' (Luke 12:47–8).

We are among those who have been given much—we have the grace of the sacraments, and the light of Christian teaching. Others, through no fault of their own, have to live without either faith or sacraments. We may observe their sins, their many sins, but we should never consider ourselves superior to them even though we may have been able, so far, to avoid these sins. Hence when we confess our temptations and passing thoughts, we are enabled to have compassion on those who sin. Only if we have compassion on them, will we be able to help them use the opportunity, as it arises, when they have a chance to turn away from sin and find hope in the Gospel.

The prophet Zephaniah spoke of the day when the proud ones of Israel would discover that there lived among them, unknown to them, a humble people who were the true heirs of the promises. 'On that day you shall not be put to shame because of the deeds by which you have rebelled against me; for then I will remove from your midst your proudly exultant ones, and you shall no longer be haughty in my holy mountain. For I will leave in the midst of you a people humble (*praus* again, in the Greek) and lowly. They shall seek refuge in the name of the LORD, those who are left in Israel; they shall do no wrong and utter no lies, nor shall there be found in their mouth a deceitful tongue. For they shall pasture and lie down, and none shall make them afraid' (Zephaniah 3:11–13).

This prophecy was literally fulfilled when the proud Pharisees were displaced by the lowly Apostles. God's people Israel were not all to suffer because of the pride of the few who vaunted themselves on being perfect, because there were enough lowly ones who knew, like the publican in the parable, that they were sinners. The Apostles, once they had been made aware of their own weakness in flying from the Cross, were given the commission to pasture the Lord's sheep, and none made them afraid. And like every passage of Scripture, there is an application to our own lives too; if we can bring ourselves to confess our frailty, the Lord will be able to use even us to feed his sheep.

Of the twelve Apostles, it is perhaps Philip who can best give us an example of meekness. Like Andrew, he was among the first to be called, and he went at once to tell others about the presence of the Christ. 'We have found him of whom Moses in the law and also the prophets wrote, Jesus of Nazareth' (John 1:45). When the Greeks ask to see Jesus, Philip goes first to tell Andrew, and lets Andrew tell the Lord (John 12:20–22). He does not put himself forward at all, he claims nothing for himself, nor does he try to convince people by his own efforts. To Nathanael he says only, 'Come and see!' Maybe the reason he stays in the background, and keeps away from too much attention is because he knows he is not very bright. He is good at accounts, yes, 'Two hundred denarii would not buy enough bread for each of them to get a little' (John 6:7), but his question to the Lord at the Last Supper betrays the fact that up to now he has had very little understanding of the significance of Our Lord's teaching. 'Philip said to him, "Lord, show us the Father, and we shall be satisfied", Jesus said to him, "Have I been with you so long, and yet you do not know me, Philip?"' (John 14:8–9)

Philip, who would not put himself forward, who had failed to understand the signs Our Lord had given, who disappeared with the others at the arrest of Jesus, became in turn one of the heroic twelve who went forth and proclaimed the Gospel to the limits of the known world. Only when we know we are weak can we be truly strong.

Of the twelve patriarchs we may take Zabulon as our guide to the virtue of meekness, and the value of the confession of trivial sins. His

Testament is meek, though his confession is not complete. Indeed it is because he cannot bring himself to make a full and complete confession that he fails, at the last, to bear a true witness to the truth.

He begins his testimony by talking about his young days, before the sale of Joseph.

1. The transcript of the words of Zabulon, of what he said to his sons before his death in the hundred and fourteenth year of his life, two years after the death of Joseph. He said to them: Listen to me, sons of Zabulon, attend to the words of your father. I am Zabulon, a welcome gift to my parents. For when I was born my father became exceedingly rich, in his flocks and his herds, since he had acquired what fell to him as a result of the particoloured rods. I am not aware, my sons, that I ever sinned in those days, except in thought, nor do I remember doing wrong except by ignoring Joseph, when I kept silent about my brothers, and I did not tell my father what had happened. I wept much over Joseph, but in secret, for I was afraid of my brothers, because they had all agreed that they would kill anyone who revealed the secret. On the other hand, when they decided to do away with him, I pleaded with them with my tears not to do such a wicked thing.

2. Simeon, Dan, and Gad attacked Joseph intending to kill him, but Joseph fell on his face and cried to them, 'Have pity on me, my brothers, have compassion on the feelings of our father Jacob. Do not lift up your hands against me, to shed innocent blood, for I have not done you any harm. And if I have wronged you, correct me with your authority, my brothers, but do not lift up your hands to murder your own brother, for the sake of our father Jacob.' And as he was wailing, and speaking those words, I found his tears unbearable, and I too began to weep. My liver was liquified within me, and all my bowels turned to water through the emotion I felt. I wept with Joseph; my heart bounded and all the joints of my body ached, so that I could no longer stand. Joseph, when he saw how I wept with him, but that they were still intent on killing him, hid behind me, beseeching me for help. And then Reuben arrived, and

said, 'Brothers, let us not kill him, but let us throw him into one of these dry wells, the ones our fathers dug but found no water.' That is why the Lord had prevented water welling up in them, so that there might be a means of escape for Joseph. The Lord continued to do this, until they sold Joseph to the Ishmaelites.

3. I refused all share of the proceeds of the sale of Joseph, my sons—it was Simeon, Dan, Gad, and their children who took the price; they bought new shoes with it, for themselves, their wives and children. 'For this,' they said, 'is the price of the blood of our brother, so we must not eat it, but let us trample it under foot—and he thought he would be king over us! We will see what becomes of his dreams.' That is why it is written in the law of Moses that he who is unwilling to raise up seed to his brother shall have his sandal loosened, and they shall spit in his face. The brothers of Joseph were not willing to preserve the life of their brother, and the Lord loosened for them the sandals which they wore because of Joseph their brother. For when they went down to Egypt, their sandals were unloosed by Joseph's servants outside the door, and thus they did honour to Joseph, in the manner that is done to King Pharoah. Not only did they bow down before him, but they were bespattered as they fell so fast before him. So they were disgraced in the sight of the Egyptians, for after that the Egyptians came to hear of all the evil that they had done to Joseph.

4. After he had been put in the pit, my brothers sat down to eat, but I could not taste anything for two days and two nights, I was so distressed about Joseph. Judah also would not eat with them, but kept watch over the pit, terrified that Simeon and Gad would jump down and kill him. Noticing that I was not eating either, he set me to watch as well, up to the day they sold him. Joseph remained in the pit three days and three nights, so that he had not eaten when he was sold. Reuben came to hear that he had been sold while he was away, and lamented, tearing his garments. He said, 'How can I look on the face of my father Jacob?' He seized

the money and ran after the merchants, but could not find them. For they had left the main road and taken a short cut along the hollow paths. Reuben lamented and would not eat anything that day, but Dan went up to him and said, 'do not grieve, do not lament, I have thought of what to say to our father Jacob. Let us kill a wild goat, and dip Joseph's coat into its blood. Then we can send it to Jacob and say, "Can you recognise whether this is your son's coat?"' And so they did. They had taken the coat off Joseph when they prepared to sell him, and put an old slave's cloak on him. Simeon had taken the coat, and was very reluctant to give it up. He threatened to cut it up with his sword, in his fury that Joseph was still alive, and that he had not been able to kill him. But the rest of us all withstood him, telling him, 'If you do not hand it over, we will say that it was you alone who committed this crime in Israel.' So he handed it over to them, and they carried out what Dan had suggested.

One cannot help feeling that we prefer Simeon's frank admission of his guilt to Zabulon's endless excuses. It began when he claimed that he never sinned, 'except in thought', as if sins of thought were of no consequence. It is never a good idea to say that we have never sinned, even if it is true. And since 'a righteous man falls seven times' a day (Proverbs 24:16), how can anyone claim never to have sinned? What it means is that he considered trivial sins not worth mentioning. He allowed passing thoughts to become sins of thought, trivial bad habits and sins to multiply until he was so used to them that he did not notice them. From that he goes on to make excuse after excuse, trying to convince us that he was really the good one among the twelve all the time. The only sin he admits is that he did not tell Jacob what had really happened, and even that he excuses on account of fear of the other brothers. But he did take part with the others in seizing his brother, selling him and covering up for themselves afterwards— he cannot get away from the fact that, like them, he did sin. But he will not admit a great sin, because he has not been accustomed to admitting the lesser ones.

His Testament continues with good advice to his sons:

5.   And now, my boys, I tell you to keep the laws of the Lord, and have pity on your neighbour, and benevolence towards everyone, not only people but animals as well. Because of that the Lord has blessed me, and when all my brothers were ill, I alone remained healthy. The Lord knows the intentions of each of us. Have compassion in your bowels, my children, for whatsoever a man does to his neighbour, the Lord will do to him. Even the sons of my brothers became ill, and some of them died because of Joseph, for they did not have mercy in their bowels. My own sons were preserved and did not catch the disease, as you know very well. As long as we were in Canaan, I used to catch fish along the shore for our father Jacob, and although there were many who drowned in the sea, I remained unscathed.

6.   I was the first man to construct a boat to sail on the sea, for the Lord gave me the understanding and skill to do that. I laid a wooden keel below it, and set a tree upright in the middle to spread my sail. I sailed along the coast in it, and netted fish for my father's household, until the time we came to Egypt. I used to give a share of my catch for any stranger, taking pity on him. Not only a stranger, but anyone who was sick, or old, received a share of my fish, and I helped everyone whatever their needs. I called them to me and sympathised with their sorrows. That is why the Lord helped me to catch so many fish in my fishing-grounds, for he who shares with his neighbour will receive much more in return from the Lord. I was a fisherman for five years, and gave shares to every man I met, as well as providing enough for my father's entire household. I used to fish in the summer, and in the winter I looked after the sheep with my brothers.

7.   Now I will tell you something else I did. I saw a man in distress, unclothed in the winter, and I took pity on him, so I sneaked a garment out of my father's house in secrecy and gave it to the man in distress. In the same way, my children, you should have pity on everyone without distinction, and assist them out of what God has given you; give to every man with a willing heart. And if you have nothing to hand which you could give someone in need, at least have compassion on him with a pitying heart. I know that I had nothing to hand at that moment to help the one in need, so I walked along with him for seven furlongs, lamenting, and my heart was moved by my compassion for him.

Both the Blessings of Zabulon mention his successful fishing business: Jacob says that 'Zabulon shall dwell at the shore of the sea; he shall become a haven for ships, and his border shall be at Sidon' (Genesis 49:13). Moses brackets Zabulon with his brother Issachar the hunter, 'for they suck the affluence of the seas and the hidden treasures of the sand' (Deuteronomy 33:19). That implies that Zabulon is more of a trader than a fisherman, and has done extremely well for himself in association with the notoriously pagan merchants of Sidon. He is being rather ingenuous in stressing his role as beneficent fishmonger, not to mention stealing his father's property to relieve the poor—but then, St Francis did that.

He continues, repeating himself:

8.   Have compassion, my children, on every man and show him pity, so that the Lord will have compassion and pity on you. For on the last of the days God will send his compassion to the earth, and where he finds those with compassion and pity, he will dwell in him. For as much as a man has compassion on his neighbour, so much does the Lord on him (cf. Matthew 6:14). When we went down into Egypt, Joseph bore no hatred against us, and when he saw me he was merciful. Consider his example, and do not bear hatred, my children, love one another and let none of you remember the offences of his brother. Such behaviour would break up unity and tear apart any family, it would plunge your hearts into confusion. For the one who bears hatred does not possess a heart of compassion.

9.   Think about the storm waters: look, if they are channelled together they can sweep away stones, timber, sand, and everything else, but if they are diverted into many streams, the earth absorbs them and they come to nothing. In the same way,

if you are divided, you will come to nothing. Do not split into two parties, for everything that the Lord has made should have a single head. He has given us two shoulders, hands, feet, yes, but all our limbs are directed by one head. I have discovered from the writings of my ancestors that the time will come when you will be divided in Israel; you will follow two kings and perform all sorts of abomination, worshipping every kind of idol until your enemies take you into captivity. You will suffer among the nations, enfeebled in every way, in affliction and sorrow of heart. After that you will remember the Lord and repent, and he will look upon you for he is merciful and compassionate, and does not consider the wickedness of the sons of men, for they are but flesh, and the spirits of deceit lead them astray in all their doings. And then it shall happen that the Lord himself shall rise upon you, the sun of righteousness, with healing and mercy in his wings. He will deliver the sons of men from all their captivity under the devil, and all the spirits of deceit shall be cast down. All the nations shall look upon him with envy. And you will see God in the likeness of man (cf. Philippians 2:7). He whom the Lord has chosen, Jerusalem shall be his name, yet once again you will offend against him in the wickedness of your ways, and you will be cast aside until the time of the consummation.

10. And now, my children, be not grieved that I am dying, do not be cast down because I am leaving you. I shall rise again in your midst, like a leader among his sons, and I shall rejoice in the company of my tribe, that is, as many as have kept the law of the Lord and the commandments of Zabulon their father. But upon the wicked the Lord will raise up eternal fire, and will destroy them to all generations. I am going now to my rest, as my fathers have done before me. Your part is to honour the Lord our God with all your strength, all the days of your life. And when he had said that, he fell asleep into a good rest, and his sons enclosed him in a wooden coffin. Afterwards they took him to Hebron, and buried him with his ancestors.

This passage is clearly Christian. The phrase 'the last of the days' refers to the common early Christian view that the six Days of Creation represent the six Ages of world history, and that the last one, the Day of Man, begins with the Incarnation of Our Lord, God's compassion on the earth. We live still in the Sixth Day: all that is to come is the eternal Sabbath. 'And you will see God in the likeness of man'—Zabulon quotes St Paul here, carefully using similar Greek words but not quite the same (he says *schemati anthropou*, St Paul says *homoiotati anthropon*, Philippians 2:7).

We cannot help remembering that when Compassion did come to dwell among us, and God took on the likeness of men, He told us the parable about the Pharisee who went into the temple to pray, 'God, I thank thee that I am not like other men, extortioners, unjust, adulterers, or even like this tax collector. I fast twice a week, I give tithes of all I get.' All of which was no doubt true, but it is not good form to say so, any more than Zabulon is justified by his endless excuses. The one who is justified is the one who cries out, without excuses or apologies, evasion or equivocation, 'God, be merciful to me a sinner!' (Luke 18:9–14)

Not only the secular world around us, but even many in the Church, ridicule the routine confession of small matters. There are even priests who still try to discourage frequent confession, and tell people to go away and sin some more until they have something worth confessing. As a result many people have become confused and discouraged. In particular they wonder what is the point of frequent confession, when they seem to say the same things every time, and never make any progress.

To this the first reply is with the familiar parables of the conscientious housewife and the keen gardener. No matter how often the housewife dusts her furniture and sweeps her floor, there will always be more of the same sort of dust the next day. Over and over again the gardener plucks out the little weeds that are just showing in his borders, and they are back again next week. The more often the garden is weeded, the shelves are dusted, the more attentive to detail we become. We are not satisfied until everything is sparkling and clean, not a leaf out of place, not a stray weed lurking in the shady places. In fact, we are never truly satisfied.

On the other hand the slattern who never sweeps the floor, and the lazy gardener who lets the weeds grow and seed, do not notice what is going on; they remain contented as squalour and entanglements build up around them. Other people will notice, but if we are not conscientious in our housework and gardening, we will not. So it is with the state of the soul: if we are conscientious in weeding out every speck as soon as it arises we will never be satisfied with ourselves, but will come back again and again to make sure it is not growing again. But if we are negligent, and allow things to grow and fester, we never notice, although others around us certainly will.

There is an important difference, of course, between being conscientious and being scrupulous. The conscientious soul is totally confident in the love of God, and is eager, for that very love, to co-operate with grace as much as possible. The scrupulous soul is either racked by the fear of God, or is caught up in such pride that she cannot admit that she is less than perfect. A confessor will know how to advise such a one: the loving conscientious soul needs less advice.

Frequent confession, therefore, is as beneficial as frequent housekeeping. And the fact that it is the same incipient sins, the same distracting thoughts and temptations, every time, is merely a factor of the human condition. Although we are potentially the victim of all eight of Cassian's viruses, in practice each of us is usually only affected by one or two. The sins we commit by inadvertence or habit are always the same. If one came to confession with a different sin every week it could only be deliberate. Those who are striving for perfection will have the humility, the meekness, to admit that they are sinners, and could fall into any sort of sin, but they will not be setting out on purpose to sample every sin mentioned in the Catechism.

Step Six

LONGANIMITY

The Patriarch Dan, Prophet Jonah and Apostle Simon

Do you do well to be angry?   (Jonah 4:4)

The sixth degree of humility is that a monk be content with the meanest and worst of everything, and esteem himself, in regard to the work that is given him, as a bad and unworthy workman, saying to himself with the prophet: *I am brought to nothing; I am all ignorance; I am become as a dumb beast before thee; yet am I ever close to thee.*

RB 7

Cassian makes this his seventh step: 'if we be content with the lowest position, and consider ourselves lazy and unworthy servants in all our responsibilities' (*Monastic Institutes*, IV, 39).

Both have alluded to Our Lord's words, 'So also you, when you have done all that is commanded you, say, "We are unworthy servants; we have only done what was our duty"', with perhaps also an echo of the rebuke, 'You wicked and lazy servant', in the parable of the talents (Luke 17:10; Matthew 25:23,26).

It is being content with our lot that leads us to the virtue of *longanimity*, for which there is no simple modern equivalent. It is more than patience, more than endurance: it is not merely forcing ourselves with gritted teeth to put up with insult, derision all day long; it is really feeling contented, with cultivating a placid spirit that is not disturbed or aroused by whatever happens to us. Patience may endure all things without grumbling publicly, while being silently convinced they are unjust. Longanimity accepts whatever happens as no more than our due.

St Jerome notes that the single Greek word *makrothymia* can best be expressed by two words in Latin, *patientia* and *longanimitas*, which is how both eventually appeared in the list of Fruits of the Holy Spirit (though not apparently in St Jerome's authentic Vulgate text). St Thomas explains the distinction between them: 'There are two ways in which the mind may be well disposed in evil circumstances; firstly if the mind be not disturbed by the threat of evil things, which belongs to the virtue of patience, and secondly if it be not disturbed by the deferral of good things, which belongs to that of longanimity.' (*Summa Theologiae* I-II, lxx, iii, in corp. art.; cf. St Jerome, *Commentary on Galations* ad locum; VII, 510 in Benedictine edition.)

Longanimity is exercised most when we see others being preferred before us, granted privileges and benefits which we think we deserve ourselves. Longanimity, in fact, really comes into action when we are actually suffering real injustice, but instead of crying out or shouting aloud, we remain dumb like a lamb before the slaughterhouse. In this we see at once that it is part of the imitation of Christ, for He suffered the greatest injustice in all human history without complaining or arguing, praying only for those who persecuted him, 'for they know not what they do.' Instead of expressing anger or indignation, he remained silent before his accusers. That is what we are called on to do, if we are to rise on the ladder of perfection.

But, we may say, are we not blessed if we 'hunger and thirst for righteousness'? Are we not to take part with the oppressed, to be champions of widows and orphans? Is there no room for the armed struggle in our thirst for justice? It is difficult, of course, to remain placid and long-suffering in the face of the unjust suffering of other people, however much we may aim at being so in our own case. Perhaps the question is not so much, should we try to aid others in distress, as in what way should we aid them. St James tells us, 'Religion that is pure and undefiled before God and the Father is this: to visit orphans and widows in their affliction, and to keep oneself unstained before the world' (James 1:27). We are also told by the prophet Ezechiel that the sin of Sodom which cried out to heaven for vengeance was that, 'she and her daughters had pride, surfeit of food, and prosperous ease, but did not aid the poor and needy' (Ezechiel 16:49).

There is no doubt that we are positively commanded to do all that we can to relieve unjust suffering, and for that matter even justified suffering, in others. But it does not appear that we are to do so in anger or by violence. Anger arises from jealousy, and clouds our perception, so that what we do in anger does not relieve suffering at all, but rather increases it. St James again speaks of this connection between anger and jealousy: 'What causes wars and what causes fightings among you? Is it not your passions that are at war in your members? You desire and do not have; so you kill. And you covet and cannot obtain; so you fight and wage war' (James 4:1–2).

Longanimity teaches us to be content with what we have, even when we really ought to be given more, according to the justice of this world. Longanimity, restraining us from anger, ought to enable us to give practical assistance to those who suffer, even though that means depriving ourselves of even more of what we think we are entitled to have. Rather than going away and fighting on behalf of the poor, we should share what we have with them and be close to them. The world would be horrified if we say we are not prepared to stand up and fight for social justice, but those who suffer would probably prefer a simple meal and an adequate shelter to the disruption and turmoil which war would bring upon them. Wars of 'liberation' all over Africa have done nothing to improve the lot of the poor, but have actually caused them immensely more suffering. The rich and powerful remain still powerful and rich. As long as this world lasts there will be injustice and wickedness in high places: we can never put a stop to that, but we can do our own little part in our own little corner of the world to make life more tolerable for those around us. It could be said that St Teresa of Calcutta did more for the poor than all the liberation forces of the world put together.

Longanimity does not only apply to external oppression. It also means being prepared to acknowledge our own imperfection, that we have failed in many things we set out to do, and that we do other things less well than they might have been done. In this it is the opposite of perfectionism, which can be a most irritating vice. The perfectionist is never satisfied with what he is doing but must be ever improving it and retouching it and polishing it because he cannot admit to himself that anything he produces could be less than the finest example of what he is trying to produce. This can affect the artist in particular, whether it applies to finely chiselled prose and verse, to painting and sculpture, music, architecture or any other art. But it can equally well affect the cook, the gardener, the teacher, or the liturgist.

The root of this perfectionism, of course, is pride, however much it may try to disguise itself. This pride can affect us just a much in our spiritual efforts, as we strive to attain a perfect and flawless performance of the chant, the liturgy, or even the sermon. We are always trying to prove to ourselves that we can be the very best at whatever we are trying to do, and naturally we would like other people to notice this and be impressed. When we fail, we become exceedingly angry with ourselves, and may either fall into a gloom, or strike out violently, shouting in frustrated rage. Then we need to find someone to blame for our own failure to be perfect, and rant against our parents, our teachers, our audience. That is how perfectionism differs from the loving conscientiousness we mentioned in the last chapter.

Perfectionism also demands an impossible standard among those around us. If we are to shine at whatever we have set ourselves to do, everyone associated with us must also be outstanding (only not quite so outstanding as we are ourselves, of course). If someone else makes a mistake which we imagine has marred our faultless performance, we are quick to direct our anger against them. We can even imagine that we are right to do so, and that we ought to rebuke them loudly and publicly for failing to be as perfect as we would like them to think we are.

The prophet Jonah had a very high opinion of himself, and a very low opinion of the people of Nineveh. It may well be true that the Ninevites were exceedingly wicked, and did not refrain from idolatry and Sabbath-breaking, theft and false witness, and were particularly vicious in coveting their neighbours' houses and goods. It is probably also true that Jonah was scrupulous in observing the Law of Moses, wore long tassells and broad phylacteries, and had never in his life seethed a kid in its mother's milk. In the most comic of all the books of the Old Testament, we see how Jonah flatly refused God's call to preach to the people of Niniveh, because he did not consider them worthy of his talents, and had no hope of their salvation whatever. His attempted escape to the opposite end of the Mediterranean was frustrated by the Lord with the aid of a large and co-operative fish, and Jonah was eventually forced to cry out against the city of Nineveh (Jonah 3:4).

He then sat down expecting to enjoy the spectacle of the fiery destruction of 'more than a hundred and twenty thousand persons who do not know their right hand from their left, and also much cattle.' He was utterly confident that their wickedness deserved nothing but wrath and annihilation, in contrast to his own supreme virtue. But the people repented, turned from their evil ways, and were saved. Jonah's reaction is fury, with the people, with himself, and above all with God. 'And the LORD said, "Do you do well to be angry?"' (Jonah 4:4) There follows the comedy of the gourd or castor-oil plant which springs up and provides shade for the prophet's bald head. When it withers away the next day, Jonah is furious again. 'But God said to Jonah, "Do you well to be angry for the plant?" And he said, "I do well to be angry, angry enough to die"' (Jonah 4:9).

Jonah is totally lacking in the virtue of longanimity. Had he been contented to do as the Lord said, to rejoice in the salvation of the Ninevites, and to be grateful for the shade as long as it lasted, and suffer its loss without regrets or complaints, he would have been a better prophet and a better Israelite. His fury is specifically directed against God, but it stems from his own pride. The little Book of Jonah is one of the most instructive in the canon, once we are prepared to forget about its literal meaning and concentrate on the spiritual interpretation. Nowhere is it more true that the 'letter killeth but the spirit giveth life', for if we waste our time investigating the aquatic species of the Mediterranean we have failed to understand that, like all the other parables of both Old and New Testament, it is about ourselves.

Anger against the sins of others, anger against God for forgiving them, anger against God and the world when inanimate objects fail to behave in the way that most suits our personal comfort: these are familiar in every age and in every life. We have to learn, through the Holy Spirit, how to be placid and resigned when things do not go as we would have them, and the gourd withers on the vine; how to rejoice when we see the grace of God bearing fruit in other people; how to be compassionate on those who are manifestly falling into sin, and to pray that they too may be saved.

Of the twelve Patriarchs, it is Dan who is most associated with anger, which he himself realises has grown from jealousy.

1.   A transcript of the words of Dan, which he spoke to his sons during the last days of his life. At the age of one hundred and twenty-five he called his family together and said, Listen to my words, O sons of Dan, attend to the words that proceed from the mouth of your father. I have examined my conscience and looked over my whole life, and I see that what is good and pleasing to God is truth and good deeds, what is hateful is deceit and anger, which teach men every kind of wickedness. I confess today to you, my sons, that I would have rejoiced in my heart over the death of Joseph, a man who was good and truthful, and I was delighted when he was sold, because our father had loved him more than us. The spirit of jealousy and conceit told me, 'You are his son too.' And one of the spirits of the devil conspired with me, saying, 'take this sword and destroy Joseph with it, for once he is dead, your father will love you.' That is the spirit of wrath, which persuaded me, that as a leopard devours a kid, so I should devour Joseph. But the God of Jacob my father did not leave him in my hands, for I never found him alone. Nor did he allow me to carry out this crime, which would have destroyed two of the sceptres of Israel.

2.   Now, my sons, see—I am dying, and I say to you in truth, that unless you preserve yourselves from the spirit of deceit and wrath, and devote yourselves to truth and longanimity, you will perish. There is a blindness in wrath, my sons, which prevents a man from seeing people as they really are. Even his father and mother he looks on as enemies, if he has a brother, he knows him not. A prophet of the Lord he ignores, a righteous man he will not look upon, a friend he will not recognise. The spirit of wrath entangles him in a net of lies, and shuts even the eyes of his body, blinding his understanding with deceit so that he can see only with the eyes of wrath. How does it cover his eyes? With hatred in the heart, for it gives him its own heart of hatred against his brother.

3.　Wrath is destructive, my sons, for it becomes the soul of the soul itself, and takes over the body of the wrathful man. It dominates his mind and gives its own strength to the body, so that it may do all manner of wickedness. Once the body has done all that, the soul finds excuses for what it has done, for it is unable to see truly. That is why a wrathful man, if he has any strength of body, gains a threefold power in his wrath. The first is through the ability and assistance of his servants. The second is through the wealth in which he trusts, and triumphs in wickedness. The third is through his own physical strength, so that he himself can carry out his crimes. If on the other hand the wrathful man be weak, the anger he feels will still work a twofold power, for his anger will always find ways to assist him in evil. This spirit of wrath ever walks at the right side of Satan, accompanied by deceit, so that a man's actions are full of cruelty and lies.

4.　You should, therefore, understand the power of wrath, for it is futile. First of all it stirs you up to words, then it stimulates the angry man to action, and confuses his understanding with bitter jealousy, until it overwhelms his soul with mighty wrath. Whenever someone speaks against you, let it not move you to anger. And if anyone praises you and calls you good, do not be elated, and do not let it change you, either towards joy or pomposity. For first of all praise delights your ears, and so it excites your thoughts until you believe the provocation, so that eventually an angry man comes to think he is right to be angry. If you should happen to suffer any detraction or loss, my children, be not disturbed, for that spirit of wrath will make you grieve over what you have lost until your longing turns to anger. Whether you suffer loss willingly or no, do not let it depress you, otherwise sorrow will give birth to anger and deceit. It is a double evil, this anger and deceit; for they accompany each other in order to throw your thoughts into confusion. Once your mind is confused like that, the Lord can find no place there, and the devil triumphs over it.

5.　Keep the commandments of the Lord, my sons, and follow his law. Turn away from wrath, and hate falsehood, so that the

Lord may dwell within you, and the devil may flee away from you. Speak the truth, each to other, and never fall into disputes and quarrels, but be at peace, at one with the God of peace; never let strife be strong against you. Love the Lord with all your soul, and your neighbour in a heart of truth. I know that in the latter days you will turn away from the Lord, you will be wrathful with Levi, and strive against Judah. But you will not prevail against them. The angel of the Lord will be their guide, for it is in them that Israel will be established. But you, when you fall away from the Lord, will be walking in every sort of evil, taking part in the abominations of the nations, committing fornication with women of wickedness, and embracing every sort of evil wished upon you by the spirits of evil. I have read in the book of the just man Enoch that Satan will be your ruler, and that all the spirits of lust and pride will submit themselves to Levi so that they can sit beside him and thus make him commit sin in the sight of the Lord. My own descendants will come close to Levi, and join in his sins in every way. The sons of Judah also will be avaritious and grasp after the goods of others like lions. For this reason you will be taken away into captivity along with them, and there you will suffer all the plagues of Egypt, and all the depravity of the nations. When you return to the Lord, he will have pity on you, and will lead you back to his holy place, proclaiming peace for you. Then shall the salvation of the Lord arise for you, out of Judah and Levi, and he will wage war against the devil, and he will grant you an avenging triumph against your enemies. He will liberate the captives of the devil, the souls of the just, and will turn unbelieving hearts back to the Lord, and to those who call upon him he will grant everlasting peace. The holy ones will find rest in Eden, and the just will rejoice in the new Jerusalem, which shall exist for God's glory for ever. No longer will Jerusalem be desolate, no longer will Israel be in captivity, for the Lord will be in their midst. He will dwell among men, and he, the Holy One of Israel will be king over them, in lowliness and poverty. He who believes in him will reign in truth, in the heavens.

6. And now, my children, fear the Lord, and keep yourselves away from Satan and his spirits. Draw near to God, and to the Angel who intercedes for you, for he is the mediator between God and man, for peace in Israel. He will stand against the kingdom of the Enemy, which is why the Enemy strives to overthrow all those who call upon the Lord. I know that on the day when Israel finds faith, the kingdom of the Enemy will be brought to an end at once. The Angel of Peace will strengthen Israel, so that he may not come to an evil end. For even in the time of the iniquity of Israel, the Lord will not withdraw from him, but he will follow close after the nation who does his will, for he does not look on any of the angels as he does on him. His name will be in every place of Israel, but he will be the Saviour among the Gentiles. So keep yourselves from every sort of evil deed, my children, and cast away wrath and deceit. Embrace truth and longanimity, and pass on to your children all that you have heard from your father. Thus the Saviour of the Nations will receive you, for he is truthful and long-suffering, meek and humble, and will teach the law of God by his actions. Turn away from every sort of sin, and adhere to the righteousness that comes from the law of the Lord, and your descendants will find salvation for ever. Bury me now near my fathers.

7. So saying, he embraced them, and fell into his age-long sleep. His sons buried him, but later they took up his bones to lie near Abraham, Isaac and Jacob. But as Dan had foretold to them, they became forgetful of the law of their God and were estranged from the land which they had been allotted, from the nation of Israel and from their fatherland. Thus it came to pass.

The patriarch Dan shows us how jealousy leads to deceit and wrath. Once we start imagining that another is better loved than we are, or that someone else has greater advantages in life, we lose sight of reality. Everything conspires to increase the delusion, so that jealousy grows and in its turn it causes anger. We manage to convince ourselves that we have every right to be angry, and even that it is up to us to put right injustice by violence and wrath. The ultimate self-deception is Dan's idea that if he killed the favourite son Joseph, his father would transfer his affections to him, the murderer.

The cure for deceit is truthfulness, a real love for the Truth, who is revealed not as an abstract idea but as a person, the Word made Flesh, who is the Way, the Truth and the Life. The cure for anger is longanimity, accepting placidly what happens around us, and 'the God of peace will be with you all' (Romans 15:33). Dan in his old age is represented as knowing all this: he makes no attempt to justify himself, but openly admits his sin and warns his children against following his example. Nevertheless, the blessing given him by Jacob is rather ambiguous: 'Dan shall judge his people as one of the tribes of Israel, Dan shall be a serpent in the way, a viper by the path, that bites the horse's heels so that his rider falls backwards. I wait for thy salvation, O LORD' (Genesis 49: 16–18). The implication is that Dan is unreliable: he is still one of the Twelve, he does still hold his place among the tribes, but he is dangerous. Moses thought the same: 'Dan is a lion's whelp that leaps from Bashan' (Deuteronomy 33:22). Notoriously, Dan is the one tribe omitted from the list of those who are to be saved in the Apocalypse (Apocalypse 7:4–8). Anger has no place in the Kingdom of Heaven.

Anger is one of the eight deadly viruses that lurk in every human heart, and can so easily break out into virulent manifestations. Cassian, naturally, writes much about it, and deals with the question of those who claim their anger is 'righteous'. He also makes the connection between anger and deceit, as anger blindfolds us so that we cannot see the truth about ourselves or others.

> A monk who is aiming at perfection, and desires to compete legitimately in the spiritual contest, must be a stranger to all taint of anger and wrath, and listen to what the Vessel of Election said to him: 'Let all anger, indignation, violence and blasphemy be eliminated from among you along with all ill-will' (Ephesians 4:31). When he says 'let all anger be eliminated from among you', he makes no exception as if it could ever be needful or useful for us ... Whatever the reason for the passion of anger arising, it blinds the eyes of the mind, and puts a pernicious beam into the faculty

of sight like a dangerous cataract, blocking the light of the sun of justice. It makes no difference whether our eyes are covered with a golden blindfold or one of lead, or any metal you choose; the value of the metal doesn't alter the quality of blindness.

True, we have the healthy instinct of anger given us for a valid reason, for which alone it is useful and healthy to feel anger, that is when we are aroused to combat the evil passions of our own hearts, and are indignant that our secret thoughts turn to things which we would be ashamed to do or even speak of before men. In the presence of the angels, and in the sight of God who penetrates all things, we are afraid and tremble because nothing can remain hidden in our consciences.

Indeed we may be indignant at anger itself, when it grows against our brother, and we may angrily drive out its deadly urgings, allowing it no hidden foothold in the depths of our hearts. The prophet teaches us to be angry in this sense, of driving anger out of his feelings so as not to desire retribution against his own enemies or those shown him by God, when he says, 'be angry and sin not' (Psalm 4:5).

We are therefore commanded to be angry in a right sense, against our own selves and the evil thoughts that occur to us, and not to sin, that is not to let them come to effect. The following verse clearly explains what this means: 'You that speak in your hearts, be smitten upon your beds' (Psalm 4:5). That is, whatever you imagine in your hearts, as sudden sly thoughts creep in, you should expel by wise consideration and eliminate all the turmoil and emotion of anger; as if lying quietly on your beds, improve and correct yourselves by a saving compunction. St Paul too quotes this verse as a witness, 'Be angry and sin not', saying, 'Let not the sun go down upon your anger, and give no place to the devil' (Ephesians 4:26). If it is evil to let the sun set on our anger, and anger gives the devil immediate entrance into our hearts, how are we previously commanded to anger when it says

'Be ye angry and sin not'? Does it not clearly mean to be
angry with your vices and your wrath, lest Christ the Sun of
Righteousness begin to set with your connivance because of
the anger which darkens your minds, until with his departure
you make space for the devil in your hearts?

Monastic Institutes, VIII, 5–8

Now in the preceding passages, Cassian does seem to give legitimacy
to anger or impatience against ourselves when we fail to avoid sin and
practise perfect virtue. Perhaps we should distinguish between anger
against sin in itself, against evil and wickedness in low places, and the
fruitless anger against our own selves which stems from pride. We may
feel anger legitimately against the devil and all his works, but that is not
at all the same thing as feeling anger against wicked men, against sinners,
even including ourselves. It is very easy to imagine that in a particular
instance we are consumed with 'righteous indignation', when we see
others committing loathly crimes or setting themselves deliberately
against God. But we are commanded to 'judge not, that you be not
judged' (Matthew 7:1), and reminded that 'God sent the Son into the
world, not to condemn the world, but that the world might be saved
through him' (John 3:17). The words 'judge' and 'condemn' in these two
passages are the same in the Greek, *krinein*. St Paul is quite firm with
us, only God has the right to judge and to condemn: 'Beloved, never
avenge yourselves, but leave it to the wrath of God; for it is written,
"Vengeance is mine, I will repay, says the Lord"' (Romans 12:19, cf.
Deuteronomy 32:35).

This is why only Our Lord is entitled to cleanse the Temple, for
he alone can see into hearts and minds, can judge rightly and punish
accordingly. Of him alone can it truly be said, 'Zeal for thy house will
consume me', and when the Jews demand a sign to show the authority
he has, he refers cryptically to his own death and resurrection (John
2:13–22). They fail to understand, but the disciples eventually do
realise that he is telling them that his authority is the authority of God
himself. We do not have that authority, and therefore we may never
show such zeal, nor take it upon ourselves to display the semblance
of anger.

Cassian continues to consider the restraint of anger from our thoughts as well as our words and actions:

> Now if we want to gain that pitch of perfection and its divine reward, as it is said, 'Blessed are the clean of heart, for they shall see God' (Matthew 5:8), we must not only eliminate anger from our actions, but also eradicate it from our thoughts. There is not much point in restraining words of wrath, or violent deeds, if God from whom no secrets are hid can see anger in our hearts. The Gospel teaches us to cut away the very roots of vice more than its fruits, for they will never grow again once the roots have been torn up. The mind can truly persevere in holiness and patience once this vice has been uprooted from the depths of our hearts, not just from our superficial words and works. To stop us committing murder, we must cut away anger and hatred, for the crime of murder could never be conceived without them. 'He who is angry with his brother is answerable to the court', and 'he who hates his brother is a murderer' (Matthew 5:22; I John 3:15). Since he longs in his heart to kill, although in the eyes of men his hand and sword have not been seen to shed blood, in the eyes of the Lord his anger convicts him of murder. God gives each man his reward or punishment, not only for actions put into effect, but also for his desires and aspirations ...
>
> An athlete of Christ who competes lawfully must eradicate the emotion of anger. The best remedy for this disease is to begin by believing that we are never justified in being angry, whether for a good or bad reason, understanding that we would quickly lose any light of discernment, any steadfastness of purpose, honour itself and the guidance of righteousness, if the principal light of our hearts were shrouded in such darkness. Moreover, while the spirit of wrath dwells in our hearts the purity of our minds would be disturbed, and we could never become temples of the Holy Spirit. Finally, we should consider that

we could not even lawfully pray if the prayers we offered to
God were ill-tempered.

Monastic Institutes, VIII, 19, 21

It is easy to see how this applies to our thoughts and feelings about
other people, whether they are really wicked or merely misguided, but
it can apply equally to our own pursuit of virtue. Anger, which should be
directed at sin itself, is so easily turned against ourselves when humility
teaches us not to be so surprised at our failings. We promise ourselves
glibly that we will never sin again, sometimes remembering to add 'with
the help of thy grace', but usually meaning 'by my own unaided efforts'.
We set out day after day, week after week, with the intention of being
absolutely sinless in thought, word, deed and omission, to do in every
case what seems to be the most perfect thing. And if we fail, and we
are certainly going to fail, we become very angry indeed, angry with
ourselves, angry with God, angry with other people.

When people come back regularly to the confessional, and have to
admit to the same boring and humiliating vices as last time, they are
liable to say 'I hate myself for this', when what they really mean is 'I love
myself so much that I am furious with myself for letting myself down,
and spoiling the image I have of my own sanctity and virtue'. They are
then tempted to blame God, remembering the clause 'with the help of
thy grace', and complain that God has let them down. They imply that if
they have sinned again it is God's fault for not stopping them. If only he
had given us the grace we asked for, we would not have sinned. In fact,
since we have so often asked for it, he should have shielded us from all
temptations. If we have sinned again, therefore, it is all God's fault. We
can even begin to blame God for our character, with all its defects, and
claim that 'God made me like this, so whatever I feel like doing is right
for me'. We easily forget that our human nature is damaged, corrupted
by original sin, and that the defects in our character are not part of our
God-given nature at all. He came to set us free from the effects of original
sin, but it takes a lifetime to do it. Once again, we need patience as well
as longanimity to accept that we have not yet achieved perfection. Hope
and faith reassure us that we are on the way of perfection but we still
have some distance to go.

Perhaps because we have understood part of the doctrine of original sin, we can also find it in ourselves to be angry with other people and blame them for our sins. We are taught by the psychologists to blame our parents for all our problems, and they to blame our grandparents, and so on back to Eve. We can also blame those involved in our education and upbringing, and those who first led us into sin. We can be very angry indeed with those around us whose thoughtless chatter has disturbed our profound meditation, whose insensitive gift of chocolates and wine has interrupted our faultless observance of Lent. When we find ourselves falling back into the same boring sins week after week, instead of meekly acknowledging that we are still in need of God's forgiveness and healing, we strike out in anger in all directions, furious that we have let ourselves down again, and desperate to blame someone.

Now we can see the difference between being conscientious and being scrupulous. Scruples really derive from pride, and foster anger. We are scrupulous if we are more concerned with our own self-image as paragons of virtue than we really are about the love of God and neighbour. Scruples lead us to be frightened of God and to despise our neighbour. The scrupulous soul is never at rest, never contented. But St Benedict says we should be content, even if we find ourselves to be the meanest and worst of everything. We are not to grumble over our failures, and seek to apportion blame for them, but we are to be content for God to find us as we are, and unabashed when other people see us in our true light. That is part of longanimity.

One of Our Lord's apostles was known as the 'Zealot'. Simon, the son of Alphaeus, the brother of James and Joset and Jude, had two nicknames which seem to mean the same thing, the 'Canaanite' and the 'Zealot'. That is all we know about him, apart from his family connection with Our Lord, since it seems that Mary the mother of James the Less and Joset was a close relation ('sister') of Our Lady (Mark 15:40, cf. John 19:25). The name 'Canaanite' must not be confused with the former pagan inhabitants of Palestine, or even with the Syro-Phoenician woman who is insultingly called that to stress that she is an unbeliever, an idolator and an outsider (Matthew 15:22). The two names are spelt quite differently in Greek and Hebrew. 'Canaanite' as applied to Simon must derive from the Hebrew word *qana'*, meaning 'to be jealous or ardent, and therefore means much the same as the Greek word '*zelotes*'. Nevertheless, the similarity of sound between 'Qanaanite' and 'Khanaanite' is so obvious, that the nickname must have been intended to imply he was as wild and ferocious as the primitive tribes of Canaan. Jealousy, or excessive zeal, leads to anger, as we have already heard from the Patriarch Dan.

The historian Josephus tells us much about the Zealots of the first century. They were a faction among the Jewish population who bitterly resented the presence and domination of pagans in the Holy Land, and were as much opposed to the mud-blood Herod family as they were to the aggressively pagan Romans. They demonstrated their opposition by violence: assassination and random destruction at first, eventually armed insurrection. It was the zealots who provoked the Romans into the full-scale invasion of Judaea in AD 70, and the resulting sack of Jerusalem and the total demolition of its temple. In their fierce determination to drive the pagans out of the Holy Land, what they actually achieved was the permanent abolition of the unceasing sacrifice, and the dispersal of the Jews, forbidden even to reside in the Roman colony built over the ruins of Jerusalem. The zealots, therefore, left a sad memory behind them. A generation later, in the rising of bar-Kochba, they again provoked the Romans into utterly destroying the Holy City. They had not been content to leave vengeance to God, but had taken on themselves the right to judge and condemn. Because of this, they were 'estranged from the land' as the author of the Testament of Dan concluded.

In their anxiety not to endure a moderate level of injustice and inconvenience, the Zealots brought down upon their people an intolerable burden of destruction and exile. It is difficult to think of any armed uprising in human history, or any military intervention, that has not in the same way caused far more suffering than it was intended to relieve. The virtue of longanimity teaches us to endure all things, to put up with injustice, suffering and oppression in this world, content to rely upon God to put straight what the world has made crooked, and to give to each one what his actions deserve.

For ourselves, longanimity means not merely putting up with the lowest and worst place, but really believing that we deserve no better, which leads us on directly to the next step on the ladder of humility.

Step Seven

FAITH

The Patriarch Joseph, Prophet Habbakuk and Apostle Peter

But I am a worm and no man (Psalm 21:6)

The seventh degree of humility is that he should not only in his speech declare himself lower and of less account than all others, but should in his own inmost heart believe it, humbling himself and saying with the prophet: *But I am a worm and no man, a byword to all men and the laughing stock of the people. I have been lifted up only to be humbled and confounded*; and again: *It is good for me that thou hast humbled me, that I may learn thy commandments.*

RB 7

Cassian uses almost exactly the same words, 'Eighthly, if we do not merely profess with our lips that we be inferior to all others, but really believe it in our hearts' (*Monastic Institutes*, IV, 39).

In many ways this step is the most significant, marking the boundary between the largely negative aspects of humility, and the positive stages of growth in the Holy Spirit. It is also by far the most difficult to explain to a modern secular audience, or for that matter any average audience at any date. How can someone who is trying to advance in holiness day by day really believe that he is not? How can someone who practises the faith, says his prayers, attends Mass and receives the sacraments regularly, genuinely believe that he is worse in the sight of God than the notorious sinners who infest every part of the world, now as much as they ever did? If we do profess that we are worms, are we not indulging in the worst sort of hypocrisy, pretending to be, in effect, 'humbler than thou'?

119

John Tauler, the great Dominican preacher, gives us an example of someone he knew who went so far as to whisper praise of his own humility to his neighbour during Vespers:

> A man shall in all sincerity rest upon his nothingness, realising that it is the only thing he can claim properly as his own, everything besides being not his own. Let him consider as an evil thing whatsoever he has or does on his own account, including his own self. Once as I was in choir alongside of a holy brother of ours, who was a man to whom God had granted many signs of sanctity, and whose holy life was full of marvels of grace—this brother whispered to me from the bottom of his heart: 'Brother, believe what I tell thee—I am the greatest and the foulest sinner in the whole world.' Let every one of us say the same in all sincerity. For I say to you, that if God bestowed upon the worst sinner the graces He has granted me, he would have become a great saint.
>
> Tauler, *Sermons and Conferences*, pp. 468–9

At first sight this seems unreal and even disturbing. Surely whatever the brother felt about himself, it would have been more seemly to keep quiet about it, especially in choir. Was it that the words slipped out unconsciously, 'from the bottom of his heart'? We hear of something similar in the life of St Philip Neri, who was overheard to murmur 'I am without hope', which prompted two kindly Dominicans to offer him consolation and spiritual advice. Eventually the saint grinned and said, 'I am without hope in myself, but I have every confidence in God.'

That, then, is the clue as to how we are to tackle this step on the ladder of humility: we must abandon all hope in ourselves, while being totally and supremely confident in the love of God. Rather than waste time thinking about ourselves, we should be filled with an awareness of God's grace that makes it possible for us to forget our own poor efforts at spiritual growth and be conscious only of the work the Holy Spirit is doing through us. We should not pretend that great things are not being done through us, or insult the Holy Spirit by asserting that they are worthless. Good works can, and are, being done through us, but we need to be constantly aware that they are not ours to claim, they are the works of God, and must be attributed to him alone. 'Not to us, O Lord, not to us, but to thy name give glory' (Psalm 113:9).

If our hope is entirely in God, then we can have no hope in ourselves. If all our good thoughts, words and actions are to be attributed to God, then we have nothing of our own to boast about. 'He must increase, but I must decrease' (John 3:30). In other words, what we are to cultivate is what the eighteenth-century mystics called *l'abandon à la providence divine*. This total trust in God is of course an important aspect of faith, another of the fruits of the Holy Spirit. Faith in this context means much more than awareness of and acceptance of the various points of doctrine. As St James pointed out, the Devil could easily pass any examination in knowledge of the catechism (James 2:19). No, the faith that justifies us is a complete self-surrender to God, throwing ourselves unreservedly into his arms, and allowing him to work through us in whatever way he pleases.

This sort of faith involves the recognition that we can do nothing whatsoever on our own. God's grace encompasses us: and therefore if we have been preserved from sin, it is not our achievement but the work of grace. Were that grace to be withdrawn, even for a second, we would plunge into such depravity that we would have no right ever to blame anyone else for whatever sins we see them commit. That is why we have no right to judge others, even if at present we are not conscious of any serious sin in ourselves: if we were subjected to the temptations they feel, we would fall further and faster than they. If they were granted the graces we have received, they would shine brighter and rise higher than we. Only God can judge, for he scrutinises the mind and heart, he knows exactly what temptations this one endures, what graces that one receives, and therefore what extent of co-operation with grace each of us have expressed. We are not, in this sense, our brothers' keepers, we may not judge them nor condemn them, for in the sight of God we are certainly no better than they, and are probably worse.

The cultivation of *l'abandon*, self-abandonment to divine providence, is not something we can do in a single act, as if we could surrender to God once and for all, and then rest for the remainder of our lives secure in the knowledge that we have made our submission and from now on it is up to God. No, we need to reflect continually that of ourselves we are nothing, and respond daily to the grace of God which works within us. That is why the regular practice of confession can never be left behind, our ceaseless prayers ever remind us of our utter dependence on God. Although we are aware that God is at work in us, still we must work out our salvation with fear and trembling (cf. Philippians 2:12–13). If we fail to co-operate with God's grace, all our spiritual life will disintegrate in a moment. If God withholds his grace to the extent that we find ourselves yet again falling into sin or imperfection, we still need the sacrament of penance to rebuild our confidence in him. He may have allowed us to fall in order to keep us humble, he will certainly grant us his sacramental grace in order to build us up.

Experience shows that many of those who are struggling to respond to grace, to love and serve God and neighbour, still have irritating vices they cannot shake off. Of course God could take away these vices and every shadow of temptation in an instant, and we frequently ask him to do so, but he does not, lest we be tempted to imagine that it was somehow through our own achievement that we had at last shaken off the bonds of sin. In fact we can go so far as to say that it is impossible to achieve sanctity unless we experience temptation. If a so-called saint were really totally free from any inclination to sin from birth, as some unfortunate lives of the saints suggest, they could not really be saints at all. When we read the letters and autobiographical writings of the saints we can see how long and hard they struggled against sin: St Paul's temper, St Teresa's greediness, St Augustine's weakness for women.

We must not imagine that even Our Lady did not have to struggle against temptation: sinless from conception, she had a greater freedom than we have ever known, but the challenges were still there. Perhaps her greatest difficulty was in understanding Our Lord's ministry, and why he had to go away from her: 'Son, why have you treated us so?' (Luke 2:48), 'Your mother and brethren are outside, asking for you' (Mark 3:32). She too, like all the saints, had to tread the path of self-abnegation, to remember again and again that the Lord 'has regarded the low estate of his handmaiden', to offer herself over and over as 'the handmaid of the Lord; let it be to me according to your word' (Luke 1:48, 38). The word translated 'handmaid' is in fact *doulé*, slave-girl. Our Lady describes herself in terms of the utmost abjection, for what God does in her is entirely the work of grace. How else could she be full of grace, were it not that she was empty of herself?

Of Our Lord's apostles, surely it is St Peter himself who most illustrates our need for total self-surrender to God. At the very beginning he listens to his brother Andrew and without question accepts his message that 'We have found the Messiah' (John 1:41). But soon enough he sees the power of God at work, and he falls flat on his face, crying out, 'Depart from me, for I am a sinful man, O Lord' (Luke 5:8). From then on we see him unreservedly committing himself to faith in Our Lord, even in the most extreme circumstances. When he is told to find the tax-money in a fish, he dutifully goes and hooks it (Matthew 17:27). When Our Lord, a land-dweller and carpenter, tells him to fish at the wrong time of day and on the wrong side, he throws out his nets at once. 'Master, we toiled all night and took nothing! But at your word I will let down the nets' (Luke 5:5; cf. John 21:6). At the sight of the Lord he is ready to step out of his boat and walk across the water (Matthew 14:29), though when he tries it again he finds himself splashing through shallow water and getting his cloak wet (John 21:6)!

Peter's profession of faith is recorded for us on two separate occasions, as an indication that in fact he, like the rest of us, had to renew his declaration of faith again and again. In the synagogue at Capernaum, he listens as Our Lord preaches to the crowd, and sees a flock of five thousand who had been eating out of his hand gradually melt away, muttering, 'This is a hard saying; who can listen to it?' Only twelve remain, and when Jesus asks them gently, 'Do you also wish to go away?' Simon Peter answered him, 'Lord, to whom shall we go? You have the words of eternal life' (John 6:60–68). And again, in Caesarea Philippi, it is Simon who proclaims the faith of them all, 'You are the Christ, the Son of the living God' (Matthew 16:16).

Each time, there is an immediate challenge to that faith. 'Did I not choose you, the twelve, and one of you is a devil?' says Jesus at Capernaum. We know which one, but at the time none of the apostles did. Peter has indeed been called and chosen, but he cannot be sure that he is not the devil. 'And they were very sorrowful, and began to say to him one after another, "Is it I, Lord?"' (Matthew 26:22) At Caesarea Philippi, Simon Peter cannot bear the prophecy of the Passion, '"God forbid, Lord! This shall never happen to you." But he turned and said to Peter, "Get behind me, Satan! You are a hindrance to me; for you are not on the side of God, but of men"' (Matthew 16:22–3). And Peter must have turned away muttering, 'and I am a worm and no man.'

Yet there is a promise as well as a challenge. 'Do not be afraid, henceforth you will be fishers of men' (Luke 5:10). 'You are Peter, and on this rock I will build my church' (Matthew 16:18). It was the prophet Habbakuk who foretold the fishing of men, 'Thou makest men like the fish of the sea, like crawling things that have no ruler. He brings all of them up with a hook, he drags them out with his net' (Habbakuk 1:14–15). We may be worms, crawling things in the dark, we cannot bring ourselves up, but he drags us out into the light. That is why, as the prophet continues, 'He whose soul is not upright in him shall fail, but the righteous shall live by his faith' (Habbakuk 2:4). By trusting in God alone, never in our own powers, we shall live. But in order to live, we must be prepared to die. And when the worm dies, the fish is caught.

'Follow me', says the Lord. 'If any man would come after me, let him deny himself and take up his cross and follow me. For whoever would save his life will lose it, and whoever loses his life for my sake will find it' (Matthew 16:24–5). So Peter was tested and challenged at the last. '"Lord, why cannot I follow you now? I will lay down my life for you." Jesus answered, "Will you lay down your life for me? Truly, truly, I say to you, the cock will not crow, till you have denied me three times."' (John 13:37–8).

Abandonment to divine providence is not total until we have abandoned our own righteousness utterly, abandoned our own integrity, every shred of self-respect. We stand before the Lord claiming nothing, holding nothing. Only then can he truly fill us. Peter's last remnant of pride in himself had to be shattered by the horror and shame of the denial. He had rashly followed St John into the Praetorium, so pleased with himself that he had not run away into hiding like the rest of them, and now he is cowed by the idle remarks of a servant girl so that he betrays his master, not once like Judas but three times. As the cock crows, Peter slinks away, knowing at last that he is truly a worm and no man.

And so he meets Our Lord again by the lakeside. Pope Benedict XVI analyses the threefold question and answer that respond to the threefold denial:

> In Greek, the word *phileo* means the love of friendship, tender but not all-encompassing; instead the word *agapao* means love without reserve, total and unconditional. Jesus asks Peter the first time: 'Simon, ... do you love me (*agapas me*) with this total and unconditional love?' (John 21:15–17)
>
> Prior to the experience of betrayal, the Apostle certainly would have said: 'I love you (*agapo se*) unconditionally.' Now that he has known the bitter sadness of infidelity, the drama of his own weakness, he says with humility: 'Lord, you know that I love you (*philo se*), that is, I love you with my poor human love.' Christ insists: 'Simon, do you love me with this total love that I want?' And Peter repeats the response of his humble human love: '*Kyrie, philo se*, Lord, I love you as I am able to love you.' The third time Jesus only says to Simon: '*Phileis me*? Do you love me?'
>
> Simon understands that his poor love is enough for Jesus, it is the only one of which he is capable; nonetheless he is grieved that the Lord spoke to him in this way. He thus replies: 'Lord, you know everything, you know that I love you (*philo se*).'
>
> This is to say that Jesus has put himself on the level of Peter, rather than Peter on Jesus' level! It is exactly this divine conformity that gives hope to the Disciple, who experienced the pain of infidelity.
>
> Benedict XVI PP, *Christ and his Church*
> (London: CTS, 2007), pp. 48–9.

In this we see the entire mystery of the Incarnation. We cannot climb up to God, so he puts himself on our level. On the Cross he shocked the world by quoting the beginning of Psalm 21, 'My God, my God, why hast thou forsaken me?' So he identifies himself with us, and we can follow him through the rest of the Psalm, even to the extent of making his words our own, 'I am a worm and no man' (Psalm 21:1,6). (It has been pointed out that 150 verses separate that first cry from the Cross from the last, 'Into thy hand I commit my spirit' (Psalm 30:5), and that maybe we should read all the intervening verses as part of Our Lord's prayer on our behalf.)

In the appearance by the lakeside, there is again a promise and a challenge, 'Feed my lambs, tend my sheep'. Now that Peter has passed this seventh step on the ladder of humility, he can be entrusted with the pastoral care of the universal Church. But even now he needs to be checked and rebuked once more: he ventures to ask of St John the Evangelist, 'what about this man?' He is given no answer; it is not his concern, 'What is that to you? Follow me' (John 21:20–22).

Once we know that we are 'lower and of less account than all others', we need have no further questions, no further anxieties. It is a moment of liberation, for we surrender entirely to God and allow him to direct us and guide us. Whatever happens, of good or ill, we know that he can bring good out of it, as long as we continue to acknowledge our dependence on his grace. Others stand before God and God alone can judge them, whether they are saints like St John, or sinners like the woman taken in adultery. 'Neither do I condemn you ... What is that to you? ... Follow me ... feed my sheep.' We are to feed the sheep and tend the lambs, but we may not judge them nor condemn them. When we see the sheep going astray we must follow them into the wilderness, search them out and bring them rejoicing home, but we may not consider ourselves superior to them, or forget how easily we ourselves might have strayed even further were it not for the grace of God that encompasses us.

All the saints, in one way or another, illustrate this same point, this same principle of self-abandonment to Divine providence. Otherwise they would not have been saints. We may think of the Little Way of St Thérèse, the self-abnegation of Blessed Charles de Foucauld, the lonely journey in the darkness of despondency travelled by St Teresa of Calcutta. Saints may give the impression of cheerful confidence, but that is only because their confidence is not in themselves but entirely in God. In him we can indeed be confident, nothing need ever make us anxious, nothing can shake our assurance of his love and his grace, precisely because we can have no trust whatsoever in our own. *Nada te turbe*, said St Teresa, 'Let naught disturb thee; Naught fright thee ever; All things are passing; God changeth never. Patience e'er conquers; With God for thine own Thou nothing dost lack—He sufficeth alone! *Dios solo basta*. (St Teresa's Bookmark, trans. Benedictines of Stanbrook, *Minor Works of St Teresa* (London 1913), p. 57.)

Continuing to look at the Twelve Patriarchs, we find that this attitude of serene trust in God is the characteristic of Joseph himself. The one who was wronged by all the others is the one who is utterly confident in the power of God to put all things right. He claims nothing for himself, and refuses in any way to incriminate any of his brothers. So he begins:

1. A transcript of the Testament of Joseph. When he was about to die, he summoned his sons and his brothers, and said to them, My brothers, and my children, listen to Joseph, the favourite of Israel; my sons, pay attention to the words of my mouth. I have seen in my life destruction and death, and I was not led astray, but remained in the truth of the Lord. My brothers here hated me, but the Lord loved me—they wished to destroy me, but the God of my fathers preserved me. They plunged me into the pit, but the Most High drew me out. I was sold as a slave, and the Master of all set me free. I was taken away into captivity, and his powerful hand came to my assistance. I was constrained by hunger, and the Lord fed me. I was alone, and God consoled me. I was in weakness, and the Most High came to my aid. I was in prison, and the Saviour brought me joy; in bonds, and he freed me; in the midst of slander, and he vindicated me; ill-spoken of by the Egyptians, and he delivered me; I was a slave, and he exalted me.

Joseph continues to tell us at great length of the wiles of Potiphar's wife, who went so far as to promise that she would forsake idolatry and force all the Egyptians to worship Joseph's God if he would agree with her. He pointed out that the Lord does not want that sort of forced service. During all these long arguments and temptations, Joseph's one refuge was his absolute confidence in God.

2. So it was that the chief officer of Pharoah entrusted me with his household. I had to contend with a shameless woman, who tried to induce me to sin with her. But the God of Israel my father preserved me from that burning flame. I was thrown into prison, I was flogged, I was derided, but the Lord brought me into favour with the warder. You see, the Lord never abandons those who fear him, neither in darkness, nor in bonds, in distress nor in necessity. God is not ashamed like man, nor does he show any fear like a son of man; he is not enfeebled like a mortal nor is he discouraged. He is at our side wherever we are, and in various ways he brings us consolation. He is swift to stand aside and allow the thoughts of our hearts to show themselves. During ten temptations he demonstrated my quality, and throughout them all I was long-suffering. Such longanimity is a great healer, and endurance brings many good things.

3. How many times did that Egyptian woman threaten me with death? And how many times, after she had handed me over to the torturers, did she call me back and make me promises? When I did not consent to lie with her, she said to me, 'You can be my master, over everything in my house, if only you will give yourself to me; you can be the lord of us all.' But I kept in mind the words of the fathers of my father Jacob, and I went into my private room and there prayed to the Lord. I fasted during those seven years, but to the Egyptians I seemed to be eating well. For those who fast for the sake of God are granted a healthy appearance. When my master gave me wine, I did not drink it, and when I fasted for three days together I accepted my victuals and gave them to the poor and weak. I used to rise early before the Lord, and I wept for the sake of the Egyptian woman, Memphia, for she troubled me greatly and without ceasing. She would come to me in the night, as if she were watching over me. To begin with, she had no son of her own, and she pretended that she wanted to treat me as her son. So I prayed to the Lord, and she did bear a son. Up to that time she had embraced me as a child, and I did not understand. But at length she tried to induce me to fornication, and when I realised that, I was distressed to the point of death. When she had left me, I came to myself and grieved about her for many days, now that I had understood her wiles and her scheming. I recounted to her the words of the Most High, in the hope that she would forsake her evil desires.

4. On many occasions she spoke, flattering me as if I were a holy man, and deceitfully spoke in praise of my temperance in front of her husband, although in private she desired to debauch me. In public she glorified me as a man of temperance, but in secret she said to me, 'Do not be afraid of my husband, for he is convinced of your chastity. Even if someone tells him about us, he will not believe it.' During all this I slept on the ground, and besought God to deliver me from her scheming. When she failed to achieve anything, she came back to me under cover of wanting instruction, to learn the word of the Lord. She told me, 'If you like, I will abandon my idols; simply give in to me, and I will persuade my husband also to turn away from idolatry, and we will walk in the way of your Lord.' But I told her, 'The Lord does not desire the worship of the unclean, neither does he take delight in adultery, but he delights in the pure of heart, and those who worship him with undefiled lips.' But she remained obstinate, still yearning to fulfil her desires. I applied myself to fasting and prayer, that the Lord might deliver me from her.

5. On another occasion she said to me, 'If you do not wish to commit adultery, I will kill my husband with poison, and then I can take you for my husband.' When I heard that, I tore my garments and said, 'Woman, have respect for God, and do not do such a wicked thing. Otherwise you will be destroyed, for believe me, I myself will tell everyone about your plan.' She was frightened then, and begged me not to tell anyone of her wickedness, and so she withdrew. Still she wooed me with gifts, and sent me all sorts of things which delight the sons of men.

6. Then she sent me a dish which had been concocted with something magical. When the eunuch who brought it to me

came in, I looked up and saw a terrible figure offering me a sword upon a plate. So I understood that she was plotting my destruction. I went out and wept, and did not taste either that food or any other which she sent me. A day later she came to me and recognised the dish. She said, 'Why have you not eaten from that dish?' I replied, 'Because you stuffed it with deadly magic. How can you say, "I will not go near the idols, but only to the Lord"? Now you must know that the God of my father revealed your wickedness to me through an angel. I have kept this, so that I can show it to you, in the hope that you would see it and repent. But in order that you may know that over those who serve God in chastity the scheming of the wicked has no power, look, I'll take some of it and eat it in front of you.' And as I said that, I said a prayer, 'O God of my fathers, O angel of Abraham, be with me', and I ate it. When she saw that, she fell on her face at my feet, crying, but I made her rise and warned her, till she swore she would never again do such a wicked thing.

7.   Nevertheless her heart was still bent on evil, and she looked around for a way to lead me into sin, so she groaned aloud and fell down in a faint. Her husband saw this, and asked her, 'Why have you had fallen on your face?' And she replied, 'I am suffering from a pain in my heart, and I collapsed because of shortness of breath.' So he gave her medicine, though she was not really ill. Then she found an opportunity when her husband was away to burst in on me and cried out, 'I shall hang myself, or throw myself down a well or off a cliff unless you agree to take me.' I understood that it was a spirit from the devil that had so disturbed her, so I prayed to the Lord, and said to her, 'Why are you so troubled and disturbed, so blinded by sin? Remember that if you do kill yourself, it will be Asitho, your husband's mistress, your rival, who will ill-treat your children and blot out all memory of you from the earth.' She replied, 'If only you would love me, that would be enough. You would safeguard my life and that of my children, and I would have the

hope of achieving my desires.' I did not know that she spoke thus at God's prompting, not her own. For if anyone suffers from obsession with an evil desire, and is enslaved to it, as she was, then even if she hear something good she would turn it towards that desire, through the passion that dominates her.

8.   Now, my children, I must tell you that it was about the sixth hour when she left me. I fell on my knees towards the Lord, in prayer all the rest of the day, and all the night. I rose at dawn weeping and begging to be delivered from her. Eventually she grasped hold of my cloak, and dragged me forcibly towards her. When I realised that she was beside herself, and had a firm grip on my cloak, I shook it off and left it, to escape naked. Then she informed on me to her husband, and her husband threw me into captivity in his own house. On the next day, after flogging me, he sent me to Pharoah's prison. Once I was in bonds, the Egyptian woman fell ill from grief, because she could hear how I sang hymns to the Lord in the house of darkness, and in joy I glorified God alone with a glad voice, for through this outcome I had been delivered from the Egyptian woman.

9.   She sent messages to me often, saying 'Be so good as to consent to my desires, and I will liberate you from your bonds, and bring you up out of darkness.' I did not have the slightest inclination to yield to her. For God has a greater love for one who fasts in a pit of darkness, through chastity, than one who feasts at leisure in a royal chamber. One who preserves chastity is also desirous of glory; the Most High knows what is expedient for him, and grants him all these things, as he did to me. Although she was ill, she came to visit me at unsuitable times, and heard my voice when I was praying; I recognised her grunting, and I kept silence. For when I had been living in her house she used to uncover her arms, even her breasts and legs, to make me fall for her. She was indeed very beautiful, and adorned herself exceedingly to seduce me. But God ever preserved me from all that she tried to do.

Joseph trusts, therefore, not in his own integrity or his own powers of resistance, but entirely on the grace of God. This same confidence in God leads him to his extraordinary docility in the face of injustice, and his concern for the reputation of his brothers above his own. More than once, it appears, the Ishmaelites suspected that he was not what he seemed, but he continued to tell them he was a slave, so as not to bring disrepute on his brothers. Potiphar's wife detected that he was free-born, and liked the look of him when he was stripped, which is why she persuaded Potiphar to redeem him.

10. So now, my children, observe how much is achieved by perseverance in prayer with fasting. If you are steadfast in seeking for chastity and purity, with prayer and fasting in humility of heart, the Lord will dwell among you, for he is a lover of chastity. Wherever the Most High dwells, even if you are subjected to envy, deception and false accusation, if you are chaste, the Lord who remains with you will not only preserve you from evil, but will exalt you and give you glory, as he did to me. For he works together with all men, whether in action, in word, or in thought. My brothers know how much our father loved me, but I was not elated in my heart, for although I was very young I had the fear of God in mind. I knew that all things pass away, and I restrained myself, and respected my brothers. Out of respect for them I was silent when they sold me, and I did not tell the Ishmaelites that I was the son of Jacob, a great and powerful man.

11. For your part, therefore, have respect for God in all your actions, and honour your brothers. For everyone who observes the law of God will be loved by him. When I came to Indokolpita, with the Ishmaelites, they asked me, 'Are you a slave?' and I told them I was a slave at home, so as not to bring disrepute on my brothers. Their leader said to me, 'You are no slave, your appearance reveals that much about you,' and he threatened to kill me. I told him that I was their slave. But once we had arrived in Egypt, they argued about who would have the profit of my sale. Eventually all agreed that since I was in Egypt they would leave me with the dealer they traded with, until they were returning home with their merchandise. The Lord gave me favour in the eyes of the dealer, and he entrusted me with his house. And the Lord blessed him through my hands, and enriched him with gold and silver. I remained with him for three months and five days.

12. Then it happened that Memphia, Potiphar's wife, came by in a covered chariot with great pomp, for her eunuchs had told her about me. She spoke to her husband about the dealer, saying that he had become rich through the help of a young Hebrew, and that they were saying they had secretly stolen him from the land of Canaan. 'Now', she said, 'do what is right for him and take that youth away to be your own steward, then the God of the Hebrews will bless you, for there is a grace from heaven upon him.'

13. Potiphar was convinced by her story, and ordered the dealer to be brought to him. He said to him, 'What is this I hear, that you are stealing people from the land of the Hebrews, and selling them as slaves?' The dealer fell on his face and entreated him, saying, 'I assure you, master, I do not know what you are talking about.' He replied, 'Then where did this Hebrew servant of your come from?' He answered, 'The Ishmaelites deposited him with me until they should return.' But Potiphar did not believe him, and ordered him to be stripped and flogged. While this was going on, Potiphar said, 'Bring the boy to me.' I was brought into his presence, and did obeisance to the lord of the eunuchs—for he was the third in rank after Pharoah, and was responsible for all the eunuchs; he had wives and concubines and children. He led me away from the dealer and asked, 'Are you a slave, or free?' I told him, 'A slave.' He replied, 'Whose slave are you?' and I said, 'Of the Ishmaelites.' He asked me again, 'How did you become their slave?' and I said, 'They bought me from the land of Chanaan.' He did not believe me, but said 'You are lying', and ordered me to be stripped and flogged as well.

14. Memphia watched me being flogged, through the window, for her house was nearby, and she sent word to her husband, saying, 'Your judgment is unjust, for you are punishing a free man who has been stolen as if he were a criminal.' Since I had said nothing while being beaten, he ordered me to be kept safely, 'until', as he said, 'the masters of the boy arrive'. His wife said to him, 'Why are you detaining this noble born youth who has been taken capture? It would be better to redeem him, and he could serve you.' What she wanted was to look at me, for she was tempted to sin, but I was quite unaware of all that. So Potiphar said to her, 'Egyptian law does not allow one to take away another's goods without proof,' which he said for the sake of the dealer, 'and the boy must remain confined'.

15. Twenty-four days later the Ishmaelites came back. They had heard that my father Jacob was grieving about me, and said to me, 'Why did you say about yourself that you were a slave? Look, we have found out that you are the son of a great man in the land of Canaan. Your father is grieving about you in sackcloth and ashes.' When I heard that I grieved within me, I was wrung to the heart, and once again I was ready to weep: but I restrained myself, so as not to bring shame on my brothers. I said, 'I know nothing, I am a slave.' Then they were eager to sell me, so that I would not be found in their hands. They were afraid that Jacob would come and wreak vengeance on them to their peril, for they had heard that he was a great man, in the sight of the Lord and of men. Then the dealer begged them, 'Release me from the power of Potiphar.' So they approached me and asked me, saying, 'Tell him that we bought you for money, and so he will let us go.'

16. Memphia spoke to her husband, 'Buy the lad, since I heard them say they are selling him.' He sent an eunuch to the Ishmaelites to ask them to sell me, but the eunuch was not prepared to treat with them, and came away again. He had enquired of them, and reported to his mistress that they were asking an excessive price for a young slave. So she sent another eunuch, instructing him,

'Even if they ask two *mnas* of gold, give it to them. Do not be sparing with gold, just buy the boy and bring him back.' So for me he gave them eighty gold pieces, though he told the Egyptian woman he had given a hundred for me. I observed this, but kept quiet about it, so that the eunuch would not get into trouble.

Joseph points the moral by exhorting his sons to love one another:

17. You see, my children, what I endured rather than shame my brothers. You therefore should love one another, and with longanimity conceal each others' faults. For God rejoices in brotherly concord, and in the decisions of a heart that is tested in love (cf. Ecclesiasticus 25:1). When my brothers arrived in Egypt, they were astonished when they discovered that I had given them back their money, and that I had never reproached them; that I had encouraged them and after the death of Jacob my father I had shown them even greater love; and that I had carried out everything he had asked me to do and more. I did not permit them to be inconvenienced in the slightest. Whatever was in my possession I shared with them. Their sons I treated as my sons, my sons as their servants. Their hearts were as my heart, their sorrows my sorrow, their weakness my distress. My lands were their lands, my advice their counsel. I did not exalt myself over them in pride despite my worldly glory, but I dwelt among them as one of the least.

18. Now if you yourselves, my children, walk according to the commandments of the Lord, he will exalt you because of it, and he will bless you with good things for ever. If anyone attempt to do you wrong, you should pray for him with a kindly heart, and you will be delivered from all evil by the Lord. You can see for yourselves that it was because of my patient endurance that I was able to take the daughter of the priest of Heliopolis as my wife, and I was given a hundred talents of gold along with her. The Lord himself made them all my slaves; he gave me beauty, as a flower above the fair ones of Israel, and he has preserved me into my old age in strength and handsomeness, so that in all things I resemble Jacob.

Joseph concludes his Testament, one of the longest in the collection, with a vision of the Mystic Adoration of the Lamb, with clear references to the Apocalypse of St John, and like several other of the Testaments urges the family to honour Judah and Levi, for it is from them that the Lamb will arise.

19. Listen, my children, to the dream I have seen. I saw twelve harts grazing, and nine of them were frightened off, and three remained, but on the following day, they too were scattered. Then I saw the three harts become three lambs, they bleated to the Lord, and the Lord led them out to a fertile and well-watered place, he led them from darkness into light. And there they bleated to the Lord until the other nine harts were brought back to them, and these also became like twelve sheep, and after a short time they multiplied and became great flocks. Then I looked again and saw twelve bulls, suckled by one cow, which filled the sea with her milk so that the twelve sheep and numberless flocks drank from it. And the horns of the twelfth bull were lifted up to heaven, and became as a wall for the sheep, and between his two horns grew another horn. And I saw a calf which circled them twelve times, and became a helpmate to the bulls. And I saw that, in the midst of the horns, out of Judah was born a Virgin, and she had a robe of fine linen. And from her proceeded a Lamb without spot, and on his right hand was one like a lion. And all the beasts rushed together against him, and the Lamb conquered them all, and destroyed them till they were trampled underfoot. And the angels rejoiced over him, as did all humankind and the whole earth. These things will come to pass in their own time, in the last days. But you, my children, keep the commandments of the Lord; revere Judah and Levi, for from their line will arise over you the Lamb of God who takes away the sins of the world. By grace he will save all the nations as well as Israel. His kingdom will be an eternal Kingdom, which shall never pass away. My own kingdom will come to its end in you, like an orchard fence (cf. Psalm 78/79:1), which is no longer noticed after the harvest.

20. I know that after my death the Egyptians will afflict you, but God will avenge you, and will lead you into the land promised to your fathers. But take my bones up with you, for as long as my bones are carried along with you the Lord will be with you in light, while the devil will shed darkness over the Egyptians. Take your mother Asyneth along with you as well, and bury her beside Bilhah, by the hippodrome near Rachel.

And when he had said this, he stretched out his feet and fell into his age-long sleep. And all Israel lamented him, and all Egypt, with a great lamentation. For he shared the griefs of the Egyptians as if they were his own members, and he did good to them, assisting them in all his works and counsels and activity. And when the sons of Israel came out of Egypt they brought the bones of Joseph with them, and buried him in Hebron with his fathers. And the years of his life were one hundred and ten.

One thing that seems clear throughout the Testament of Joseph is that it is a fundamentally Christian document, expressing an astonishing degree of forgiveness, tolerance and humility, which can surely not be attributed to any pre-Christian writer. Joseph, in fact is presented as a type of Christ, who 'as a sheep led to the slaughter or a lamb before its shearer is dumb, so he opens not his mouth' (Acts 8:32, Isaiah 53:7–8). The emptiness before God that Joseph expresses, that total dependence on grace, is the mind of Christ Jesus, who 'emptied himself, taking the form of a servant, being born in the likeness of men' (Philippians 2:7). Although Christ is the incarnate God, he makes himself like a slave; so must we be, claiming nothing whatsoever for ourselves, but relying with full confidence on the grace of God who does great things for us and through us. 'Whoever would be great among you must be your servant, and whoever would be first among you must be slave of all' (Mark 10:43–4).

In all this, the Testament of Joseph differs from the picture of him we find in the Old Testament. There he is praised, and amply rewarded for the injustice he has suffered. Jacob blesses him at length, as we would expect, given that the previous thirteen chapters of Genesis have been the story of Joseph, and that after his sufferings he had become one of the most powerful men in Egypt (Genesis 49:22–6):

Joseph is a fruitful bough, a fruitful bough by a spring; his branches run over the wall. The archers fiercely attacked him, shot at him and harassed him sorely; yet his bow remained unmoved, his arms were made agile by the hands of the Mighty One of Jacob (by the name of the Shepherd, the Rock of Israel), by the God of your father who will help you, by God Almighty who will bless you with blessings of heaven above, blessings of the deep that couches beneath, blessings of the breasts and of the womb. The blessings of your father are mighty beyond the blessings of the eternal mountains, the bounties of the everlasting hills; may they be on the head of Joseph, and on the brow of him who was separate from his brothers.

Moses is slightly more sparing with his blessings, for centuries have passed, but since Joseph has divided into two large and powerful tribes, they also are amply blessed with riches and prosperity in this world as a tangible reward for virtue (Deuteronomy 33:13–17):

And of Joseph he said, 'Blessed by the Lord be his land, with the choicest gifts of heaven above, and of the deep that couches beneath, with the choicest fruits of the sun, and the rich yield of the months, with the finest produce of the ancient mountains, and the abundance of the everlasting hills, with the best gifts of the earth and its fulness, and the favour of him that dwelt in the bush. Let these come upon the head of Joseph, and upon the crown of the head of him that is prince among his brothers. His firstling bull has majesty, and his horns are the horns of a wild ox; with them he shall push the peoples, all of them to the ends of the earth; such are the ten thousands of Ephraim, and such are the thousands of Manasseh.'

These promises of earthly glory can only be accepted if we follow the Church Fathers in looking for a spiritual or allegorical meaning. Virtue is not to be rewarded in this life, nor should we look for any visible prosperity in this world, but if we look towards the real 'everlasting hills', there is a promise and a fulfilment beyond all the prophecies of Jacob and Moses. Yet that is not at present our concern: our concern is to surrender ourselves to the love of God, 'grant that I may love thee always, and then do with me what thou wilt.'

It is only when we know that we have nothing to offer that God can work freely through us. We are to be clean pipes through which the water of life can flow: the more hollow and empty we are the faster and more clear the flow of water. If we do see the results of that gush of the Holy Spirit, we can rejoice in the good works that God does through us, once we know that they are his good works, not ours. This is how the saints were able to live with the awareness that 'he who has mighty has done great things for me', simply because they know that 'he has regarded the low estate of his handmaiden' (Luke 1:49, 48).

Good works are the tangible proof of our faith, as St James teaches us so clearly (James 2), not because we are enabled by faith to do anything of our own, but because faith means relying totally on God to work through us, as St Paul teaches equally clearly (Galatians 3). To despise these works would be to despise God's gifts, his work—but to claim them as our own would be equally arrogant in despite of the God who gives us the grace to do them.

Cassian discusses this attitude of recognising our own nothingness in the face of great works being done through us, quoting a great catena of texts from the Scriptures to show how this is the consistent teaching of both Old and New Testaments:

> It is possible for us to evade the clutches of this evil spirit if whenever we become aware that we have advanced in any virtue, we repeat what St Paul says, 'It is not I, but the grace of God within me; by the grace of God I am what I am' (I Corinthians 15:10), and 'it is God who enables us both to will and to perform our good desires' (Philippians 2:13). The Saviour Himself also says, 'He who abides in me and I in him, he will bear much fruit; for without me you can achieve nothing' (John 15:5). Also, 'Unless the Lord build the house, they labour in vain that build it. Unless the Lord keep guard over the city, in vain does the sentry keep watch', and again,

'It is vain for you to rise before dawn' (Psalm 126/127:1–2, LXX), and 'Victory is not to the willing, nor to the swift, but to God who has mercy' (Romans 9:16). No one who is still clothed in the flesh which wars against the spirit, however 'willing or swift' he be, can display such an ideal will or effort that he can attain that prize of victory and trophy of pure integrity, unless he be protected by the mercy of God, and so be fit to arrive at his great desire, the goal for which he is running. 'For every good gift, every perfect gift comes from above, descending from the Father of lights' (James 1:17), and 'What do you have that you were not given? And if you have been given it, how can you boast as if it were not a gift?' (I Corinthians 4:7).

(Monastic Institutes, XII, 9–10)

If we are trying to love God and neighbour, we cannot pretend that we do not, occasionally, become aware that we are practising the faith more, being more devout, avoiding sin more than many around us. We may observe, and hear others acclaiming, that there are some things we are doing well, some words we have spoken that help unfold the love of God to others, some actions we do that relieve the sum of human suffering. To claim them as our own would be fatuous: all this is God's work. He gives us the virtues, he gives us the thoughts, the words, the actions by which we 'let your light so shine before men, that they may see your good works and give glory to your Father in heaven' (Matthew 5:16).

It is very difficult to preserve due modesty and humility when the world speaks well of us, and everyone acclaims us for our words or actions. That is why, in the loving Providence of God, the world can be relied upon to speak evil of us. Whatever we say, whatever we do, the world will find something to criticise, something to blame. It is very noticeable in the case of the last two Popes: the media of the world delighted in heaping scorn and rebuke on them, whatever they said or did. 'Blessed are you when men revile you and persecute you and utter all kinds of evil against you falsely on my account. Rejoice and be glad, for your reward is great in heaven' (Matthew 5:1–12).

It is also part of God's loving Providence that he does not allow us to be free of sin, free of humiliating vices that keep us coming back to the confessional, and remind us constantly that we are incapable of avoiding sin except by his grace. Because we cannot fail to be aware of our constant lapses from virtue, we cannot fail to remember that we are, still, worms and no men.

Step Eight

BENIGNITY

The Patriarch Asher, Prophet Hosea and Apostle Thomas

I led them with cords of compassion, with the bands of love

(Hosea 11:4)

'The eighth degree of humility', according to St Benedict, 'is that a monk do nothing except what is commended by the common rule of the monastery and the example of his superiors' (*RB* 7).

Cassian puts the same sentiment slightly lower down his ladder: 'Sixthly if we do nothing on our own initiative but follow the common rule and the general custom' (*Monastic Institutes*, IV, 39).

As in almost every point of the Rule of St Benedict, and the Institutes of St Cassian, it is possible to apply the text to everyone, not just nuns and monks. Following the 'general rule and common custom' is the best way to live in any family, school or college, place of work, society, institute or association of any kind. If we are always determined to do things our way, determined to be different and stand out from the crowd, not only does this display an intolerable degree of pride, but it also makes life difficult for those around us. The accusation of 'being singular' is the traditional way of pointing out to a brother or sister that they are out of step with the rest of the community; in a family it is more often just, 'We don't do that', or 'It's not our way'. Trying to adapt oneself to the little customs and mannerisms of the others is part of our way of showing that we want to live in charity with them. Setting out to be different is a breach of charity.

Except, of course, when the others are hastening away from God on the wrong path. Then we do have to be different, even to the point of martyrdom. The discernment necessary to distinguish between appropriate conformity and a betrayal of the Gospel is often difficult indeed. In times of persecution, there are many who were happy to drift along with the general mood, 'for fellowship's sake', and by no means all of them are really malicious or truly traitors to the faith. Only a few see clearly, that the powers of this world may go thus far and no further, here their proud waves shall be stayed.

This then is the challenge, to follow the customs and rules of those around us, when it is necessary for charity, or to stand firm for the Gospel and the faith of Christ when it is necessary for the Truth. For this we need Discernment, one of the great gifts of the Holy Spirit, which may be matched with Benignity, one of the fruits of the same Spirit, which enables us to live harmoniously with others. *Benignitas* is the Latin translation of St Paul's *chrestotes*, the word deriving from the adjective *chrestos*, which originally means 'useful' or 'serviceable', and so naturally came to mean beneficial, kindly, or generous. It did not escape the notice of the early Fathers that it is almost impossible to distinguish the sound of the word *chrestos* from that of *christos,* Christ, the Anointed One. In fact even in the New Testament, the Apostles were unable to resist the pun. St Paul tells us, 'be kind to one another, tenderhearted, forgiving one another, as God in Christ forgave you' (Ephesians 4:32). St Peter in his turn quotes the Septuagint Greek version of the Psalms, 'for you have tasted the kindness of the Lord' (I Peter 2:3, cf. Psalm 33/34:9), which sounds exactly as if he were saying 'you have tasted that Christ is the Lord.' In both cases, the word translated 'kind' is *chrestos*.

Christ is the kindly one, the one who comes to share our life, to sanctify every aspect of our being. He conforms to the manners and customs of his people, observing not only the letter of the Law of Moses but also the traditional ways of those around him, 'for it is fitting for us to fulfil all righteousness' (Matthew 3:15). That makes it all the more startling when he breaks with those traditions, speaking to the Samaritan woman at the well, cleansing the Temple, inviting his disciples to eat his Body and drink his Blood. Whatever we do, however we associate with other people, our model must always be Christ, our question always how would Christ have me behave in this situation. If we are to follow Christ, we must decide at every turn what is the right way to follow Him, at what point we should refuse to conform ourselves to the powers of this world, and at what point we should submit to our lawful superiors. The choice is not often easy. But if we are careful to conform to the little, trivial, traditional customs of those around us, to demonstrate our wish to live in harmony with them and to follow their ways, then our witness will be all the more powerful when we have to take a stand for righteousness and truth. It is precisely because St Thomas More was such a good servant to the King that his witness to serving God first was so powerful.

We may think that once we have agreed to live in a particular community, be it a religious house, a family, a place of work, a club or society, then all we have to do is to do as we are told, and generally fit in with what everyone else is doing. The alternative is 'singularity'. And to a large extent, this is true. Particularly if we have chosen the community to join, we have made our decision in the light of what we know about it, we trust it to be acting properly, and that its rules and superiors can be trusted to direct us the right way. I repeat, this applies to a sports club as much as to a monastery. Obviously in the case of a family we have no choice: we are born into it, or its new members are born around us, we have little choice in whom we live with. The same could apply in a regiment or ship, more particularly in a prison or hospital. Some institutions are thrust upon us, others we select with care and make our own. But in all communities and institutions of all kinds there needs to be a recognisable authority, someone with the right to command, and there needs to be a rule of life to make it tolerable to live and work together.

Not all rules are written down. St Benedict himself has distinguished between 'rule' and 'customs', for customs grow up of their own accord, and often without anyone consciously intending to begin them. Yet if we ignore the customs of the house it can have just as devastating an effect on the community as if we were contradicting a direct written or spoken order. Customs are, by definition, unwritten. Often they are so trivial and casual that it would seem absurd to go to the lengths of writing them down. It is little things like whether we put the place mats away in the cupboard or stack them on top of the sideboard, whether we wear our belts fastened on the left or the right, whether we give the cat her milk in the dining room or only in the kitchen. We can all recognise moments and memories of family or community life when conforming to the trivial and insignificant manners of behaviour can make a difference between harmony and conflict. No one would dream of making these things a matter of obedience, but if we ignore them and persist in being different, then we are indicating that we do not really want to be part of this family, this community, this club. We do not really feel at home here—and if we indicate that, then everyone else is made to feel a little uncomfortable.

Such things are not the matters of which crises of conscience are made. Little community customs do not impinge on faith or morals, and we cannot say that doing things this way or that way could be morally right or wrong. Except in so far as it is always morally right to be kind and considerate to others, and being inconsiderate and rude is a breach of charity, and therefore wrong.

Very different, therefore, are the occasions when in conscience it is necessary to refuse to obey, and to break away from society, community or family. At the time when Henry VIII was forcing all religious to swear that he was the head of the Church, in most cases priors and abbesses simply commanded their subjects to swear, and to obey the king. Most monks and nuns dutifully swore the oath, and if anyone raised a question about it they were told simply that they were bound to obey their lawful superiors. We know of few, very few, who realised the limits of holy obedience and refused. When brave superiors gave a lead, as in the London Charterhouse or among the Brigettines of Sheen, others followed suit, even to martyrdom. But most signed away their faith and their integrity, and when it came a few years later to signing away their vocations, they did so without a murmur. That was not a matter of rule or custom but of faith. Knowing the difference is crucial.

Those who are docile and obedient in following the laws and customs of their house or family are often those with the integrity to know when they should refuse to obey on a matter of conscience. Those who are well known to be fractious and difficult will not be taken seriously if they suddenly decide to take a stand on some matter of real importance. Even when the Catholic faith and religious life is being destroyed, the virtue of kindness or benignity still demands conformity to the little politenesses of daily life. Martyrs speak with courtesy and consideration to their persecutors, for in this way they can be truly Christ-like, imitating him who said to Judas, 'Friend, why are you here?' (Matthew 26:50)

If we rely on our own intelligence and our own natural skills in discernment to enable us to make the decision between right and wrong, to distinguish lawful custom from unlawful commands, we shall certainly get it wrong. Knowing how to act, what to say, in every situation, so as to display the kindness of Christ, is not something we can cultivate for ourselves, no purely natural virtue: it is a gift of God, a work of grace, like all the gifts and fruits of the Holy Spirit. Our guide in the decisions of life, in the trivial decisions of every day or the great crises of life and death, can only be the Holy Spirit. It is the Holy Spirit who speaks to our conscience, instructing, reproving, soothing, accusing, at every moment showing us what we should be doing and how. But it takes time and attention to prayer if we are to accustom ourselves to hearing the voice of the Holy Spirit.

Discernment, therefore, is one of the essential virtues. We hear much about that from Cassian, or rather from Abba Moyses whom he remembers teaching thus:

> I remember that when I was young, and living in the Thebaïd where St Antony dwelt, one night the elders gathered to ask him about the grace of perfection. Their discussion went on from evening to dawn, and the whole night was occupied in this greatest of questions ... Each one put forward his opinion as he was minded to do ... After the greater part of the night had been taken up in the debate, the blessed Antony finally took a part.
>
> 'All these things which you have mentioned are indeed necessary, and profitable for those who thirst for God and long to reach him, but long experience of many events has shown that we cannot attribute the supreme grace to any of these. Time and time again I have seen men suddenly deceived and overthrown, although they had practised fasting and watching with diligence, withdrawn into marvellous solitude, undertaken to renounce all property to the extent that they

would keep back not even so much as a day's livelihood or a single denarius, and performed works of mercy with whole-hearted devotion. But after all this they were unable ever to bring the work they had begun to a fitting conclusion, and all their great fervour and admirable way of life came to a bad end. Now we can discover the principal path to God if only we analyse accurately what was the cause of their fall and delusion. They abounded in the practice of virtue, but discretion alone was lacking, so that they were unable to persevere to the end. No other cause can be found for their fall except that they were insufficiently instructed by their elders, and unable to acquire the virtue of discretion. It is discretion which avoids extremes on either side and leads the monk to advance along the royal road, neither puffed up on the right by his own virtue, that is surpassing the reasonable degree of self-denial by foolishly presuming on his excessive zeal; nor deviating to vices on the left, through laxity in his obligations, that is allowing the opposite spirit to make him slack and tepid on the excuse of looking after his health. It is this discretion which the Gospel calls the eye and lamp of the body, in Our Saviour's words, "The light of thy body is thy eye. If thy eye be single, thy whole body shall be lightsome. But if thy eye be evil, thy whole body shall be darksome" (Matthew 6:22–3). Discerning all the thoughts of a man and his deeds, it examines all that is to be done and sheds light on it. If a man have the evil eye, meaning that it is bad in judgment and ignorant, deceived and deluded by overconfidence, it will make our whole body darkness. It darkens the mind totally, and all our actions are obscured by the blindness of vice and confusion. "If then the light that is in thee," he goes on, "be darkness; the darkness itself how great shall it be!" (Matthew 6:23). Let no one doubt that if our heart's judgment is erroneous, sunk in the darkness of ignorance, all our thoughts and works will become entangled in the greater darkness of sin once they have deviated from the guidance of discretion.

'Saul was the first to be chosen by God as worthy to rule the people of Israel, but he did not possess this gift of discretion at all, and "his whole body being darksome", was eventually deprived of his kingdom. His light was turned to darkness and error, so that he was deceived into imagining that his own sacrifice would be more acceptable to God than obedience to the command of Samuel (I Kings (I Samuel) 15). Through an action which he had hoped would appease the divine majesty, he incurred nothing but blame. In the same way it was failure of discretion that misled Achab, King of Israel, after God had graciously granted him a splendid military victory; he thought his own compassion to be better than the execution of God's severe commandment, which in his own eyes he considered to be a cruel order. Softened by this thought he chose to temper his bloody triumph with mercy, but for this inappropriate mercy he incurred the inevitable sentence of death, as if his whole body too had become darksome (III Kings (I Kings) 20).

'This discretion is not only the "light of the body" but is described by St Paul as the sun, when he says, "Let not the sun go down upon your anger" (Ephesians 4:26). That this is the guiding principle of our life is shown in the text, "Those who have no guidance fall like leaves" (Proverbs 11:14, LXX). It is appropriately called "counsel" without which as scripture tells us, we may not do anything at all. Not even the spiritual wine, which "may cheer the heart of man" (Psalm 103/104:15) may we imbibe without moderation, as in "Do all things with counsel, drink wine with counsel" (Proverbs 31:3, LXX).'

Thus blessed Antony and all the others agreed in the opinion that it is discretion which leads a valiant monk on a sure path to God, and preserves from corruption the virtues that they had mentioned before. With discretion one can mount with little effort to the pinnacles of achievement; without it so many have failed to attain the height of perfection, despite their endless toil. It is discretion that begets all virtues, preserves them and governs them.

Collations, II, 2–4

In many places in the Scriptures, God's people are confronted with the choice of whether to serve him, or not. Joshua, after completing the long journey of the Exodus, and clearing the land before the Children of Israel, offered them one last choice: 'Now therefore fear the LORD, and serve him in sincerity and in faithfulness; put away the gods which your fathers served beyond the River, and in Egypt, and serve the LORD. And if you be unwilling to serve the LORD, choose this day whom you will serve, whether the gods your fathers served in the region beyond the River, or the gods of the Amorites in whose land you dwell; but as for me and my house, we will serve the LORD' (Joshua 24:14–15).

The prophet Jeremiah describes the choice between the way of life, following the Lord, and the way of death, in a passage so similar to the first Psalm that we instinctively read them together: 'Blessed is the man who walks not in the counsel of the wicked, ... The wicked are not so, but are like chaff which the wind blows away' (Psalm 1:1,4, cf. Jeremiah 17:5–8). Jeremiah returns to the theme often, for instance 'Thus says the LORD, behold I set before you the way of life and the way of death' (Jeremiah 21:8). That Psalm was set at the beginning of the Psalter to set the tone for the entire cycle of poems, to introduce us to a theme which in one way or other runs right through to the end of the 150th. If we serve the Lord, the God of Israel, we shall walk on the way of life; but if we follow any other path, it leads only to destruction. And Our Lord warns us that 'the gate is wide and the way is easy that leads to destruction, and those who enter by it are many. For the gate is narrow and the way is hard, that leads to life, and those who find it are few' (Matthew 7:13–14). The early Christian document known as the Epistle of Barnabas develops the same image of the two ways, and it remains a commonplace of Christian preaching.

If we are to find the way of life, we must be single-minded in our pursuit of it, not wavering from side to side like the Israelites whom Elijah taunted, 'How long will you go limping, with two different opinions?' (III Kings (I Kings) 18:21) Nor can we be luke-warm, like the Laodiceans in the Apocalypse (Apocalypse 3:15–16). We need to be single-minded and whole-hearted, determined to follow the way of the Lord at all times, and the Lord will guide us in all our decisions.

The Patriarch Asher made this the theme of his Testament, urging his family not to be 'two-faced' but 'single-faced', for 'all things are paired, one opposite to the other.'

1.   The transcript of the Testament of Asher, which he spoke to his sons in the one hundred and twenty-fifth year of his life. While still in good health, he said to them, Listen, children of Asher, to your father, and I will reveal to you everything that is right in the sight of God. Two ways has God given to the sons of men, two counsels, two actions and two situations and two goals. That is why all things are twofold, one opposite to the other (cf. Ecclesiasticus 33:14–15). The two ways are those of good and evil. In these lie the two counsels in our breasts, by which we make our choice. For if a soul is willing to walk in the way of goodness, she will do all her actions in righteousness, and if she should sin, she repents at once. When a soul thinks of what is right, she casts away wickedness, she is quick to avoid evil, and tears up sin by the roots. But when her thoughts incline to evil, all her works will be wicked, she thrusts good away and embraces evil, so that the man is so dominated by the devil that even if he should chance to do some good, he will turn it to wrong. Whenever he begins to do something right, the goal of his actions lead him to commit wrong. The treasury of the devil is full of the poison of that evil spirit.

2.   It may happen that a soul declare that she has turned away from the good, in favour of evil, and the goal of her action draws her away to wrong. It is possible that a man is pitiless towards anyone who helps him, but he is two-faced, and the end result is evil. Or a man may be so fond of the sinner that he joins him in sin, and chooses to die in his sins because of him. In such a case it is obvious that he is two-faced, and all he does is evil. Even though there be love, it is corrupt, and conceals the evil. It may well have a reputation for goodness, but the end of its actions is wickedness. A man may be a thief, a swindler, a robber, a miser, and still take pity on the poor, but this also is two-faced, and the whole is evil. A man may defraud his neighbour and incite God

to anger; he defies the Most High, but he takes pity on the poor. He sets aside the law of the Lord, and provokes Him, yet he gives relief to the poor. He defiles his soul, but displays a splendid body; he destroys many, and has pity on few. This also is two-faced, and entirely evil. Another may be an adulterer or a fornicator, though he is abstemious in his eating; he commits sin while fasting, and through the power which his riches give him he seduces many, writing his own commandments out of the abundance of his wickedness. This also is two-faced, and the whole is evil. They are like swine or hares, which have half the requirements for being clean, but in truth are classed as unclean. So has God spoken in the tablets of heaven.

3.　You, therefore, my sons, be not two-faced like them, following both good and evil, but cling to goodness alone, for God reposes in it, and men desire it. Flee from wickedness, and banish the devil by your good works. The two-faced do not serve God but their own desires, and therefore are most pleasing to the devil and to men who are like him.

4.　Good men, who are single-faced, are righteous in the sight of God, even if the two-faced consider they are sinners. For there are many who put a stop to the wicked, and thus perform a double deed, something evil as well as good, but the whole result is good, for they eradicate evil and destroy it. A man may hate an almsgiver who is wicked, an adulterer who fasts, and this is two-faced, but the end result is good, for he is imitating the Lord, not tolerating what seems to be good along with the undoubted evil. Another man may be unwilling to celebrate a feastday along with the profligate, lest he defile his body, and besmirch his soul; this also is two-faced, but the whole is good. For such men are like harts and hinds, which appear to be unclean because they live in the wilderness, but they are entirely clean. They act out of zeal for God, holding aloof from those whom God himself hates and forbids in his commandments, and keeping evil away from the good.

5. See now, my children, how everything is twofold, one against the other, and one concealed beneath the other. In possessions there is excess, in celebrations, drunkenness, in laughter there is grief, in a wedding feast extravagance. Death succeeds to life, disgrace to glory, night to day, and light to darkness. But all things are under the day, all righteousness under life, all wickedness under death, and therefore eternal life succeeds to death. It is not possible to say that the Truth lies (cf. Isaiah 5:20), or that righteousness is unjust, for all Truth is under the light (cf. John 3:21), just as all creation is under God. All these things I have learnt in my lifetime, and I have not been deceived in following the Truth of the Lord. I have sought out the commands of the Most High, and with all my strength I have pursued what is good with a single face.

All truth is under the light, says Asher, referring to but not exactly quoting St John, who speaks so often about 'the true light that enlightens every man' (John 1:9). He concludes with the exhortation:

6. Pay attention now, my children, to the commands of the Lord, following the truth with a single face, for the two-faced will be punished in two ways. For they both do evil and applaud those who do so (cf. Romans 1:32), in imitation of the spirits of deceit, and striving against mankind. Observe the law of the Lord, my children, and do not treat evil as if it were good. Look to what is truly good, and pursue it in all the commandments of the Lord. Turn back towards him, and find your repose in Him, for the destiny of men shows forth their righteousness. Distinguish the angels of God from the angels of Satan. When a disturbed soul departs, it is tormented by the unclean spirit, which it has been serving by its evil desires and deeds. But if a soul is at rest, it will recognise the angel of peace, who will escort it into life.

7. O my children, be not like Sodom, which failed to recognise the angels of the Lord, and has been destroyed forever. I know that you will fall into sin, and be handed over into the hands of your enemies. Your land will be laid waste, they will overthrow your holy places, and you will be dispersed to the four corners of the earth. In exile you will be brought to nothing, like undrinkable water, until the Most High looks upon the earth. He will come himself, as a man, eating and drinking among men (cf. Matthew 11:19), and he will crush the head of the Serpent, through water. He will save Israel and all the nations, Godhead in hiding as man (cf. Isaiah 45:15). Tell your own children these things, O my children, that they may not refuse to believe Him. For I have read in the tablets of heaven that in disbelief you will refuse to believe in Him, and without reverence you will not show Him reverence, obeying not the commandments of God but those of men, and so destroyed in wickedness. That is why you will be scattered, like Gad and Dan my brothers, who will not know their own lands, nor their tribes and languages. But the Lord will gather you together in faith, because of his great mercy, and for the sake of Abraham, Isaac and Jacob.

8.   And when he had said these things, he instructed them, saying, 'Bury me in Hebron'. And so he died, falling into a peaceful sleep. And after that his sons did as he had instructed them, they took up his body to Hebron and buried it with his fathers.

Now we are not to suppose that Asher, or any of the orthodox Jewish or Christian writers, place the two ways, the two spirits, on an equality. When Joshua offered his people the choice between serving the Lord and the gods of the Amorites, he is not suggesting that there is any real choice: the pagan gods are either deceitful demons, or they do not exist at all. No good can come of serving them, for they have no power to benefit us even in this world. Those who follow them find nothing but futility, 'like chaff which the wind drives away' (Psalm 1:4). A very large proportion of the Old Testament is occupied with emphasising this point. In the histories again and again we see God's people making the wrong choice, turning away from the Truth towards the Baals and the Astartes, worshipping on every high hill and under every spreading tree. In so doing they doom themselves to utter futility. Nothing goes well for them: the prophets are even able to appeal to the evidence of their material prosperity or poverty in this world as a proof that the pagan gods are worthless (e.g. Haggai 1:5–11). The psalmist optimistically says, 'I have been young, and now am old; yet I have not seen the righteous forsaken or his children begging bread' (Psalm 36/37:25).

Maybe it is because of this pledge that the one who rightly discerns between good and evil shall never be found 'begging for bread' that the only blessing Jacob gives to Asher is the brief verse, 'Asher's food shall be rich, and he shall yield royal dainties' (Genesis 49:20). Moses is more expansive on Asher, although we have heard nothing about him to justify the praise: 'Blessed above sons be Asher; let him be the favourite of his brothers, and let him dip his foot in oil. Your bars shall be iron and bronze, and as your days, so shall your strength be' (Deuteronomy 33:24–5). The promise of prosperity probably has more to do with the subsequent fortunes of the tribe of Asher, settled in the north of the Holy Land, on the fertile coast north of Mount Carmel, than with the character of the patriarch himself, who does not feature as an individual at all in the Book of Genesis. Yet we should not forget that Asher does get one mention in the New Testament (Luke 2:36–8):

> And there was a prophetess, Anna, the daughter of Phanuel, of the tribe of Asher; she was of great age, having lived with her husband seven years from her virginity, and as a widow till she was eighty-four. She did not depart from the temple, worshipping with fasting and prayer night and day. And coming up at that very hour she gave thanks to God, and spoke of him to all who were looking for the redemption of Jerusalem.

It cannot be irrelevant that the tribe of Asher is mentioned here. Anna is obviously a woman of discernment, but her discernment is directed by God: she is sent by just at the right moment, and she perceives that this Child is the one who is to redeem Jerusalem. Therefore the prophecies concerning Asher must be fulfilled in Christ: he is the one who provides us with the rich food, the royal dainties of the Blessed Sacrament; he is the first among many brothers, and he is the Christ, the one anointed with oil. He shatters the iron bars and his strength is eternal, as are his days. Although we do not hear the words that Anna spoke in the Gospel, the message is surely that all the blessings promised to her ancestor are fulfilled in this Child, who is the heir to all the promises of Israel.

The fulfilment of these promises is not of this world, for Christ is to be rejected by his brothers, to live without rich food, without precious oil save only to prepare him beforehand for his burial; he is imprisoned behind iron bars and in bronze chains, and his strength fails him as the Day turns to Night. In the Old Testament it is the book of Job that makes the obvious point that devoutly serving the Lord does not always lead to prosperity in this world, and that righteous men do indeed suffer. The provisional answer to Job is simply the appearance of the Lord to declare that he is master of creation, and that in him all things will be resolved. The definitive answer is of course in the New Testament, that God himself comes to share the injustice of this world, and by sharing it triumphs over it.

Yet we can never set the Old Testament against the New, as the shallow-minded have been doing ever since the days of Marcion and Tatian. The God revealed in the Old Testament is none other than the Father of Our Lord Jesus Christ, who yearns for his people with all the tenderness of the mother hen over her chicks. The prophet Hosea, possibly because of the tragedy of his own life, sees most clearly how much God loves his people (Hosea 6:3–4, 11:1–4, 8–9):

> Let us know, let us press on to know the LORD; his going forth is as sure as the dawn; he will come to us as the showers, as the spring rains that water the earth. What shall I do with you, O Ephraim? What shall I do with you, O Judah? … When Israel was a child I loved him, and out of Egypt I called my son. The more I called them, the more they went from me; they kept sacrificing to the Baals, and burning incense to idols. Yet it was I who taught Ephraim to walk, I took them up in my arms; but they did not know that I healed them. I led them with cords of compassion, with the bands of love, and I became to them as one who eases the yoke on their jaws, and I bent down to them and fed them … How can I

give you up. O Ephraim! How can I hand you over, O Israel!
… My heart recoils within me, my compassion grows warm
and tender. I will not execute my fierce anger, I will not again
destroy Ephraim; for I am God and not man, the Holy One
in your midst, and I will not come to destroy.

The God who speaks through Hosea is revealed as one who cares for
his people more than they can ever understand. No matter how many
times they drift away from him, he is always ready to call them back, to
receive them once again, to heal them. The prophet truly looks forward
to the incarnate Lord who lamented, 'O Jerusalem, Jerusalem, killing
the prophets and stoning those who are sent to you! How often would I
have gathered your children together as a hen gathers her brood under
her wings, and you would not!' (Matthew 23:37)

All these disparate considerations can be brought together in the
character of the Apostle Thomas. To begin with, his very name is
significant: Pope Benedict informs us that it 'derives from a Hebrew
root, *ta'am*, which means "paired", "twin". (Benedict XVI PP, *Christ and
his Church* (London: CTS, 2007), p. 89.) His Greek name, Didymus, is
therefore a straight translation of the Hebrew. He is one of a pair: we
never meet the other one. The Patriarch Asher has quoted ben Sirach,
'Good is the opposite of evil, and life the opposite of death; so the sinner
is the opposite of the godly. Look upon all the works of the Most High;
they likewise are in pairs, one the opposite of the other' (Ecclesiasticus
33:14–15, quoted in TAsh 1). Thomas is one half, the godly one, the
chosen Apostle, the other, presumably, is the opposite, the bad one, the
sinner, rejected from the discipleship.

It is Thomas who confronts us with choices, to follow Jesus or to
walk away from him; to believe in him as Lord and God, or to refuse to
believe. When they are at risk of persecution and death if they return to
Judea, and Jesus announces that he is going there to waken Lazarus, it is
Thomas who cries out, 'Let us also go, that we may die with him' (John
11:16). To follow Our Lord means to carry the Cross, to die with him,
so that we may rise with him. 'For if we have been united with him in a
death like his, we shall certainly be united with him in a resurrection like
his' (Romans 6:5). Thomas urges us to follow where the Master leads,

not to choose for ourselves, not to make our own way but to conform to the pattern of Christ. In this he is an example of the virtue demanded by St Benedict in this eighth step, to do only what is commended by our Master.

That readiness to follow Jesus all the way is surely also indicated in the rather obtuse question Thomas puts at the Last Supper. When Jesus announces that '"you know the way where I am going", Thomas said to him, "Lord, we do not know where you are going, how can we know the way?"' The question is obtuse, yes, but it gives rise to that most astounding declaration: 'Jesus said to him, "I am the way, and the truth, and the life; no one comes to the Father, but by me"' (John 14:4–6). Here is the answer to our problem over discernment, how to find the way to where we should be going—it is resolutely to follow Jesus, to do nothing except at his prompting, at his command. If we are attentive to the Holy Spirit calling in the silence of conscience, we shall be guided at every step into the right way, so that everything we think, we say or do, is in accordance with the will of God. That is the way, the only way, to the kingdom of heaven, to be where Christ is, 'so that where I am you may be also.'

And then, most famously, Thomas emphasises the centrality of belief in the Resurrection. We call him 'doubting Thomas', and his first refusal to believe is indeed shocking, but his response is absolute: 'My Lord and my God!' (John 20:28) There is no half-measure, no compromise, nothing is left unresolved and undefined. For Thomas, if it is true, then everything is true: if Jesus of Nazareth has indeed risen from the dead, then he is truly the Lord, the God of Israel.

Thomas, like the other apostles, during most of Our Lord's ministry conforms to the manner of life of the others. Again and again in the Gospels we hear of the disciples or the apostles acting as a single group, even speaking in unison at times. As a group they run away at the Garden of Gethsemane. Thomas, like the others, conforms to what the group are doing. But he is the one who realises that it is not the group who should be followed, but the one, the Master: when the disciples say, 'Rabbi, the Jews were but now seeking to stone you, and are you going there again?', it is Thomas who stands out and exhorts them all to forget their fears and follow Jesus (John 11:8–16). When he is the odd one out, 'not with them when Jesus came', his eventual profession of faith is the most fundamental Christian creed, that Jesus Christ is Lord, to the glory of God the Father.

Step Nine

GOODNESS

The Patriarch Naphtali, Prophet Joel and Apostle James the Less

In quietness and in trust shall be your strength   (Isaiah 30:15)

'The ninth degree of humility', says St Benedict, 'is that a monk restrain his tongue and keep silence, not speaking until he is questioned. For Scripture showeth that *in much talking thou canst not avoid sin*; and that *the talkative man shall not prosper on the earth*' (*RB* 7).

Cassian also makes it his ninth, although with a slightly different emphasis: 'Ninthly if we restrain our tongue and never shout aloud' (*Monastic Institutes*, IV, 39).

The only appropriate reflection on this step on the ladder of humility should be silence, not to spend unnecessary words elaborating what needs no exposition. But somehow we must resist that easy temptation, and consider how the way to goodness is the way of silence.

The Patriarch Naphtali boasted that he could outrun the deer, referring doubtless to the brief and enigmatic blessing given him by Jacob, 'Naphtali is a hind let loose, that bears comely fawns' (Genesis 49:21). He began his testament by addressing his sons on the goodness of silence:

1.   The transcript of the Testament of Naphtali, of the instructions he gave at the time of his passing, at the age of a hundred and thirty. He gathered his sons together, on the first day of the seventh month, while he was still in good health, and he prepared for them a banquet with much to drink. After they woke in the morning, he announced to them that he was dying, but they would not believe him. Then giving praise to the Lord he confirmed it, saying, 'My

flesh has been dying since last night's dinner.' And so he began to speak, saying, 'Listen, my children, sons of Naphtali, listen to the words of your father. I am the son of Bilhah. Rachel acted astutely in giving Bilhah to Jacob instead of herself, and she conceived and gave birth to me on the knees of Rachel. That is why he called me Naphtali. Rachel loved me greatly, because I was born on her knees, and when she saw that I was delicate, she kissed me and said, 'May I see a brother for you out of my own womb after you.' That is why Joseph was so like me in every way, in answer to Rachel's prayer. Now my mother Bilhah was the daughter of Routheos, the brother of Deborah, who was Rebecca's nurse. She was born on the same day as Rachel herself. Routheos was of the same family as Abraham, a Chaldean, who was devout towards God, freeborn and of good family. He was taken prisoner, and bought by Laban, who gave him his maid Edna as his wife. She bore a daughter and he called her Zelpha, after the village in which he had been taken prisoner. After that she bore Bilhah, saying, 'My daughter is quick to action', for as soon as she was born she was eager to take the breast.

2.   Since I was quick on my feet, like a deer, my father Jacob employed me for all sorts of errands, and when he blessed me it was 'as a hind let loose'. For as the potter knows for each vessel how much clay it will need, and brings the right amount, so the Lord makes the body apt to the size of the spirit, and infuses the soul according to the capacity of the body. There is no so much as a hair too many. Every work of the Most High is made by weight and measure and rule (Wisdom 11:21). And just as the potter knows the use of each vessel (Wisdom 15:7), and its purpose, so the Lord knows the body, for what good purpose it is apt, and when it will begin to go wrong. For there is no material, no thought, that is unknown to the Lord, for he created every man in his own likeness (Hebrews 4:13). As a man's power is, such is his work; as his thoughts, such is his skill, as his choice, such is his creation, as his heart, such is his mouth, as his eye, such is his sleep, as his soul, such is his understanding, whether for the law of the Lord

or the law of the devil. As there is a difference between light and darkness, between sight and hearing, so there is a difference between man and man, between woman and woman, though it is not possible to say what the difference is between one face or form and another. God made everything in order, and it is good, the five senses in the head, and the neck linked onto the head; the hair for adornment and glory (I Corinthians 11:7, 15), the heart for understanding, the belly to enclose the stomach, the windpipe for health, the liver for anger, the gall for bitterness, the spleen for laughter, the kidneys for astuteness, the loins for power, the ribs to enclose all else, the spine for strength, and so on. Now, my children, in the same way all your works must be well ordered for good (cf. I Corinthians 14:40), in the fear of God. Do nothing disordered out of contempt, nor out of its proper time. You cannot speak to the eye and make it hear (I Corinthians 12: 16 ff.), neither if you are in darkness can you do the works of light.

3. Be not quick to spoil your actions with avarice, and do not deceive your own souls with empty arguments. It is by keeping silence, in pure hearts, that you will be able to observe the will of God, and cast off the will of the devil. The sun and the moon and the stars do not change their course (cf. Judges 5:20; Job 38:33; Jeremiah 31:35), and like them you must not change the law of God with your disordered actions. The wandering nations who have abandoned the Lord have changed their course, for they follow after wood and stone, in pursuit of the spirit of deceit. You should not be like them, my children, but you should acknowledge the Lord as Creator, in the firmament, on the earth, and in the sea, and in all that is made. Be not like Sodom (Jude 7), which changed the order of her nature. In like manner the Watchers changed the order of their nature, and the Lord cursed them at the time of the Flood, for he made the earth uninhabitable and fruitless because of them.

The advice not to deceive ourselves with empty arguments reminds us of St Paul's 'not in plausible words of wisdom', and the remainder of his warning against pagan philosophy in the first letter to the Corinthians (I Corinthians 2:4, etc.). The Testament of Naphtali contains many more allusions and half-quotations to St Paul than any of the others, though as always the author is careful not to use the identical words, which would break the illusion of antiquity.

It is easy to quote St Paul against any use of philosophy or reason at all in our thinking about God, but that would be to do him an injustice: he warns us, not against reason, the *Logos* which is the intelligence God has given to his creation, but against misusing it with twisted arguments and devilish sophistries that teach us to make the worse cause sound the better. If Paul says 'my speech and my message were not in plausible words of wisdom' (*sophias logois*, I Corinthians 2:4), he also states that one of the great gifts of the Holy Spirit is 'the utterance of wisdom' (*logos sophias*, I Corinthians 12:8), using exactly the same words. There is a true logic, and a false logic, just as there is a true wisdom and a false wisdom: we must distinguish them carefully.

In too much speaking, in complicated drawn-out arguments, it is quite possible to deceive ourselves, almost deliberately, to the extent that by arguments and persuasive subtleties we can convince ourselves that evil is really good, and that good is evil. St Paul was perfectly familiar with the sophistry of the Greeks, which enabled them to persuade themselves to approve of unspeakable vice, even though in heart and conscience they had been perfectly capable of distinguishing goodness from evil. 'Although they knew God they did not honour him as God or give thanks to him, but they became futile in their thinking and their senseless minds were darkened. Claiming to be wise they became fools, and exchanged the glory of the immortal God for images' (Romans 1:21–2).

The same misuse of subtlety and argument is so familiar in our own time that we hardly need make the point. Which brings us back to silence. It is in silence, listening to the voice of conscience in the stillness of our hearts, that we hear the authentic teaching of the Holy Spirit. When we stop talking and arguing and debating and proposing false dichotomies and propounding hard cases, we still know what the truth is, if we could only bear to listen to it. That is why ordinary people, the uneducated, the simple, still know instinctively what is right and wrong—it is the 'learned and the clever' who have so dazzled themselves with plausible words that they have lost sight of the truth. It is easy to detect the results of such a process: the arguments somehow always come down to the conclusions that fallen human nature most desires, permitting vice and crime, prohibiting worship and virtue. Clever arguments never lead to a stricter morality or a more sincere worship, except, occasionally, as steps towards a greater decadence.

The very word 'conscience' gets misused often enough. Newman tells us that the confusion arises from ignoring 'the doctrine that conscience is the voice of God, whereas it is fashionable on all hands now to consider it in one way or other a creation of man ... Conscience is not long-sighted selfishness, nor a desire to be consistent with oneself; but it is a messenger from Him, who, both in nature and in grace, speaks to us behind a veil, and teaches and rules us by His representatives. Conscience is the aboriginal Vicar of Christ, a prophet in its informations, a monarch in its peremptoriness, a priest in its blessings and anathemas' (*Difficulties*, II, 247–9). In Newman's time philosophers and journalists had already succeeded in changing the idea of conscience into meaning no more than 'the right of thinking, speaking, writing and acting, according to their judgment or humour, without any thought of God at all ... they demand what they think is an Englishman's prerogative, for each to be his own master in all things' (*ibid.* 250). With astonishing insensitivity, Newman's own words about Conscience are often taken out of context and twisted about until they appear to mean the exact opposite of what he was trying to say. His 'Letter' was written in defence of the teaching of Vatican I about the papacy, and to explain how the role of the Pope is to expound the word of God, but he goes on to say that if we hear the voice of conscience calling us to a higher and stricter path, we should follow that even should the Pope permit something less. It would never occur to Newman that we could cite 'conscience' as an authority to do something worse than the united teaching of the Church permits.

If only we could refrain from arguing ourselves into a position we know to be false but very much want to hold, and if we were to listen to the 'still small voice' of the Holy Spirit, not only would we be able to discern true goodness, but, much more importantly, we would be given the motivation to pursue it. There is little benefit in knowing the truth if we pay no attention to it: goodness comes from obeying the voice of God, and conforming ourselves to the commandments he lays upon us, whether directly in conscience or indirectly through the teaching office of the Church.

Naphtali continues, like many of his brothers, by predicting troubles to come, citing the book of Enoch, and under the guise of dreams. Levi and Judah take the first places, and Naphtali ends by looking forward to the resolution of all such troubles when God dwells with men on the earth:

4. I am telling you all this, my children, because I have read in the holy book of Enoch that even you will turn away from the Lord and walk in all the wicked ways of the nations, and behave according to all the crimes of the Sodomites. The Lord will bring you into captivity, and you will be slaves there under your enemies, and caught up in every sort of suffering and distress, until the Lord comes to liberate you all. And after you have become few in number and humble, you will return and acknowledge the Lord your God. According to his great mercy, he will bring you back to your own land. But it will happen that those who had returned to the land of their ancestors will again forget the Lord, and will behave wickedly. The Lord will disperse them across the face of the whole world, until the merciful Heart of the Lord shall come, the Man who works righteousness, and shows mercy to all those who are far off and those who are near (Ephesians 2:17).

5. It was in the fortieth year of my life that I saw, upon the Mount of Olives to the east of Jerusalem, that the sun and the moon stood still (Habakkuk 3:11). And behold, Isaac my father's father spoke to us, 'Run quickly and each of you catch hold of whatever he can. The sun and the moon will belong to whoever can catch them'. We all ran together, and Levi caught the sun, but Judah ran faster and caught the moon, and the two of them were carried up by what they had caught. Levi became as the sun, and a young man gave to him twelve palm branches. Judah shone like the moon, and under his feet were twelve peaks. Levi and Judah ran towards each other

and caught hold of each other. And behold, a bull on the earth, and it had two great horns, and on its back the wings of an eagle, and we wished to seize hold of it, but were unable. But Joseph arrived, and he was able to control it, and he was caught up into the heights with it. And I saw that I was in a garden, and behold, a holy writing was revealed to us, and it said, 'The Assyrians, the Medes, the Persians, the Elamites, the Chaldaeans, the Syrians, will each have a share in the captivity of the twelve sceptres of Israel' (cf. Acts 2:9).

6. And again, after seven days, I saw my father Jacob standing by the sea of Jamna, and all we his sons were with him. And behold, a ship came up, with sails spread, and full of mummified bodies, yet without crew or helmsman. And upon it was written, 'The Ship of Jacob'. And our father said to us, 'Let us embark on our ship'. But as we embarked a sudden storm blew up, and a mighty squall of wind, and our father, who was holding the tiller, was snatched away from us. We were whirled away by the storm and driven across the sea, and the ship began to fill with water, as every third wave broke over it, so that it fell apart. Joseph escaped in the dinghy, while the rest of us clung to ten separate planks, for Levi and Judah held onto the same one. Thus we were dispersed to the ends of the earth. But Levi put on sack cloth and entreated the Lord on our behalf, and the storm subsided, and the boat came to land as if in peace. And behold our father Jacob appeared, and we all rejoiced together.

7. I told my father these two dreams, and he said to me, 'They are bound to be fulfilled in their own time, since Israel has much to undergo'. Then my father said to me, 'I trust God that Joseph is alive, for I notice that the Lord always includes him in the number with you'. He wept, saying, 'Alas, you are alive, Joseph my son, but I cannot see you, nor can you see Jacob who begat you'. When he spoke like that he made me weep as well, and I was strongly moved to tell him that Joseph had been sold, but I was afraid of my brothers.

8. Behold, my sons, I have revealed to you the last times, when all these things will happen in Israel. It is for you to tell them to your children, so that they may stay united to Levi and Judah. For it is through Judah that salvation will arise for Israel, it is in him that Jacob will be blessed. Through his sceptre God will be made manifest, dwelling among men on the earth, to save the race of Israel and to call together the righteous from among the gentiles. If you do what is good, both men and angels will bless you. And God will be glorified among the nations because of you, and the devil will flee from you, and the wild beasts will fear you, the Lord will show you his love, and angels will minister to you. For just as when a man educates his child well, he leaves a good memory behind him, in the same way a good work is remembered by God with gratitude. But one who does not do what is good will be cursed by both men and angels. And God will be held in scorn among the nations because of him, and the devil will dwell in him as in his own vessel, and all the wild beasts will dominate him, and the Lord will hate him. For the commandments of the law are twofold, and are fulfilled with care. There is a time for commerce with your wife, and a time for abstinence for the sake of prayer (I Corinthians 7:5). There are two commandments of God (Matthew 22:39–40), but if they are not taken in the right order, they will be the cause of a great sin among men. Thus it is with all the other commandments. Be wise therefore in God, my boys, and prudent, knowing the order of his commandments, and the laws governing every action, so that the Lord may love you.

9. And after he had given them many instructions of this kind, he begged them to transfer his bones to Hebron and bury them with his fathers. They ate and drank together with glad hearts, and then he veiled his face and died. And his sons carried out all the things which Naphtali their father had asked them to do.

When the Patriarch Naphtali says, 'the devil will flee from you, and the wild beasts will fear you and angels will minister to you', there is a clear allusion to Our Lord's temptations in the desert: it is by resolutely upholding the good that he put the devil to flight, 'he was with the wild beasts, and the angels ministered to him' (Mark 1:13). The devil, 'more subtle than any other wild creature', appears with subtle arguments, winning words designed to twist the truth into falsehood, and make evil appear to be good. 'When you eat of it your eyes will be opened, and you will be like God, knowing good from evil' (Genesis 3:1, 5). Eve allowed herself to be deceived. The devil tried again with the New Adam, 'If you are the Son of God, throw yourself down, for it is written, "He will give his angels charge of you"' (Matthew 3:6). The use of selected quotations from the Scriptures, the offer of a quick route to the desirable end of popularity, reputation, and influence, and the suggestion that Our Lord's mission would be accomplished so easily if he would only do the devil's bidding and worship him—all this is the literally devilish use of subtle argument, twisted logic and empty philosophy.

Our Lord, who is the Logos himself, and knows the scriptures very much better (for he himself was their author), can refute the devil with words. For us it is better to keep silent, and not to allow ourselves to be drawn into any discussion with the devil. For 'in much talking thou canst not avoid sin' or, as the modern version has it, 'When words are many, transgression is not lacking' (Proverbs 10:19). When we are besieged by clever arguments, and subtle writers try to persuade us that the truth we have always professed is now false, when they appeal to our desire for self-indulgence with carefully thought-out rational explanations of why the Church has been wrong all these centuries, then it is better for most of us not to attempt to engage the enemy in his own terms, but simply to remain silent, content in the knowledge that to follow the voice of the Church is to hear the voice of God, and that goodness, beauty and truth are unchanging. Great theologians and philosophers may attempt on our behalf to answer the devil—we can leave the Dominicans to do that for us, all we need is the simple familiar teaching of the Catechism, and a still silent attentiveness to the inner voice of conscience.

Naphtali has given us the ultimate answer to all the debates about goodness, when he foretells the coming of 'God, dwelling among man on the earth.' For it was to be in the territory allotted to his own tribe that the Word was made flesh. 'Now he withdrew into Galilee; and leaving Nazareth he went and dwelt in Capernaum by the sea, in the territory of Zabulun and Naphtali, that what was spoken by the prophet Isaiah might be fulfilled: "The land of Zebulun and the land of Naphtali, toward the sea, across the Jordan, Galilee of the Gentiles"' (Matthew 4:12–15, cf. Isaiah 9:1). In fact, Nazareth, Caparnaum and Cana are all in Naphtali territory, as is the entire western shore of the See of Galilee; the land of Zebulun lay a bit further north towards Caesarea Philippi. That is why in the blessing which Moses gives to the tribe of Naphtali, we hear, 'O Naphtali, satisfied with favour, and full of the blessing of the LORD, possess the lake and the south' (Deuteronomy 33:23).

It is the Word of God, made incarnate in Nazareth, who sends forth his Spirit into our hearts, the Spirit who speaks in the voice of Conscience. As the prophet Joel said long before, 'It shall come to pass afterward that I will pour out my spirit on all flesh; your sons and daughters shall prophesy, your old men shall dream dreams, and your young men shall see visions. Even upon the menservants and maidservants in those days, I will pour out my spirit' (Joel 2:28–9). The Holy Spirit speaks in the conscience of every human creature, if only we have the inner stillness to listen. But if our own perception of conscience is obscured or confused, we have an external guide in the Church. It is Christ who teaches us, who sends us his apostles to teach in his name, for 'he who hears you hears me, and he who rejects you rejects me' (Luke 10:16). In the Mystical Body of Christ, which is the Church, we have a sure guide, against all the philosophers and critics and scribblers of our age.

Again, it is in silence that we can hear most clearly. Within the silence of our hearts we hear the Holy Spirit calling us, conscience becoming aware of what is good and what is bad, what is false and what is true. It is not only morals we learn from conscience, but doctrine too—which is why God's little ones often know, without much need for study, what the truth is. But we can, and should, compare what we hear within ourselves with what we hear in the Church, the teaching handed down through the ages and expounded in our own times. When we become aware that the inner voice of conscience, and the outer ear that listens to the preacher, are in perfect agreement, we have absolute certainty. If we find a conflict, we do have to pause and assess. Our first instinct should be to doubt ourselves, to presume that it is we who have not been able to discern the Holy Spirit clearly, rather than to set ourselves up immediately against the united voice of the Church. Though, of course, we should be careful to make sure that what the particular preacher is saying really is the teaching of the united Church—that is where the Catechism is such a useful tool. Again, it is often the simple people of God who can tell at once when a preacher or writer is talking nonsense, however subtle and learned his arguments. But if we have found that he is really speaking in unity with the entire Church, what arrogance it would be for us to think we know better! There are many things that might have obscured our own perception of the voice of conscience— the litter of past sins, the desire for future ones, the general confusion of mind inseparable from living in a fallen world. That is why we talk of having an 'informed' conscience, the result of careful and humble comparison of what we think we have heard internally with what we have certainly heard externally.

But having said all that, it is still the teaching of the Catholic Church that conscience is binding, even if it be erroneous (*CCC*, 1790–4). We must do all we can to inform our conscience, but in the last resort it must prevail. That is why on occasion saints have defied the teaching of authority when they were convinced that authority was wrong—the classic examples are St Joan of Arc, and Blessed Franz Jägerstatter (1907–43; see John Frain, *The Cross and the Third Reich* (Oxford, 2009), pp. 202–8).

St Paul tells us that the pagans do have the ability to discern the voice of Conscience, if only they would use it. 'When Gentiles who have not the law do by nature what the law requires, they are a law to themselves, even though they do not have the law. They show that what the law requires is written on their hearts, while their conscience also bears witness' (Romans 2:14–15). Cassian elaborates on this (Abba Serenus is speaking):

> When God created man, he gave him a complete knowledge of the law to be his by nature. Had mankind preserved this knowledge intact, as the Lord intended, it would have been quite unnecessary to give the other law which was later promulgated in written form. If the internal law had

survived within us, the gift of an external law would have been superfluous. But since, as we have seen, natural law had become deeply corrupt as a result of the free practice of sin, the strict distinctions of the Mosaic law were granted to accuse, to examine, to punish, and also, as the very words of Scripture tell us, to assist. Thus fear of immediate punishment would prevent the benefit of natural conscience being extinguished, as the Prophet said, 'He gave us the law to assist us' (Isaiah 8:20, LXX). St Paul also describes the Law as being like a tutor given to children, to teach them and watch over them, so that they would not forget and fall away from the right conduct which had been instilled into them by nature (Galatians 3:24). All the saints observed the commandments of the law without reading any of it in writing, before the law was given, before the flood indeed, which proves that a knowledge of the whole law had been instilled into mankind from the beginning of creation. How otherwise would Abel have known, before the law commanded it, that he should offer a sacrifice to God from the firstfruits of his flocks and of their richness, were he not so taught by the natural law instinctive within him? (Genesis 4:4) Or how could Noah have distinguished between clean and unclean beasts, when this legal distinction had not yet been decreed, were he not informed by natural knowledge? (Genesis 7:2) Or again, how did Enoch learn to walk with God, when no one had taught him the enlightenment of the law? (Genesis 5:22) Where did Shem and Japheth read, 'Thou shalt not uncover the nakedness of thy father,' when they walked in backwards to cover up their father's body? (Genesis 9:23, cf. Leviticus 18:7) Who warned Abraham to refuse the plunder of his enemies that he was offered, lest he earn vengeance for his pains? Or to give tithes to Melchisedek, as the Mosaic law prescribed? (Genesis 14:20,22) What inspired Abraham and Lot to offer humane assistance to wanderers and pilgrims, and to wash their feet, when the glorious commandment of the Gospel had not yet been given? (Genesis 18, 19, cf. John 13:34) Where did holy Job learn such great faith, such chaste purity, such compassion, meekness, mercy and humanity, such as we hardly see fulfilled nowadays even by those who have the Gospels by heart? Do we ever read of any saint from before the Law who transgressed any commandment of the Law? Was there any of them who did not obey, 'Hear, O Israel, the Lord our God is one Lord'? (Deuteronomy 6:4) Which of them failed to listen to 'Thou shall not make to thyself a graven thing, nor the likeness of any thing that is in heaven above, or in the earth beneath, nor of those things that are in the waters under the earth'? Was there anyone who failed to 'honour thy father and thy mother', or to keep the following commandments of the Decalogue, 'Thou shalt not kill, thou shalt not commit adultery, thou shalt not steal, thou shalt not bear false witness, thou shalt not covet thy neighbour's wife'? (Exodus 20:4–17) Did they not also keep the greater commandments which the Gospel enjoins as well as the Law?

We can be sure that God created all things perfect in their origin, and that there was no need for anything to be added to his original dispensation, as if it had been ill-considered and incomplete; nor, if everything had remained in the state and manner in which it was created, would any further disposition be necessary... Therefore, 'The Law is not made for the just, but for the unjust and disobedient, for the ungodly and for sinners, for the wicked and defiled' (I Timothy 1:9). Those who found all the salutary discipline they needed in the instinctive natural law, needed no external law to be given them in writing to support the natural law. We can see clearly from this that there was no need for a law committed to writing to be given in the beginning, for as long as natural law remained undamaged and whole, it would be superfluous. Nor could the perfection of the Gospel be given them before they observed the law, for those who would not accept that they should avenge their injuries with an equal retribution, but react to a slight slap with fists and wounding weapons, seeking the lives of their aggressors for the loss of a single tooth, would not be capable of hearing, 'If one strike thee on thy right cheek, turn to him also the other.' Nor could you say to them, 'Love your enemies' (Matthew 5:39, 44), if the most that could be hoped for is that they would love their friends and keep away from their enemies, merely refraining from hating them and being too eager to oppress them or kill them.

Collations, VIII, 23–4

When Blessed Humphrey Pritchard was arraigned before his judges in Oxford in 1589, they ridiculed him, saying that an uneducated barman could not possibly be right against the combined wisdom of the schools and the courts. 'Humphrey replied that he knew very well what it was to be a Catholic, though he could not, perhaps, explain it in the proper terms of divinity; that he knew what he was to believe, and for what he came there to die; and that he willingly died for so good a cause. With that he was thrown off the ladder, and so reposed in the Lord' (Bp Challoner, *Memoirs of Missionary Priests* (Edinburgh, 1878), I, 165). The martyr's silence before his judges, and his simple affirmation of confidence in the Church, became rapidly famous throughout Europe, and is quoted in Cardinal Bellarmine's controversial writings, which were to inspire the next generation of martyrs.

Goodness cannot always be defined and explained in the precise terminology of philosophical argument: it is recognised immediately when we see it, if we can raise our sight from the tangled words of those who think themselves clever, and look straight towards the face of God. That is why it is 'in returning and rest you shall be saved; in quietness and in trust shall be your strength' (Isaiah 30:15). Also, 'The words of the wise heard in quiet are better than the shouting of a ruler among fools' (Ecclesiastes 9:17).

There are many reasons for keeping silence, and many dangers in the unbridled tongue, as we hear from St James (James 1:19,26; 3:2,5; 4:11; 5:12):

Let every man be quick to hear, slow to speak … if any one thinks he is religious, and does not bridle his tongue but deceives his heart, this man's religion is vain … If any one makes no mistakes in what he says he is a perfect man, able to bridle the whole body also ... the tongue is a little member and boasts of great things. How great a forest is set ablaze by a small fire! ... Do not speak evil against one another, brethren. He that speaks evil against a brother or judges a brother, speaks evil against the law, and judges the law ... But above all, my brethren, do not swear, either by heaven or by earth or with any other oath but let your yes be yes and your no be no, that you may not fall under condemnation.

So there are four evils that may flow from talking too much: it may deceive the heart; it may start a false idea that spreads and causes much damage; we may fail to express the charity we owe to our fellow-sinners; and by rash swearing we may involve ourselves in perjury and condemnation.

We have already explored the danger of becoming entangled in specious arguments which are bent on proving the worse case to be the better. Another even greater danger is speaking falsehood, whether deliberately or not. A casual unguarded comment may be repeated, and grow in the repetition, until reputations are destroyed, and good works brought to nothing. Once spoken, a falsehood can never be totally retracted. We see this in the case of some of the lies being spread about Pope Pius XII—no matter how many times the truth has been explained, and the facts proved, people still repeat the old lies again and again until reality is lost. One of the books rejected by the Council of Trent is the Third Book of Esdras, which contains the memorable line often quoted as 'Great is truth, and it shall prevail.' (The actual text is 'As for the truth it endureth, and is always strong; it liveth and conquereth for evermore', III Esdras 4:38.) Unfortunately it is not true, which may be why the Church does not consider that book to be inspired Scripture! Truth is often overlaid by falsehood, and lies prosper and flourish on the earth. The only way to prevent a lie from growing is never to speak it in the first place. We may try to set straight the memory of what was really said and done in the past, but it is rare that we succeed. Even more difficult is explaining what we really meant to say, what our actions truly indicate. 'Mean it? I never said it', cried Newman (*Apologia pro*

Vita Sua, p. xv), but the world never listens to explanations, once a lie has begun to circulate.

We can also do a great deal of harm by speaking the truth, if it is something disparaging and calumnious against our neighbour. It may be perfectly true that our neighbour is a sluggard and a drunkard, but it does not often do any good to tell everyone about it. By judging another, we are laying ourselves open to judgment in our turn, for none of us can claim to be righteous before God. Better to keep silence altogether about the failings of our friends and family, and even of our neighbours and enemies. On occasions, rare occasions, it may be our responsibility to speak to them directly about their sins, and try to help them towards repentance and amendment; it is rare indeed that we have a duty to warn others against them. In most cases, the best thing to do about our neighbour's sins is to keep silent but to pray earnestly for them, in the hope that others will do us the like charity.

And finally, St James warns us against swearing. Even on the practical level, the more vigorous we are in affirming the truth of what we say, the more inclined people will be to doubt it, muttering 'methinks the lady doth protest too much.' But swearing in the name of God is something we are warned against in the Gospel as well: in effect we are challenging God to prove the truth of our claims by some miraculous intervention, which is surely 'putting the Lord our God to the test.' Our Lord himself says, 'Let what you say be simply "Yes" or "No"; anything more than this comes from the evil one' (Matthew 5:37).

St James must have been present when Our Lord spoke those words. But something we do notice about James the Less in the Gospels is that he never speaks at all. Nor do we hear anything about him, neither for good or ill, except that like the rest he ran away from the Garden of Gethsemane. He is mentioned in the lists of Apostles as James son of Alphaeus; we hear about his mother, who stood at the foot of the Cross, 'Mary, the mother of James the Less and Joses' (Mark 15:40, Matthew 27:56). St John, in his account of the Crucifixion, names 'his mother's sister, Mary of Clopas' (John 19:25), who is usually understood to be the same Mary. The association with Joses shows that James the 'less' is one of the four mentioned as 'brethren' or 'kinsmen' of the Lord, James and Joses and Simon and Jude (Mark 6:3). (Jude is elsewhere called 'Jude of

James' (Luke 6:16) which should mean the son of James, but could also mean his brother, and the traditional understanding is that there were four brothers, sons of Mary of Cleopas, and Alphaeus.) In calling James the 'less' or the 'little', the Evangelist does not necessarily imply he was less important or younger than the other James, although as St Jerome translated the word *mikros* as *minor* he has been known ever since as 'the Less'. He may conceivably have been simply smaller than the burly fisherman James son of Zebedee.

The silence of James the Less in the Gospels is more than made up in the Acts of the Apostles, as well as his Epistle. He takes a leading role in the Church in Jerusalem, and after the martyrdom of the other James, replaces him as one of the Three Pillars (Galatians 2:9). It is he who acts as secretary to the Council of Jerusalem (Acts 15), and formulates the document which resolves the debate about the extent to which Gentile converts must observe the ritual Law of Moses. Thus he shows that he knows when is 'a time to keep silence and a time to speak' (Ecclesiastes 3:7). That is wisdom, granted to few of us.

In his ninth step, Cassian says we should not 'shout aloud'. The allusion is surely to Isaiah, 'he will not cry or lift up his voice, or make it heard in the street' (Isaiah 42:2). It is again Our Lord who is offered to us as a model. He taught in obscure places, avoided the crowds, withdrew into lonely country. And before his accusers he did not defend himself, but remained silent under the cross-examination by Caiphas, and Herod, and Pilate. How are we to imitate him? It is by not defending ourselves, even when they bear false witness against us. Does it matter if the world thinks ill of us, or continues to think ill? Why should we be concerned about our own reputation, our legacy? And if we are to be silent before our accusers, so too we should not be too quick to try to cry out in public, to make a great noise in the world. As Our Lord taught in the desert, and his disciples followed him there, so most of us can best imitate him by speaking quietly, in our own churches, to those who will come there to hear us. Yes, there have been saints like St Bernardine who spoke loudly in the public streets, and they had a great following for a time, but that is a rare vocation, and it did not necessarily have a lasting effect. The silent witness of a St Pius of Pietrelcina or St John Vianney in the confessional is better remembered.

The Psalmist says, 'be still and know that I am God' (Psalm 45:11). It is only in stillness and silence that we can hear God. All the words we use in prayer are only means to an end; the thoughts and meditations produced by our imagination are but preliminaries to the real business of prayer, which is in the silence of our hearts. But how difficult it is to keep interior silence, even for a moment, let alone the half hour of silence in heaven celebrated in the Apocalypse! (Apocalypse 8:1) We are all familiar with the difficulty of banishing distractions, and how they seem to multiply the more we try to banish them. That is why often it is in very brief moments of silence that we really make contact with God.

A very great deal of grace can be packed into a brief moment. Several of the saints say, indeed, that the actual 'prayer of union' lasts only for a moment, for the twinkling of a eye, in the midst of long periods of vocal prayer and meditation and 'simple regard' and the other ways in which we try to place ourselves in God's presence. We can, as it were, catch God's eye, and that is enough: he looks at us, and we look at Him. It will take us the rest of the day or the rest of our lives to unfold what that glimpse meant, but in a flash he can tell us of his love for us and all creation, and so he enlightens us on how to perceive the truth and the beauty and the goodness which is the manifestation of his love.

Step Ten

JOY

The Patriarch Issachar, Prophet Amos and Apostle Bartholomew

When you were under the fig tree, I saw you (John 1:48)

St Benedict takes us up another step on the ladder, by telling us that 'The tenth degree of humility is that he be not ready and prompt to laughter, for it is written: *The fool lifteth up his voice in laughter'* (*RB* 7).

Cassian also makes this his tenth step: 'Tenthly if we be not easily moved to laughter' (*Monastic Institutes*, IV, 39).

Of all St Benedict's Steps, this one is surely the most implausible, the most difficult to explain in the modern world—indeed it seldom fails to raise a laugh when it is read out in a monastic refectory. These days we consider that laughter is positively a good thing, we feel we should do our best to amuse each other on all occasions with witty quips and frivolous interpolations. When we hear that the Fathers of the Church were grave and serious at all times, we find that repellent, quite remote from our own image of what sanctity should be. Many of the older spiritual writers make a point of observing that nowhere in the Gospels is it recorded that Our Lord ever laughed, and they try to make us share their feeling that laughter is at best foolish and at worst a sign of a totally unmortified soul.

This view is especially galling to the followers of St Philip Neri, the Apostle of Joy, for he seems to have been something of a practical joker, always looking for the opportunity for a humorous comment or a ludicrous penance. We expect our saint to have a twinkle in his eye, and a smile on his lips. He was notorious for enjoying little books of jokes, and reading them out at inappropriate moments. His followers, on the whole, have the same sort of frivolous reputation—Newman not only read novels but even wrote them, earning the rebuke that 'Dr Newman has degraded himself to the level of Dickens'.

But St Philip had probably read the Rule of St Benedict, and certainly used the writings of Cassian as the basis for much of his teaching. He must, therefore, have interpreted the saying about being not easily moved to laughter in a way that did not exclude his famous *allegrezza*, lightness of touch.

Cassian explains that the wrong sort of laughter is a characteristic of pride, saying that 'Pride, while it may be one single vice, has two aspects: in one they feign a serious and grave demeanour, in the other they dissolve in giggles and laughter with unrestrained licence' (*Collations*, IV, 20). The type of laughter the Fathers encourage us to try to avoid is rude, intrusive, mocking laughter, laughter at others' expense, laughter that ridicules what is good and holy. That is not at all the same thing as the gentle joyful humour expressed by many of the saints. We need to be clear about the difference, and the reason why St Benedict warns us against the laughter of the fool.

Laughter can be a cruel weapon. If we want to crush someone, to humiliate him in a destructive way, to mock him and despise him, we resort to loud and immoderate laughter. That is something which horrid children in the school playground quickly learn: how easy it is to reduce another child to tears by cruel laughter. Such laughter implies the belief that we are superior to the object of our mockery, that we have a right to dominate him and crush him. It is therefore the very opposite of that humility which we are climbing our ladder to find.

Joy, on the other hand, is gentle, and wants to share with others. The joyous saint is one who radiates joy himself, and brings joy to those he meets. There is all the difference in the world between mocking laughter and cheerful good humour. When the saints utter humorous remarks they intend to raise a quiet smile, and to create happiness around them. The proud man jokes in order to humiliate others and make them feel wretched.

Many of the saints share that characteristic of joy, which is often expressed in a humorous or light way of speaking. St Teresa of Ávila's letters are full of these touches of cheerfulness. 'I know very well that gratitude is no perfection in me—it must be my nature, for a sardine would bribe me' (*Letters*, III, 183). Even on her tedious journeys, her nuns remembered how she cheered them up: 'We waited impatiently to get rid of the crowd, and spent the *siesta* under a bridge. We drove away some pigs and took their place in the shade, thinking ourselves lucky to get such a shelter from the blazing sunshine. We bore all such trials cheerfully, for the Mother's conversation gave us fresh life. She spoke gravely, told us amusing tales, or composed verses, and very good ones too' (*Letters*, I, 35). Obviously neither the saint nor her nuns saw any contradiction between speaking gravely and telling amusing tales.

But having said that, we get the occasional glimpse of what St Teresa herself felt: 'Sometimes God seems to wish me to suffer without any interior consolation' (*Letters*, IV, 180). A saint who radiated joy around her could at times be conscious of nothing but sorrow. That is seen much more clearly in the writings of St Teresa of Calcutta as we have already seen: she shared the darkness of the lives of those she had chosen to serve, for only by embracing the darkness could she shed light into their lives.

I suspect that many saints who appeared to be cheerful, with joyous countenance, were like that to some extent—joy on the outside, but a consciousness within of nothing but sorrow. Their glory was hidden so deep within them, in the recesses of the heart, that it was only revealed at their death. Even the joyous St Philip at times said things that suggest an experience of the darkness, which St John of the Cross was to explain for his generation.

Cassian anticipated St John of the Cross by a thousand years, remembering how he and his companion asked for advice about the alternate moods of joy and sadness:

> We asked this holy man Daniel how it can happen that sometimes we could be dwelling in our cells, with great attentiveness of heart, and filled with an inexpressible joy and inner delight, so that not a word, not even a thought intruded, but prayer was pure and prompt, the thoughts full of spiritual benefits, aware that effective petitions easily winged their way to God even in sleep; and then suddenly for no apparent cause we would be filled with such anxiety

and crushed under so unreasonable a gloom that we would feel our spirits dried up, and the very cell seemed unbearable, reading intolerable, prayer itself as wavering and indistinct as a drunkard, until neither by tears nor by mental effort could we bring our thoughts back to their former path. The more urgently we applied ourselves to God, the more violently our elusive thoughts were driven to wild imaginations, so drained of spiritual benefit that neither a longing for the kingdom of heaven, nor the fear of hell could stir our intentions out of this deadly torpor. Daniel replied as follows:

'The elders have told us that the dryness of mind which you have described can have three causes. It can arise either from our own negligence, or from the attacks of the devil, or from the Lord who tests us in his wisdom. If it is from our own negligence, it is because through our fault we have been careless and lazy in times past, feeding idly on evil thoughts, and making thorns and briars sprout on the soil of our minds, till they choke us, and we become quite sterile, bereft of all spiritual benefit or contemplation.

'It may happen through the assault of the devil, for even if we have applied ourselves to good learning, the enemy is subtle enough to penetrate the mind so that we are drawn away from our best intentions either unknowingly or unwillingly.

'If it is the Lord who is testing us in his wisdom, then there can be two reasons: the first is that we are briefly abandoned by him in order that we may become aware of the weakness of our minds, in real humility, and thus avoid being at all elated by the purity of heart which we had formerly possessed as a gift on his visitation. Tested by his abandoning us, we come to understand that our own tearful efforts are quite unable to recover that state of joyful purity, for our former attentiveness of heart was conferred on us by his mercy, not by our own efforts, and can now only be begged for through his grace and the light of his countenance.

'The second reason for testing us is to demonstrate our perseverance, and the constancy of our desire, to prove our eagerness and urgency in begging the Holy Spirit to return to visit us whom he had deserted. Recognising how much effort it takes to recover that lost spiritual joy and glad purity, we may be the more careful to preserve it when we have found it, and to cherish it, for if you believe something to be easily recovered, you will take little care to preserve it.

'This shows us clearly how the grace and mercy of God are always at work in us to produce good results. If he desert us, our own studied labour will be useless, and no amount of mental strife will suffice to recover our former state without his aid. The text is fulfilled in us which says, "it is not of him that willeth, nor of him that runneth, but of God that sheweth mercy" (Romans 9:16). Grace however does not disdain to visit those who are negligent and dissolute, with a holy abundance of spiritual consolations such as those you have mentioned, for so it encourages the unworthy, awakens the slothful, and enlightens those oppressed by the darkness of ignorance. Mildly it prompts us and corrects us, penetrating into our hearts until we are persuaded by its insistence to rise out of our state of idle somnolence. Often enough when divine grace visits us we are overwhelmed by a sweet scent beyond the skill of any human perfumer, till our thoughts are so enchanted by delight that we are rapt into a spiritual maze, forgetting ourselves to be still clothed in flesh.

'King David knew how beneficial it can be that God conceal himself, or I might even say desert us, for he refused to pray that we should never be deserted by God at all, knowing how little that would profit us, or anyone striving for perfection: he did however pray that this desertion should be modified, saying, "O do not thou utterly forsake me" (Psalm 118/119:8). This is as much as to say, I know well that you customarily withdraw from your holy ones, so as to test them. In no other way could they be tempted by the enemy were they not to some extent deserted by you; therefore I do not pray that you should never desert me, for that would do me no good at all. How else could I become aware of my weakness, so as to say, "It is good for me that thou hast humbled me" (Psalm 118/119:71), or how could I gain experience in fighting, which I would surely never do if the divine protection were always over me unceasingly? The devil would never dare to assault me as long as I am sustained by your defences, and repeat that resentful accusation against both me and you, and again cry out in slander of your champions, "Doth Job fear God in vain? Hast thou not made a fence for him, and his house, and all his substance round about?" (Job 1:9–10, LXX) Nay, rather I will pray that you do not forsake me utterly, or as the Greek says, *heos sphodra,* to an extremity. It is as beneficial for me that you withdraw from me a little to prove my perseverance in longing, as it would be dangerous for you never to allow me to be deserted for the sake of my merits and of my sins. No human virtue can endure for long if it is tempted continuously without your aid, but it would swiftly fall to the power and influence of the enemy were you not aware of man's strength, and the umpire of his contests, "who will not suffer us to be tempted above that which we are able; but will make also with temptation issue, that we may be able to bear it" (I Corinthians 10:13).

'We find something similar in the Book of Judges, where it speaks mystically about the extermination of the spiritual enemies that threatened Israel, "These are the nations which the Lord left, that by them he might instruct Israel ..., that they might learn to fight with their enemies", and a little further on, "The Lord left them, that he might try Israel by them, whether they would hear the commandments of the Lord, which he had commanded their fathers by the hand of Moses, or not" (Judges 3:1–4). It was not that God grudged peace to the Israelites, or planned evil for them, but he preserved their enemies for their own benefit; thus through being always under pressure from the attacks of these foes they might never imagine they could do without the help of God, and through meditating on this always and through prayer they would be safe from complacency, and never lose the skill and practice of warfare. For it often happens that ease and prosperity overthrow those who could not be defeated by adversity.'

Collations, IV, 2–6

Sorrow, therefore, can have a positive aspect. But it is never good in itself, and only does good if we co-operate with grace, allowing the experience of the absence of sensible joy to mortify us, to detach us from material things and earthly concerns, and to unite us with the passion of Christ and the woes of the world he came to deliver. To 'embrace the darkness' may be an important part of our spiritual progress—to reject it, and to clamour unceasingly for joy shows that we are still unmortified, still clinging to our own self-esteem and our own self-aggrandisement. That is why attachment to joy and laughter can indeed be an obstacle on the way of perfection.

True spiritual joy is a gift from God, and should be welcomed and treasured, though we cannot cling to it or claim it as a right. Even when it overlays an interior of sorrow, joy goes always with simplicity of heart. The joyous ones see things straightforwardly, without too many complications. We are reminded of the Apostle Bartholomew, who is usually considered to be the same as Nathanael, 'an Israelite indeed, in whom is no guile'. His approach to the Lord is very simple, direct and open: he goes from a scornful rejection of anything that comes from Nazareth to full acceptance of the divinity of Our Lord. Philip had told him that they had found 'him of whom Moses in the law and also the prophets wrote, Jesus of Nazareth, the son of Joseph.' Nathanael finds that difficult to believe—and indeed he is quite right. Jesus was not born in Nazareth; he was not the son of Joseph. What Nathanael perceives is the truth about who the Father of Our Lord really is, and where he comes from: 'Rabbi, you are the Son of God! You are the King of Israel!'

An Israelite in whom is no guile, Nathanael is blessed for his simplicity. He has asked Our Lord how he knew him, and the answer was the enigmatic, 'I saw you under the fig tree.' As so often in St John's Gospel there are layers of meaning. There must have been some decisive moment in Nathanael's life, some great decision for God taken while he was meditating under a fig tree. But Our Lord had already seen him under the fig tree in the Garden of Eden. The call of Nathanael, Bartholomew, to be one of the Lord's Apostles was already in the mind of God from the beginning of creation (John 1:45–51).

Nathanael calls Our Lord 'King of Israel', not 'of Judah'; and he in turn is called 'an Israelite'. There is naturally a reference here to the North Kingdom, the Kingdom of the Ten Tribes including Bethsaida, where Philip finds Nathanael, and of course Nazareth. Nathanael was tempted to laugh at Nazareth. But his laughter is turned to true joy when he finds the fulfilment of the prophecies, Jesus of Bethlehem, the Son of God. Our Lord immediately reminds him, and us, of the original Israel, the new name given to Jacob, who had seen the angels of God ascending and descending on a ladder whose top reached to heaven (Genesis 28:12). Our ascent of the steps of humility is of course based on that same Ladder, as St Benedict makes explicit: 'we must set up a ladder of our ascending actions like unto that which Jacob saw in his vision, whereon angels appeared to him ascending and descending' (*RB* 7).

Simplicity is the theme of the Testament of the Patriarch Issachar, who comes across as the nicest of the twelve brothers. He was the fifth son of Jacob, born as a result of the curious and rather disreputable episode of the mandragora or mandrakes (Genesis 30:14–18). Because Rachel had given Leah two mandrakes (described as 'fruits' or 'apples') she herself was eventually to have two sons, but Leah could have had two more herself had she not been so avaricious.

1. A transcript of the words of Issachar. He called his sons and said to them, Listen, my children, to your father Issachar, pay attention to the words of one beloved by the Lord. I was the fifth son born to Jacob, in exchange for the mandrakes. When Reuben my brother brought some mandrakes in from the countryside, Rachel was the first to see him, and she took them from him. Reuben burst into tears, and my mother Leah came out when she heard him crying. Mandrakes are a sort of sweet-smelling fruit, which grow in the land of Aram, high up, below the waterfalls. Rachel said, 'I will not give them to you, I will keep them, to compensate me for children. For the Lord has overlooked me, and I have born no children for Jacob'. Now there were two mandrakes.

Leah said, 'Is it not enough for you that you have stolen away the husband of my virginity, must you take these as well?' Rachel replied, 'Very well, Jacob may come to you tonight in exchange for your son's mandrakes.' But Leah said to her, 'Do not be so proud and arrogant: Jacob is mine, I am the wife he married in his youth.' 'How so?' replied Rachel, 'I was the first to be engaged to him, it was for my sake that he served our father fourteen years. What shall I do to you? Deceit and wickedness have multiplied among men, deceit has taken over the world. Were it not for that, you would never have even seen Jacob's face. You are not his wife, it was through deceit that you were brought in instead of me. My father tricked me, and moved me away that night and did not let Jacob see me. If I had been there, it would never have happened. Take one of the mandrakes', concluded Rachel, 'and in exchange for one of them he may sleep with you for one night.' So Jacob came to Leah, and she conceived, and I was born. She called me Issachar because of the exchange.

2.   Then an angel of the Lord appeared to Jacob, and told him that Rachel would bear two children, because she despised commerce with her husband and preferred to remain chaste. If Leah my mother had given up both fruit instead of wanting to sleep with Jacob, she would have born eight sons; as it is she bore six, and Rachel two, for the Lord looked upon her after the mandrakes. He saw that it was for the sake of children that she wanted to lie with Jacob, not out of lust. In the morning Rachel offered the mandrakes to Jacob, and so the Lord heard Rachel, because of them. Although she desired them she did not eat them, but laid them up in the temple of the Lord, bringing them to the one who was at that time the high priest.

Possibly because of this connection with fruit, Issachar grew up to be a farmer. But again we are reminded of the Garden of Eden. He continues:

3.   When I grew up, my sons, I walked in righteousness of heart, and tended the farm of my fathers and my brothers; I brought

the produce of the fields in season, and my father blessed me, seeing that I walked in simplicity before him. I was not anxious about my work, nor was I harsh and overbearing towards my neighbour. I did not revile against any man, nor wish the death of any, but walked in simplicity of sight. I did not marry a wife until I was thirty-five, for my work had sapped my strength, and I knew nothing of the desire of women. After work I fell asleep at once, and my father was always glad to see my simplicity. Of all that my labours produced, I offered the first to the Lord through his priest, the next to my father, only then for myself. And the Lord multiplied his benefits in my hands. Jacob my father also knew that God worked through my simplicity, so that I was able to give the good things of the earth to all the poor and needy, in simplicity of heart.

4. Listen therefore to me, my children, and walk in simplicity of heart, for I know that in such is all the Lord's delight. The man of simplicity desires not gold, hates not his neighbour, has no longing for strange foods, wishes not for fine clothing, does not set his heart on long life, but simply accepts the will of God. And the spirits of deceit have no hold over him. He does not take pleasure in the beauty of women, so as not to defile his thoughts in dissipation; no jealousy creeps into his thoughts, nor does envy infect his mind, neither does he plot excess of acquisition. He walks in directness of life, and sees all things in simplicity, never led astray by the evil glances of this world's deceits, lest he look at any of the Lord's commands in a distorted manner.

This whole treatise on simplicity is in fact an elaboration of the words of Our Lord in the Gospel, 'If your eye is sound, your whole body will be full of light; but if your eye be not sound, your whole body will be full of darkness' (Matthew 6:22). The words translated 'eye' and 'sound' also mean 'intention', and 'simple'—it is a difficult phrase to translate, as indeed the Testament of Issachar is difficult to render into the language of a people who do not value simplicity. But this simplicity is the key to joy, to blissful innocence and an innocent's blessing. Issachar continues:

5. So again, my children, keep the law of God and possess simplicity, walk in innocence, without scrutinising the commandments of the Lord, or the deeds of your neighbour. Love the Lord, and love your neighbour, have pity on the poor and the weak. Bend your back to the plough, and work the land with effort, so that from every field you may bring gifts to the Lord with thanksgiving. The Lord will bless you in the firstfruits of your land as he has blessed all the saints from Abel until now. For no other share is granted you other than the fatness of the land, whose fruits you gain by your labours. For our father Jacob blessed me with the blessing of earth and firstfruits. It was Levi and Judah whom the Lord glorified among the sons of Jacob, for the Lord granted portions to them, to one he gave the priesthood, to the other the kingship. Obey them, therefore, and walk in the simplicity of your father. But it was to Gad that it was given to overcome the trials that were to come on Israel.

Again there is an obvious reference here to the two great commandments of the Gospel, although we are also reminded of the protestations of the good man Job. Issachar might be thought a little bit too complacent about his own virtue, when he goes on to prophecy that his descendants will fall away, but can still be redeemed:

6. You should know, my children, that in the last days your descendants will depart from the ways of simplicity and attach themselves to avarice; leaving innocence behind, they will draw near to wickedness; abandoning the commandments of the Lord, they will adhere to the devil. They will no longer be farmers, but will follow after their own evil thoughts, and so they will be dispersed among the nations, and will be slaves to their enemies. Tell your children these things, so that if they sin, they may turn at once towards the Lord, for he is merciful and compassionate towards them, and will bring them back to their land.

7. I am now one hundred and twenty-two years old, and I do not know of any mortal sin in me, Apart from my wife, I have known no other woman. I have not committed fornication through indulging my eyes, I have never drunk wine to excess. I have never coveted what is dear to my neighbour, there has been no deceit in my heart, and no lie has ever passed my lips. I have shown compassion to every man in distress, and I have shared my bread with the poor. I have not eaten alone, I have not taken away my neighbour's landmark. All my days I have practised piety, and I have preserved the truth. I have loved the Lord with all my might, and I have likewise loved all men as much as my own sons. Do this as well, my children, and all the spirits of Belial will flee from you, nothing that evil men can do will overpower you, and you shall tame all the beasts of the field, for you will have with you the God of heaven and earth, and he will walk among men in simplicity of heart.

And saying this, he commanded his sons to take him to Hebron, and bury him there in the cave beside his fathers. So he stretched out his feet and died, in a graceful old age; he was sound in every limb, and while still strong he fell into his long sleep.

Dear Issachar seems to have forgotten that, like the rest of the brothers, he agreed to capture Joseph and sell him as a slave. In the blessing given him by Jacob he does not come out quite so well: 'Issachar is a strong ass, crouching between the sheepfolds; he saw that a resting place was good, and that the land was pleasant; so he bowed his shoulder to bear, and became a slave at forced labour' (Genesis 49:14–15). The idyllic pastoral image we found in the Testament now seems much less attractive. His farming now reminds us of the curse of Adam, 'cursed is the ground because of you, in toil you shall eat of it all the days of your life' (Genesis 3:17). But that is the Old Testament: in the light of the Gospel the curse has become a blessing, which is why the Christian writer of the Testaments is able to find joy in the simple life of the farmer.

Moses combines Issachar with Zebulun, in the joint blessing we have already quoted, 'Rejoice, Zebulun, in your going out, and Issachar in your tents. They shall call peoples to their mountain; there they offer right sacrifices; for they suck the affluence of the seas and the hidden treasures of the land' (Deuteronomy 33:18–19). Zebulun, we remember was the fisherman; Issachar the tender of the land. Here is already a prophecy of the joy which will come in the light of the Redeemer, when the right sacrifices can be offered. In this context we may go back to the passage we translated as 'bring gifts to the Lord with thanksgiving' and remember the word for 'thanksgiving' is *eucharistia*—it may be that already it has become a technical term, and that Issachar is summoning us to render our thanks in the context of the sacrifice of the Mass.

The prophet Amos came, like Issachar, from an agricultural background, and with all the force and vigour of a simple rustic denounces the decadence and crimes of the city dwellers. 'I am no prophet,' he declaims, 'nor a prophet's son; but I am a herdsman, and a dresser of sycamore trees, and the LORD took me from following the flock, and the LORD said to me, "Go, prophesy to my people Israel"' (Amos 7:14–15).

There was a strong tradition among God's people that the country life is best, that the rustic who lives in simplicity is much closer to the love of God and neighbour than those who live by trade and extortion and violence, hemmed in within their proud city walls. More specifically, it is better to be a herdsman and a nomad, like Abel and Abraham, wandering freely over the face of the earth, following the flocks and herds to wherever they can find pasture, rather than an arable farmer like Cain who encloses his fields with hedges and fences and tries to control what grows on his land. The nomad was always suspicious of the settler, and both were very dubious about the city-dweller. Amos, like King David, was predominantly a shepherd (it is not at all clear why he also used to dress sycamore trees), and the image of the Shepherd King, the Good Shepherd, is central to both Old and New Testaments. As a result, when Amos has had his fill of denunciations, and the crimes of Israel and Judah have been condemned along with those of their pagan neighbours, he concludes with a promise of peaceful prosperity in the countryside: '"Behold, the days are coming," says the LORD, "when the ploughman shall overtake the reaper and the treader of grapes him who sows the seed; the mountains shall drip sweet wine, and all the hills shall flow with it"' (Amos 9:13).

Joy, then comes with the simplicity of rural life. Amos preferred the sycamore tree, but it was under the fig tree that the Lord found

Nathanael, an Israelite indeed in whom is no guile. It is by sitting peacefully under the fig tree that we can become aware of the presence of God. Moses promised his people 'a land of wheat and barley, of vines and fig trees' (Deuteronomy 8:8), and it became a proverb in Israel that prosperity and happiness was when 'they shall sit every man under his vine and under his fig tree' (Micah 4:4, cf. I Kings 4:25, II Kings 18:31; Zechariah 3:10 etc.). It is true that there is also a tradition of exalting the Holy City, the prophecy of the new and eternal Jerusalem, but more often the bliss to come is described in pastoral terms. 'I am the Good Shepherd, I know my own and my own know me' (John 10:14).

In the Testament of Issachar we heard him say that 'God worked through my simplicity', which reminds us at once of the words of Our Lady, 'He has regarded the low estate of his handmaiden … he who is mighty has done great things for me' (Luke 1:48–9). It is precisely because she knows her simplicity and lowliness that God is able to work through her for the salvation of the world. And so she rejoices in God her Saviour: joy is her characteristic, even though she too had to bear a sword of sorrow through her heart.

This may be why the very earliest of all Christian hymns to Our Lady celebrates her joy. There are three lines addressed to her in that very curious poem, the *Sibylline Oracles*, which certainly took its present form in the reign of the Emperor Hadrian (*c.* AD 136), and which we may translate prosaically as:

'Rejoice, O maiden, and be glad, for he who made heaven and earth has given you the joy of the ages; within you will he dwell, and he will be your everlasting light' (*Sibylline Oracles*, III, 722–5).

The Angel's first greeting to Mary was *Ave*, 'rejoice', and joy has been her gift to the world ever since. Painters love to show her waiting patiently for the angel to arrive; some even depict her under a fig tree, but more usually she is shown indoors, in contemplation while engaged in the simple activity of spinning. St Bernard, who is another of the great and serious saints with a sense of humour, tells us that 'Mary, as a most prudent virgin, had her door closed, not however against angels, but only to men' (St Bernard, *Sermons for the Seasons* I, p. 96).

The prayer of contemplation begins, according to some authors, with the 'prayer of simple regard'. It is by stripping away all the complications of earthly life, eliminating all the multitude of worries and concerns and issues, that we come to sit quietly before the Lord and are ready to hear him speak. Under our spiritual fig tree, we should not be afraid to remain quite still, doing nothing in particular, thinking nothing in particular, just waiting on the Lord. We may find it best when we pray to 'go into your room, and shut the door' (Matthew 6:6), to keep out the anxieties of men; the angels will be able to enter easily enough. If our minds and hearts are full of business, churning over the choices and the problems of our own lives and the lives of those around us, then we shall not be able to hear the voice of the angel saying, 'rejoice!' nor shall we be able to receive the message of joy which Our Lord wants to give us.

In quietness and simplicity, then, is our joy. It is a joy that needs no loud and immoderate laughter, that excludes all mockery and scorn of others: our laughter is the innocent laughter of unfallen creation, when the world was new and unstained: 'when the morning stars sang together, and all the sons of God shouted for joy' (Job 38:7).

Humility, therefore, is one step nearer when we can laugh in simplicity, in the peaceful possession of our own vine and fig tree, in the radiance of the light of God, in the image of Mary. The mocking laughter which St Benedict excludes can have no place in true joy, and the tranquillity of a heart that engages in the simple regard of God is not easily moved away to lesser things. All earthly songs are nothing, once we have joined the Morning Star in her song of joy.

> *Another version of the Sybilline verses:*
> Maiden, rejoice for mirth!
> Hear the maker of all, heaven above, and earth.
> (O hear him call!)
> Maiden, rejoice, for joy!
> He gives joy without end—come, O redeemer boy!
> (And an angel send!)
> Maiden, rejoice, for light!
> Light in you shall abide, shining with clearest sight.
> (At this Christmas tide.)

Step Eleven

PEACE

The Patriarch Gad, Prophet Nahum and Apostle James the Great

A soft answer turns away wrath, but a harsh word stirs up anger

(Proverbs 15:1)

At first sight, St Benedict's penultimate step appears to be rather a repetition of the last two put together: 'The eleventh degree of humility is that a monk, when he speaks, do so gently and without laughter, humbly and seriously, in few and sensible words, and without clamour. It is written: *A man is known by the fewness of his words*' (*RB* 7). That is effectively the sum of Cassian's ninth and tenth steps, on silence and not being easily moved to laughter, which we have already noticed. The only one of his steps that we have not yet noticed is his fifth, 'if we not only refrain from injuring others, but bear injury ourselves without grieving or complaining' (*Monastic Institutes*, IV, 39), which is in turn equivalent to St Benedict's sixth and seventh. All of which reminds us that any description of the spiritual life is to a large extent relative. There is no single clear road map of the Way to Perfection, since the Holy Spirit leads us in different ways and at different speeds. 'Pray as you can and don't try to pray as you can't.' St Benedict was certainly well acquainted with Cassian, and often quotes him word for word: the fact that he arranges his steps differently shows that he was also well acquainted with this principle that different people advance towards God in different ways, taking the various steps in different orders.

Nevertheless, it is also true that the Holy Spirit can bring together different texts and show us a common meaning. What St Benedict's eleventh and Cassian's fifth steps have in common is the gift of placidity or peace, the third of the fruits of the Holy Spirit. Peace, along with joy and love, reflects 'the mind of a man as it is ordained in itself', as St Thomas teaches us. 'The perfection of joy is peace, in two aspects: firstly with regard to remaining quiet despite external disturbances, … secondly with regard to the calming of transitory passions' (*Summa Theologiae* I-II, lxx, *in corp. art*). We are not to be excitable, loud and garrulous; neither are we to be disturbed by what happens around us, not murmuring or complaining. Again, we are reminded that it is good to be content with few words, again we are warned against speaking at great length to little effect. We continue to model ourselves on Our Lord: 'He will not cry out or lift up his voice, or make it heard in the street' (Isaiah 42:2).

Perhaps the first difficulty is to distinguish between this spiritual peacefulness and rank insensitivity. Some external events are genuinely disturbing, and it would seem callous not to be affected by them. Some emotions and passions are integral to our human nature, and it would be inhuman not to feel them. Our Lord was not insensitive to the griefs or the joys of those around him. 'When he saw the crowds he had compassion on them, because they were harassed and helpless, like sheep without a shepherd' (Matthew 9:36). Many times we are told he 'had compassion', either on the sick or on the ignorant, using a very strong Greek word (*splanchnizesthai*) which implies that he felt their grief in his bowels. A similar word in the Benedictus is rendered 'the tender mercy of our God', where the Douai version has 'through the bowels of the mercy of our God' (Luke 1:78). Our Lord bears our grief and carries our sorrows with human emotions; the Sacred Heart is wounded, and bleeds with human sympathy for the woes of the world.

At the tears of Martha and Mary, Jesus himself wept. 'When Jesus saw her weeping, and the Jews who came with her also weeping, he was deeply moved in spirit and troubled; and he said, "Where have you laid him?" They said to him, "Lord, come and see." Jesus wept. So the Jews said, "See how he loved him!"' (John 11:35) If Our Lord had shown no emotion at all, or confronted their grief with a cheerful carefree grin it would not have shown love. No matter how confident we are in the love of God, how full of hope for the future, it is little less than cruel to confront mourners with jollity and sing happy frivolous songs at a funeral.

Our Lord rebukes those who refuse to respond to the emotions of others: 'like children sitting in the marketplaces and calling to their playmates, "We piped to you, and you did not dance; we wailed, and you did not mourn"' (Matthew 11:16–17). The Pharisees might have prided themselves on being indifferent to emotion, holding aloof from the joys or the sorrows of those around them. Not so Our Lord and his disciples—indeed that was made a reproach against them, 'behold a glutton and a drunkard, a friend of tax collectors and sinners!' (Matthew 11:19) It is perfectly possible to lull ourselves into a state of indifference to all around us, and persuade ourselves that this is being 'detached' and 'deeply spiritual', but that is not Our Lord's way, nor the way of the Gospel.

The possession of inner peace, therefore, does not exclude an outward sharing in the turmoil of worldly emotions, any more than it means going placidly and unconcerned amidst the horrors of human suffering. The peace Christ offers is quite different from what the world calls peace. 'Peace I leave with you; my peace I give to you; not as the world gives do I give to you. Let not your hearts be troubled, neither let them be afraid ... I have said this to you that in me you may have peace. In the world you have tribulation; but be of good cheer; I have overcome the world' (John 14:27, 16:33).

By 'peace', what the world expects is the absence of physical threat, and a prosperous state of society in which no one is at a much greater disadvantage than any other. Peace in this sense is usually coupled with justice, given that the most obvious cause of the disruption of worldly peace is the resentment built up among those who suffer injustice, or who imagine that they do. Many holy men and women make great efforts towards this sort of peace and justice, and it is right that they do so: we should not ignore the search for worldly peace and justice, for the Kingdom of Heaven must be reflected in the state of human society if we are to be true to the Gospel. But we will certainly be disappointed if we expect that the preaching of the Gospel will inevitably lead to the realisation of an ideal Christian society in this world. No matter how hard we try to express our love for neighbour in tangible terms, in works of charity both among those close to us and on the national scale, we will never succeed in eradicating injustice and conflict as long as this world lasts. Yet we must not give up on the attempt, any more than we can give up on our efforts to avoid sin and to teach others virtue. The angels sang of 'peace on earth', but it is only 'for men of good will' (Luke 2:14). Given the amount of ill-will there is in the world, we need not be surprised when Our Lord warns us, 'Do you think that I have come to give peace on earth? No, I tell you, but rather division' (Luke 12:51). The history of the Church bears out the fulfilment of that prophecy in every age.

The peace that Our Lord offers us is different. It is an interior peace, sometimes hidden so deep in the interior of our hearts that we are quite unaware of it ourselves. Many are the saints who have cried out in agony, accusing God of abandoning them, only to discover that he was concealed in their hearts all the time. So the Psalmist cried out, 'My God, my God, why hast thou forsaken me', and worked through the prayer 'But thou, O Lord, be not far off!' to the realisation that 'the afflicted shall eat and be satisfied; those who seek him shall praise the LORD!' (Psalm 21/22: 1, 19, 26) Our Lord made that psalm his own on the Cross, for he came to share our grief and our perplexity, and to lead us to that assurance and that hope. As long as there is war, suffering and injustice in the world, it is the lot of all Christians to share that suffering, to bear their part in compassion with Christ's little ones. Those who have the vocation of caring for the sick and distressed, for prisoners and strangers on the earth, must share their griefs in order truly to care for them. It would be a strange sort of 'compassion' that walked serenely through the battlefield and the ward oblivious to suffering, condescending from a great height of complacency to give cold consolation to those in grief. *Com-passion* means literally suffering along with the sufferer. Hence the desolation felt by Mother Teresa of Calcutta, which we have mentioned before, bringing her close to the desolate for whom she had offered her life.

But just as we should share the griefs of those who grieve, so we must share the joys of those who rejoice. Hence the joyous lightness of touch displayed by St Francis and St Philip Neri. They were able to join in the sports and the frivolities of the young people they were sent to convert, earning the same rebuke from the Pharisees that Our Lord himself earned. The *Fioretti* of St Francis, and the *Primo processo* of St Philip give many examples of the way in which they could share the joy of those around them. Perhaps it is their rapport with birds and beasts that best show their joyous and apparently frivolous nature. 'And as he went on his way, with great fervour, St Francis lifted up his eyes, and saw on some trees by the wayside a great multitude of birds; and being much surprised, he said to his companions, "Wait for me here by the way, whilst I go and preach to my little sisters the birds", and entering into the field, he began to preach to the birds which were on the ground and suddenly all those also on the trees came round him, and all listened while St Francis preached to them, and did not fly away until he had given them his blessing' (*Little Flowers*, I, 16). St Philip also had a way with birds: people often gave him birds, and he was particularly gentle with them. Zazzara found a fallen fledgling once, 'and brought it to show Philip, who said, "Don't strangle it, don't hurt it—open the window and let it go." Then a bit later he asked me what I'd done with it, and I said I'd let it go, and he answered that he wished he'd kept it to bring up, because it was so tiny, "it won't know where to go"' (*Primo processo* I, 65). Loys Ames remembered he had given some birds to St Philip, 'two goldfinches and a canary, and the Father put me in charge of looking after them. Then one day, among others, I went to check on the birds after dinner, and looking at the goldfinch's cage I saw that it was open (I don't know who opened it), and looking around for the goldfinch I found it on the Father's beard, it was pecking at his beard, and singing. The Father asked me, "does it do this with you, this bird?" and I said it didn't. Then the father waved it away a few times and the bird kept coming back, sometimes to his feet, sometimes to his beard, behaving in the same way. After I had looked after the others—there were two canaries, one which Master Ludovico had given him, and the other from me, and the father said to me, "pick up the cage and see if it flies back there". And I picked up the cage, and it went back there of its own accord' (*Primo processo* I, 249). It was presumably the same goldfinch that flew out of its cage when St Philip opened the door, and went into the next room where someone was lying ill (it was a domestic of the elder Cardinal Borromeo, probably Costanzo Tassoni). It flew straight to the sick man's mouth; he laughed, and the bird flew back to its cage. St Philip told it, 'go over there', and it went back to the sick man again, and so returned (*Primo processo* I, 251).

Now all this fits in perfectly well with St Benedict's injunction to speak 'gently and without laughter, humbly and seriously, in few and sensible words, and without clamour.' The laughter he discourages is the raucous mocking laughter that is designed to hurt and humiliate others; the gentle humour of the saints is designed to humiliate themselves and to edify others. When others were scandalised, and denounced them for being frivolous, they accepted the rebuke with gentleness and kindness. That is the mark of humility—the proud man would be indignant and resentful at the gibes of the Pharisees, just as the proud man would be too dignified to play with a pet bird, or to show any feeling of distress in the face of the sufferings of others.

St John the Evangelist is the first saint recorded to have kept a pet. Cassian records how Abba Abraham told the famous story:

> Once upon a time the holy evangelist John was gently stroking a pet partridge, when he suddenly saw someone coming towards him in search of wisdom, and dressed as a hunter. The latter was astonished to find a man of so great a reputation engaged in such a trivial pastime, and asked, 'Are you really that John whose fame and repute have brought me here with such an eager desire to meet you? Why are you engaged in such a ridiculous pursuit?' St John replied, 'What are you carrying in your hand?' 'My bow,' he said. 'But why do you not always keep it strung as you carry it about?' He answered, 'It would not do, because if it were always bent and tensed it would slacken and lose its strength, and so become perished. Then if I needed to shoot an arrow effectively at some game, it would be unable to supply enough force, having lost its power through being kept tensed too long.' 'Then do not take offence, young man,' said St John, 'at my brief moment of recreation. Unless we relax the rigour of our purpose from time to time by some remission, we will be unable to draw on the power of the spirit when it is needed, since uninterrupted austerity would weaken it.'
>
> *Collations*, XXIV, 21

Humility knows when to rest and when to be busy, when to give time to friends and when to attend entirely to God. It is humility that makes St Paul say, 'I have become all things to all men', just as in the fulness of time God himself is to 'be everything to everyone' (I Corinthians 9:22, 15:27). The saint shares the condition of those to whom he is sent, just as Christ came to share our condition. That means sharing joy and grief, tears and laughter, but it does not mean that we are overwhelmed by them, or that we give ourselves up to nothing but grief on the one side or jollity on the other. Surely that is what St Benedict meant, for it is certainly what we see in the life and writings of so many of his best-known followers. St Bernard, St Aelred, Blosius, Baker, Chapman and van Zeller all write with a gentle humour which is never mocking; their letters displaying a concern to sympathise when necessary, to congratulate when appropriate.

Peace, tranquillity and serenity is truly a gift of God, and it remains with us even while we are able to share in the suffering or the joy of those around us. It is not something we can be expected to manufacture for ourselves. Left on our own, our lives are full of strife, conflict and jealousy. Even the greatest saints have had to struggle to 'bear injury without grieving or complaining' as Cassian put it. It is far easier to find examples of those who have not yet achieved this step of humility than those who have. Some saints, like St Jerome, were noted for their ill temper and quick anger, though those who write the lives of saints always try to gloss over these aspects of their subjects, or to pretend that they only pretended to be angry in order to edify others. In reality, saints are saints precisely because they repent of their sins and accept the grace of God which is more than sufficient for them (cf. II Corinthians 12:9).

Our Lord's twelve Apostles were all too eager to assert their own importance, and to expect special treatment. 'He asked them, "What were you discussing on the way?" But they were silent; for on the way they had discussed with one another who was the greatest' (Mark 9:33–4). Of the Twelve, it seems to have been James and John who were the most liable to assert themselves, just as they were the most aggressive— presumably James, the 'great', being the older, was the leader in their exploits. Our Lord named them Boanerges, 'that is, sons of thunder' (Mark 3:17), which implies he knew their boisterous nature from of old.

They are the two who, when they saw how a Samaritan village refused entry to Our Lord and his disciples, asked him, 'Lord, do you want us to bid fire come down from heaven and consume them?' (Luke 9:54) In the original text, Our Lord's rebuke to them was 'you do not know what manner of spirit you are of, for the Son of Man came not to destroy men's lives but to save them'. Despite that, they continue to squabble over priority, even persuading their mother to speak for them: 'and kneeling before him she asked him for something. And he said to her, "What do you want?" She said to him, "Command that these two sons of mine may sit, one at your right hand, and one at your left, in your kingdom." But Jesus answered, "You do not know what you are asking. Are you able to drink the cup that I am to drink?" They said to him, "We are able"' (Matthew 20:20–22). In St Mark's version they ask for themselves (Mark 10:35–9).

All this out of context seems like simple self-aggrandisement, but we should note that immediately before their mother made this request, Our Lord had been speaking about his approaching Passion, of how he will be 'mocked and scourged and crucified, and raised on the third day' (Matthew 20:19; Mark 10:34). They must know, therefore, even their mother must be aware, that the places on his right hand and his left are for those who will be crucified with him, and so to enter into his glory. When they answer, 'yes, we can', to the invitation to drink the cup, they must have been at least partially aware of what they are saying, but in their longing for the places of honour they are prepared to accept even the Cross.

The other apostles were understandably 'indignant at James and John' (Mark. 10:41), but despite that they are chosen three times for a privileged position. They, with Peter, are the witnesses when the daughter of Jairus is raised (Mark 5:37), when Our Lord is transfigured (Mark 9:2), and during his Agony in the Garden (Mark 14:33). It is clear that James is one of the leaders of the Apostles, despite the fact that he wanted to be. And he leads them in one thing more—he is the first to be killed for the sake of the Kingdom of Heaven, to drink the cup of which he heard Our Lord pray that it might pass him by (Acts 12:2). Then at last this Son of Thunder was at peace. But his subsequent reputation was as the great warrior who led the armies of Christian Spain in the *reconquista.* Peace he may have found, but not as the world gives it, for St James the *Matamoros* is celebrated as a fighter and a conqueror.

There is a long tradition of glorifying war for the sake of righteousness, and the debate still continues over whether warfare can ever be justified. St Augustine and St Thomas Aquinas give us clear principles to apply, though their application in any particular case is difficult if not impossible. The fierce little prophet Nahum had no doubts: he rejoiced over the destruction of Nineveh with no reservations. 'The LORD is a jealous God and avenging, the LORD is avenging and wrathful; the LORD takes vengeance on his adversaries and keeps wrath for his enemies' (Nahum 1:2). Throughout the next three chapters he does not relent in his grim jubilation over the discomforture of his foes, 'Desolate! Desolation and ruin! ... Woe to the bloody city! ... Wasted is Nineveh, who will bemoan her? ... All who hear the news of you clap their hands over you' (Nahum 2:10; 3:1, 7, 19).

To be fair, the kings of Nineveh had been exceedingly wicked, and the tyranny of their rule had brought grief and suffering throughout the Middle East as much as some of the terrible organisations of our own time. But the Scriptures are inspired as a whole, and we may not take one passage in isolation. We must read the prophet Nahum in his context, as one of the Twelve, collected by the inspiration of the Holy Spirit into the same book as the story of Jonah. The men of Nineveh 'repented at the preaching of Jonah' (Luke 11:32), and the Lord said to him, 'should I not pity Nineveh, that great city, in which there are more than a hundred and twenty thousand persons who do not know their right hand from their left, and also much cattle?' (Jonah 4:11) Nearly all the prophets tell us that the Lord is a God of mercy and compassion. 'He is gracious and merciful, slow to anger, and abounding in steadfast love, and repents of evil', says Joel (Joel 2:13). Ezekiel speaks in his name, 'Have I any pleasure in the death of the wicked, says the LORD God, and not rather that he should turn from his way and live?' (Ezekiel 18:23) The savage exultation of Nahum is given to us as an example of the first reaction of fallen man against his enemies; the other prophets show us how God would have us respond. In the same way the fiercer passages of the Psalms are intended to stimulate us to read the other side of the story, and hear the Gospel message of forgiveness and healing. To read

Nahum alone would give us a very distorted theology of grace, just as reading Ecclesiastes alone would leave us without hope. These books show us just how desperate our condition would be if we did not have the revelation of God's love for us. All the same, when St Peter asked the crowds, 'Which of the prophets did not your fathers persecute?' (Acts 7:52) the simple answer would be 'Nahum'.

The patriarch Gad gives us a more refined account of how hatred leads to violence and strife, and how necessary it is to repent. The fiercest of the twelve sons of Jacob, he was accustomed to killing wild animals with his bare hands. When he was attacked he attacked vigorously in return, as Jacob remarked (making a play on the word for raiding party, *gedud*), 'Raiders shall raid Gad, but he shall raid at their heels' (Genesis 49:19). He despised Joseph because he was weak, and hated him because he had informed Jacob on Gad and his brothers. This, it appears, is the 'ill report' that Joseph brought to their father (Genesis 37:2). Hatred leads to anger, anger to violence, so Gad warns his family not to follow his example.

1.   The transcript of the Testament of Gad, which he spoke to his sons in the one hundred and twenty-fifth year of his life. Hear me, my sons: I was the ninth son of Jacob, and I was courageous in looking after the flocks. I watched the sheep by night, and when the wolf came down on the fold, or the lion, the leopard or the bear, I would run after it and grasp its feet in my hand, I would whirl it around like a stone from a sling; that is how I killed them. Joseph did tend the sheep with us for a month, but he was young, and became unwell because of the heat. So he went back to his father in Hebron, and lazed there with him, because his father loved him. And Joseph told our father that the sons of Zilpah and Bilhah were killing the best sheep and eating them, without the knowledge of Reuben or Judah. He knew that I had rescued a lamb from the jaws of a bear, and I killed the bear, and sacrificed the lamb, which I was sorry for, but it could not have lived. Then we ate it together. But Joseph told our father. I was angry with Joseph for that reason, until the day we sold him into Egypt, and the spirit of hatred was in me. I was unwilling to take notice

of Joseph, neither to look at him nor listen to him. He rebuked us to our face, because we had eaten some of the flock without permission from Judah, and our father believed everything that Joseph told him.

2.   So now I confess my sin to you, my children, for I often resolved to kill Joseph, and hated him from my very soul, with no feelings of compassion towards him. Because of his dreams also I hated him even more, and wanted to tear him away from the land of the living, as a calf tears up the grass from the ground. So Simeon and I sold Joseph to the Ishmaelites for thirty gold pieces. We hid ten pieces, and showed the remaining twenty to the others. Thus through avarice I was confirmed in my wish for his destruction, † though the God of my fathers delivered him from my hands, and so I did not do what was abominable in Israel.

3.   So now, my boys, hear the word of Truth, and do what is right, observe the whole law of the Most High. Do not roam about with the spirit of hatred, for it brings evil upon all men's works. When a man hates, all that he does is abominable, and even if he does observe the law of the Lord he cannot praise him; even if he fears the Lord and wants to do right, he cannot love him. For hatred corrupts the truth, and makes a man jealous of one who acts with righteousness; he embraces slander and loves arrogance. Hatred blinds a man's soul, which is what happened to me when I looked at Joseph.

Here we have moved well away from the 'righteousness of the Scribes and the Pharisees'. Gad has become aware that there is no benefit in observing the rest of the Law, or in trying to do good, if we cherish hatred in our hearts. As long as we hate our brother, we are unable to love God or to praise him. St John tells us the same: 'He who hates his brother is in the darkness and walks in the darkness ... anyone who hates his brother is a murderer, and you know that no murderer has eternal life abiding in him ... If anyone says, 'I love God,' and hates his brother, he is a liar' (I John 2:9, 3:15, 4:20). In this passage, of course,

St John is passing on faithfully the message he heard from the Lord, 'But I say to you that everyone who is angry with his brother shall be liable to judgment' (Matthew 5:22). The whole of the Testament of Gad is steeped in the revelation of the Gospel, which has put an end to the fierce anger of such as Nahum. 'You have heard that it was said, "You shall love your neighbour and hate your enemy". But I say to you, love your enemies and pray for those who persecute you' (Matthew 5:43–4).

Gad continues at some length on how hatred is evil:

4. Guard yourselves against hatred, my children, for it leads to sin against the Lord himself. If you are unwilling to listen to his commandment about the love of neighbour, you are sinning against God. If your brother should happen to stumble, you are quick to tell everyone about it, eager that he should be put on trial for what he has done, and be punished by death. If he should be a slave, you accuse him to his master, and press charges against him in all his distress, in the hope that he will be put to death. For hatred works together with murder, and when it sees one making progress in doing good, or hears about him, it is always deprived of strength. Just as love longs to give life even to the dead, and is eager to come to the assistance of those under sentence of death, in the same way hatred desires to kill those who are alive, and does not allow even those who sin in small matters to live. The spirit of hatred, because of its narrowness of soul, works together with Satan in every way to cause the death of men, but the spirit of love in greatness of heart works together with the law of God for the salvation of mankind.

5. Hatred is evil, for it keeps close company with lies and speaks against the truth; it makes much of little things, turns light to darkness, and sweet it calls bitter. Hatred is experienced in calumny, it stirs up wrath and incites men to strife and pride, with every abundance of evil, and it fills the heart with poison from the devil. This I tell you from my own experience, so that you may flee from this devilish hatred and cling to the love of the Lord. Righteousness drives out hatred, humility destroys hatred, for a man who is righteous and humble is ashamed to do what is unjust, not because another person is observing him, but because of his own conscience, for the Lord searches his thoughts. He does not accuse a holy man, for the fear of the Most High dwells within him. One who fears the Lord does not offend him, nor is he willing to wrong any man in any way, even in thought. I learnt this at last after I had repented about Joseph. True repentance from God destroys disobedience, puts darkness to flight, enlightens the eyes and brings wisdom to the soul (cf. II Corinthians 7:10). It leads the understanding towards salvation. I did not learn this from men, but through repentance I came to know how to accept those who rebuked me. God afflicted me with a disease of the liver, and had not the prayers of my father Jacob assisted me, my spirit would soon have departed from me (Wisdom 11:17). For it is through the parts by which a man sins that he is punished. Since it was my liver that was set against Joseph without pity, I suffered without mercy in my liver, and bore my punishment for ten years, for that was the length of time I had plotted against Joseph until the day he was sold.

'Humility destroys hatred', and Gad eventually finds peace, after he had repented about Joseph. After much suffering, Gad recovered through the prayers of his father Jacob, and concludes his testimony by urging his children to peace and harmony:

6. So now, my sons, I beg you, let each of you love his neighbour; banish hatred from your hearts, love each other in deed and word and thought. As long as I was in my father's presence I spoke smooth words to Joseph, but once I had gone away from him, the spirit of hatred darkened my understanding, and stirred up my soul to his destruction. Love one another with your whole heart, and if anyone sin against you, speak words of peace to him (cf. Matthew 18:15, Luke 17:3), banish the poison of hatred and do not store up rancour in your hearts. If he admits his sin and repents, forgive him; if he denies it, do not dispute with him, lest he perjure himself and thus commit a second sin. Let no one else hear your secrets in conflict, lest he hate you and become an enemy, and work a great injustice against you. For he will often speak deceitfully to you, or meddle with you for evil, having drawn his poison from you. If he denies it, and is ashamed when he is found out, keep quiet about it, and do not lead him on. Then the one who was denying it will repent, so as not to interfere with you again; indeed he will respect you and fear you, and so make peace with you. Even if he is shameless and persists in his malice, still forgive him from your heart, and allow God to avenge you (cf. Romans 12:19).

7.   If someone prospers more than you, do not be grieved, but pray for him that he will prosper even more. Maybe that will be for your own advantage too. And if someone is even more exalted, do not be jealous, but remember that all flesh must die. Sing a hymn to the Lord (James 1:5), for it is he who grants to all men what is good and beneficial to them. Examine the judgments of the Lord, and he will shine upon you and grant peace to your thoughts. If anyone become rich through his crimes, like my uncle Esau, do not envy him, but accept the boundaries laid down by the Lord. Either the Lord will take him away in his sins, or he will forgive him after repentance, or he will reserve him, impenitent, for eternal punishment. The poor man who bears no grudge gives thanks to the Lord for all things, will be enriched by him in every way, for he does not have the distractions of evil men. Drive out hatred, then, from your souls, and love one another in the goodness of your hearts.

8.   Say these things to your children, and tell them to honour Judah and Levi, for it is from them that the Lord will arise as the Saviour of Israel. I know that at the end your descendants will rebel against him, and resist the Lord through every kind of wickedness, evil and corruption.

    Gad was silent for a moment, then he said to them, My children, obey your father, and bury me near my ancestors. And he drew up his feet and fell asleep in peace. Five years later they carried him away and buried him in Hebron, with his fathers.

In the blessings of Moses, Gad still retains his reputation as a fierce warrior and slayer of wild beasts. 'Blessed be he who enlarges Gad! Gad couches like a lion, he tears the arm, and the crown of the head. He chose the best of the land for himself, for there a commander's portion was reserved; and he came to the heads of the people, with Israel he executed the commands and just decrees of the LORD' (Deuteronomy 33:20—21). Although the children of Israel had not yet crossed the Jordan into the Promised Land, the tribe of Gad, along with Reuben and half the tribe of Manasseh, had already carved out a territory for themselves on the east bank, in the lands wrested from Sihon, king of the Amorites, and Og the king of Bashan. Moses permitted this, on condition that the fighting men of the two and a half tribes agreed to support the other tribes in their conquest of Canaan, hence the reference to 'executing the commands and just decrees of the LORD.' There remained some tension between the east and west bank tribes, and the eastern side was early lost to Israel, but it was in the territory of Gad that John the Baptist began his ministry.

The Testament of Gad is an important witness to how well the early Church had understood the teaching of Our Lord. A patriarch who had historically been associated with war and revenge, is presented as one who preaches repentance, forgiveness, and reconciliation. He fulfils now the instruction of Cassian, 'not only to refrain from injuring others, but to bear injury ourselves without grieving or complaining' (*Monastic Institutes*, IV, 39). Whether or not he had any real grounds for complaint against Joseph who brought the ill report of him to their father, he knows now that he should 'not resist one who is evil, but if any one strike you on the right cheek, turn to him the other also' (Matthew 5:39).

This we see also in Gad's counsel that if one who offends us will not admit his fault, we should not press the point, nor defend ourselves, but let the matter go. Even if we are clearly in the right, it seldom does any good to emphasise the point. Far better to bear the reproach, and accept the injury. 'Blessed are you when men revile you and persecute you and utter all kinds of evil against you falsely on my account' (Matthew 5:11). The inner peace which is Christ's gift to us is better preserved if we accept injury quietly and calmly, rather than standing up for our rights and fighting our cause. St Francis de Sales frequently advised his correspondents to have nothing to do with lawsuits, even when they were certainly in the right, because the disturbance and distraction caused by getting involved in such matters would be fatal to the devout life. Lawsuits can be more distracting than sickness or bereavement, he writes, 'How many people we have seen at peace in the thorns of sicknesses and loss of friends, who lose interior peace in the worry of exterior lawsuits' (St Francis de Sales, *Letters to Persons in the World* V, 1, p. 215).

St Benedict's advice is that when we speak, we should do so 'gently and without laughter, humbly and seriously, in few and sensible words, and without clamour.' Learning not to react to injury, calumny or angry words by repaying them in the same kind is an essential step towards humility. We should not mock those who accuse us, turning them into objects of ridicule as a means of crushing them, but we should speak to them or about them gently and 'without clamour.' It is the same advice that St Paul gave to the Romans: 'Bless those who persecute you, bless and do not curse them.' But it does not exclude a proper sharing in their feelings, for he continues, 'Rejoice with those who rejoice, weep with those who weep' (Romans 12:14–15). We are not supposed to be callous and insensitive towards those who suffer, neither should we be cold and forbidding towards those who are filled with gladness, but we should not be so carried away by our emotions that we lose sight of the presence of God. When we sin we can be confident that God will accept our repentance and our penance; in the same way when others sin against us we should be as compassionate and forgiving towards them as God is towards us. In this way not only shall we be assured of the love of God in eternity, but rewarded even in this life with serenity and an interior peace. 'A soft answer turns away wrath, but a harsh word stirs up anger' (Proverbs 15:1).

Step Twelve

CHARITY

The Patriarch Benjamin, Prophet Micah and Apostle John

This I command you, to love one another   (John 15:17)

It is with charity that St Benedict reaches the top of his ladder.

> The twelfth degree of humility is that a monk should not only be humble of heart, but should also in his behaviour always manifest his humility to those who look upon him. That is to say, whether he is at the Work of God, in the oratory, in the monastery, in the garden, on the road, in the fields, or anywhere else, and whether sitting, walking, or standing, he should always have his head bowed and his eyes downcast, pondering always the guilt of his sins, and considering that he is about to be brought before the dread judgment seat of God. Let him constantly say in his heart what was said with downcast eyes by the publican in the Gospel: *Lord, I a sinner am not worthy to raise mine eyes to heaven*; and again with the prophet: *I am bowed down and humbled on every side*.
>
> Then, when all these degrees of humility have been climbed, the monk will presently come to that perfect love of God which casts out all fear; whereby he will begin to observe without labour, as though naturally and by habit, all those precepts which formerly he did not observe without fear: no longer for fear of hell, but for love of Christ and through good habit and delight in virtue. And this will the Lord deign to show forth by the power of his Spirit in his workman now cleansed from vice and from sin.
>
> *RB* 7

Cassian, more succinctly, makes charity the landing above his last step: 'True humility may be detected by these signs and others like them, and when it is possessed in truth it will swiftly bring you to that charity which drives out fear. At this level of excellence all these things which at first you observed out of fear of punishment, you may now embrace quite naturally and without effort. No longer will you be moved by the recollection and dread of suffering, but by the love of goodness in itself and joy in virtue' (*Monastic Institutes*, IV, 39).

If the fear of the Lord was the first stage of wisdom, the culmination of wisdom is nothing less than the love of God, 'not that we loved God but that he loved us and sent his Son to be the expiation for our sins' (I John 4:10). Once we know how much God loves us, we in turn can love him, 'when you sit in your house and when you walk by the way, and when you lie down, and when you rise' (Deuteronomy 6:7). By his choice of words in describing the condition of fear, St Benedict invites us to remember that text about love, so that our fear may be cast out by love. That love for God in turn drives us to love our neighbour—'for the love of Christ controls us' (II Corinthians 5:14, better translated as 'compels us'). It is the perfection of charity which finally drives out fear (I John 4:18).

St John the Evangelist is above all the apostle of charity. In his life he is shown to be the 'disciple whom Jesus loved', and in his writings he repeats the commandment of love again and again. He is someone who was close to the Lord from the time of his baptism in the Jordan— indeed, since his mother is described as a sister of the Mother of the Lord, they must have known each other in childhood. John had listened attentively to what the Lord said, and alone among the disciples had dared to remain in the Praetorium after Peter had fled, had dared to stand at the foot of the Cross. He more than any other knew, in Christ's sacrifice on the Cross, what is the meaning of the love God has for us. He pondered over what Our Lord had said, and remembered it, ready to repeat it and eventually to write it down. His own message, repeated many times in the Epistles, is always the same as that of his Master, 'little children, love one another.' St Jerome tells us:

> The blessed Evangelist John lived at Ephesus into extreme
> old age, and could only with difficulty be carried to church

by his disciples; he was unable to speak at any length, and the only phrase he was able to utter was nothing more than 'Little children, love one another.' Eventually his disciples, and the others who were there, became tired of always hearing the same thing, and said, 'Master, why do you keep saying that?' And John replied, in a manner worthy of himself, 'Because that is the Lord's commandment, and if you do just that, it is enough.'

Jerome, *Commentary on Galatians*, VI, 10;
Benedictine Edition VII, 529

There can be no serious doubt that the Gospel and the Epistles of John are by John the son of Zebedee—the commonly held opinion to the contrary is based on the prejudiced view of cynical nineteenth-century writers, who were unable to believe in the divinity of Christ, and unwilling to accept the love of God and neighbour, and therefore could not believe that anyone who knew Jesus personally could have written so movingly about the love of the Word of God made flesh. Indeed, St Irenaeus, who was personally acquainted with St John's disciple Polycarp, affirms that John wrote the Gospel, the Epistles, and the Apocalypse as well. All this has been exhaustively demonstrated by Canon John Redford in his book, *Who was John?* (St Pauls, London 2008).

The new commandment is that we should love one another, as Christ has loved us. That means being prepared to empty ourselves of rank and dignity, to 'assume the condition of a slave', and to lay down our lives for each other. There is no limit to the love which God has lavished upon us: there can be no limit to our love for each other. This is no easy commandment: indeed when we compare ourselves to the model held up for us, the model of Christ himself, we can say no more than, 'Depart from me, for I am a sinful man' (Luke 5:8), or 'God, be merciful to me, a sinner!' (Luke 18:13) We have nothing to offer of ourselves, we can do nothing for God, nor for our neighbour, but we are totally dependent on grace.

That is why the earthly model held up for us in the Gospel is St Mary Magdalen, who did nothing but sit at the Lord's feet and listen to him, as St Luke tells us (Luke 10:39). All the bustle and good works done by Martha are only of transitory value, for Mary's love will continue in eternity when all need for cooking and cleaning and mending has ceased.

St John Cassian, as always, has a passage to enlighten us, from the discourses of Abba Moyses:

> A parable of this state of mind can be found in the Gospels, beautifully demonstrated in Martha and Mary. Martha was busy at a holy and useful service, waiting on Our Lord Himself and His disciples, while Mary was only intent on spiritual learning, sitting at the feet of Jesus which she had kissed and anointed with ointment during her holy confession—she it was whom the Lord commended for she had chosen the better part which could not be taken away from her. For when Martha was hard at work, distracted by her loving care for the provisions, and saw that she alone was unequal to such a great service, she begged Our Lord for her sister's help, saying, 'hast thou no care that my sister hath left me alone to serve? Speak to her therefore, that she help me.' She was not calling her to do something disreputable, but to a praiseworthy service. But what does she hear from Our Lord? 'Martha, Martha, thou art careful and art troubled about many things. But one thing is necessary. Mary hath chosen the best part, which shall not be taken from her' (Luke 10:40–42). You see that Our Lord places the chief good in simple sight, that is divine contemplation. We can therefore see that other virtues, no matter how necessary and useful we deem them, are to be placed in the second rank, for they are all subservient to this one. When Our Lord says 'thou art careful and art troubled about many things; but one thing is necessary', he places the supreme good not in actual good works, however praiseworthy and profitable, but in the contemplation of himself, which is simple and one. When he says few things are needed for perfect bliss, he means that our gaze is firstly fixed on the consideration of a few holy things. One who is already proficient in this contemplation

progresses, with God's help, to the vision of what he calls the One, that is the vision of God alone. He passes beyond the deeds and wonderful service of the saints to feed on the beauty and wisdom of God alone. Mary, therefore, has 'chosen the best part, and it shall not be taken from her'. We must observe this carefully—when he says 'Mary hath chosen the best part', he may well be silent about Martha, and certainly does not appear to rebuke her, but in praising the one he does imply that the other is inferior. And when he says, 'it shall not be taken away from her', he shows that the ministry of the other one can be taken away. Physical good works cannot really endure in a man, but he shows us that Mary's devotion can never be brought to an end.'

Collations, I, 8

We may note that Cassian took it for granted that Mary at Bethany was the woman who had previously washed Our Lord's feet—the early Church identified both with Mary Magdalen, as was the constant tradition until the biblical critics got to work! Cassian's companion Germanus was more concerned about how we can fulfil the demands of charity to our neighbour, if we are so wrapped up in contemplation of the Lord. Moyses continues:

It is impossible for any man who dwells in this frail flesh to be completely attentive to God and, as you put it, totally wrapt in contemplation of Him. But we should be aware of the object on which the intention of our minds is to be fixed, and what should be the goal to which we must ever redirect our sight. When the mind attains this, it is glad, and when it is distracted it sighs in disappointment. It knows itself to have fallen away from the supreme good to the extent that it finds itself losing sight of this contemplation, so that it considers even a momentary distraction from the contemplation of Christ to be as bad as infidelity! When our attention wanders away from him, even for a moment, we have to turn back the eyes of our heart and apply our minds to him again straightaway. The whole matter rests in the inner part of the soul. Once the devil has been expelled, and the vices find no further dominion there, the Kingdom of God will be established within us, as the Gospel says, 'The Kingdom of God cometh not with observation. Neither shall they say: Behold here, or behold there. For lo, the kingdom of God is within you' (Luke 17:20–1) ... The kingdom of heaven can be understood in three ways. It can mean that heaven will reign, or that the saints will have dominion over others, ... or finally that in heaven, we shall reign with the Lord. ...

The contemplation of God can be conceived in various ways. God may be acknowledged in wonder at His nature, beyond our understanding, though this wonder remains veiled while we hope for the promise to be fulfilled. He may also be perceived in the magnificence of his creation, or in recognition of his justice, or through the guidance of his daily providence. He may be contemplated when with an open mind we consider what he has done through his saints over the generations, or in fearful awe we admire the powerful authority with which he controls and directs all things, and the vastness of his knowledge and perception from which no secrets of the heart are hid; when we reflect that he counts and knows the sands of the sea and the number of its waves; when we contemplate in wonder that his knowledge extends to every drop of rain, the hours and the days of the centuries, all things past and yet to come; when we consider how inconceivable is his mercy and forbearance, tolerating the countless crimes committed in his sight minute by minute; when we perceive how he calls and chooses us in his loving grace, when we had no merits of our own before; when we are lost in admiration of the frequent occasions of salvation he offers to those to be adopted as his sons; how he ordained our birth so that from the cradle we could be taught about his grace and instructed in his laws, and how he himself overthrew our enemy needing nothing but our assent, and strengthened us for eternal happiness and rewards to come;

and finally, how in his wisdom he took on the Incarnation to save us, and distributed his wonderful Mysteries among all the nations. And there are countless other grounds for contemplation, which come to mind depending on the quality of our life and the purity of our hearts, by which God may be perceived in a pure sight, and may be retained.

Collations, I, 13, 15

If we are full of the contemplation of the love of God, our practical love of neighbour will be fulfilled without our having to make a conscious effort. That is why St Benedict and Cassian can say, 'all these things which at first you observed out of fear of punishment, you may now embrace quite naturally and without effort.' We do not have to stop and think 'this is what I ought to do, and I will force myself to do it against my lower inclinations', but the love of God will enable us to do what is right, and will prevent us from doing what is wrong, without our having to think about it. In this way, the performance of works of charity will not interrupt our contemplation of God at all. Then Martha will be able to serve our meals promptly and keep a tidy household, without being 'anxious and troubled'. We can see that in the lives of many of the great mystics, who were extremely practical in their daily contact with the people they served. St Catherine of Genoa worked efficiently as a hospital matron, St John of the Cross had a talent for designing land irrigation schemes, St Teresa was busy in the kitchen. St John the Evangelist himself was an efficient fisherman, and businesslike in sorting, counting and no doubt marketing his fish. On an occasion when others would remember only the most sublime matters, he remembered the prosaic detail that there were exactly one hundred and fifty-three fish in the net (John 21:11).

Throughout the Scriptures, in the Old Testament as much as in the New, the love of God is promised as the solution to all the woes of the world. We are reminded, we need to be continually reminded, that it is our own sins, our own pride and stupidity, that have brought suffering upon us, and many of the prophets expand on this theme in an attempt to bring home to the stiff-necked children of God just how far they have wandered away from the right path, how little grounds for complaint they have when their own actions bring suffering upon them. But once this message has been heard and understood, we hear the resolution of all difficulties: it is the love of God.

In all the prophets (except of course Nahum) the conclusion is a promise of forgiveness and restoration. It is Micah who asks (Micah 7:18–20):

> Who is a God like thee, pardoning iniquity and passing over transgression for the remnant of his inheritance? He does not retain his anger for ever because he delights in steadfast love. He will again have compassion upon us, he will tread our iniquities under foot. Thou wilt cast all our sins into the depths of the sea. Thou wilt show faithfulness to Jacob and steadfast love to Abraham, as thou hast sworn to our fathers from the days of old.

Micah does not only tell us of the forgiveness and compassion of God, he also tells us where it will be made manifest on earth. 'But you, O Bethlehem Ephrathah, who are little to be among the clans of Judah, from you shall come forth for me one who is to be ruler in Israel, whose origin is from old, from ancient days' (Micah 5:2). God's love for us is no abstract idea, but a living person, born for us in Bethlehem.

The little town of Bethlehem may have been in the territory of Judah, and the birthplace of King David, but long before that it had been the place where Rachel died, giving birth to her second son, that she names Benoni, but his father named him Benjamin (Gen. 35:16–20). Benjamin was the last and most favoured of the twelve sons of Jacob, the child of promise and of old age. But he is also the Old Testament type or representative of the contemplative life. 'There is Benjamin, a youth, in ecstacy of mind', sings the Psalmist (Psalm 67:28), or at least he does in the original version. The psalm speaks of a triumphant liturgical procession, in which the other tribes are represented marching and singing, even 'in the midst of young damsels playing on timbrels'. And amidst all this jubilant celebration it is the youth Benjamin who stands silent, in ecstacy, the one who gives all his attention to God like Mary Magdalen at the feet of Jesus. From this text, in the version used by the Church for most of her history, derive the great mystical treatises of Richard of St Victor, *Benjamin Major* and *Minor*. Richard also works through a catalogue of virtues, typified by the other eleven patriarchs and their sister Dinah, before devoting himself to a study of contemplative prayer.

Benjamin appears in a very different character in different places of the Scriptures. We get the impression in Genesis that he is something of a spoilt darling, pampered both by his father and his brother Joseph, who insists on teasing him with the episode of the cup hidden in his bag, before overfeeding him at the great reconciliation banquet. Perhaps this is why the tribe of Benjamin turns out to be rather wild and disreputable. However in his Testament, he does speak more than any others about the love of God and the love of neighbour. Like St John, he urges his children to love one another. He begins, as we have always to begin, with the need for compassion and the forgiveness of wrongs, reminding his sons of how ready Joseph was to forgive his brothers:

1.   A copy of the words of Benjamin, which he spoke to his sons at the age of 125. He kissed them and said, Just as Isaac was born to Abraham at the age of an hundred years, so I to Jacob. Since Rachel died in giving birth to me, I never received her milk, but was suckled by Bilhah, her maid. Rachel was sterile for twelve years after she had born Joseph, until she prayed to the Lord with fasting for twelve days, and then she conceived and bore me. Our father loved Rachel greatly, and longed to have two sons by her. That is why I was named the Son of Days, that is *Ben-iamim*.

2.   So when I came into Egypt, and Joseph my brother recognised me, he said to me, 'What did they tell my father when they sold me?' I told him that they had dipped your coat in blood, and sent it to him with the message, 'See whether this be your son's coat.' And he said to me, 'Yes, brother. When they had pulled off my coat, they handed me to the Ishmaelites. They gave me a loincloth—hit me and told me to run. One of them was beating me with a cane, when a lion attacked him, and killed him. That is why those who were with him were afraid, and sold me on to their companions,

and they did not lie when they said these things. Joseph wanted
to keep from me what our brothers had done, so he called his
brothers over and said to them, 'Do not tell my father what you
have done to me, but tell Benjamin what I have suggested. Such
shall your thoughts be, let not these words come into the heart
of my father.'

3.   Now you, my sons, must love the God of heaven and earth,
and keep his commandments, in imitation of that good and holy
man Joseph. Your minds must be intent on the good, as you know
mine is. He who has a good intention sees all things rightly. Fear
the Lord, and love your neighbour. If the spirits of Belial were to
assail you with all manner of evil cruelties, you would assuredly
not be overwhelmed by them, any more than happened to Joseph
my brother. There were so many people determined to destroy
him, but God watched over him. He who fears God and loves his
neighbour cannot be wounded by the aery spirits of Belial, for
he is protected by the fear of God. Neither the desires of men
nor of beasts can dominate him, for he is assisted by that love
of the Lord which he shows to his neighbour. Joseph entreated
our father Jacob to pray for his brothers, so that the Lord would
not hold against them the sin, the evil they had plotted against
Joseph. This is what Jacob exclaimed, 'Oh Joseph, my son, you
have conquered the feelings of your father Jacob.' He embraced
him and remained two hours kissing him, saying, 'the prophecies
of heaven will be fulfilled in you, the prophecies about the Lamb
of God and the Saviour of the world, for he will be handed over,
the innocent on behalf of the guilty, he will die, the sinless for the
ungodly, in the blood of the Covenant, for the salvation of Israel
and of the Gentiles; he shall overthrow Belial and his minions.'

4.   Observe, my children, the end of a virtuous man; imitate his
compassion, with a good intent, that you also may wear crowns
of glory. The good man does not have an eye of darkness, for
he has mercy on all, even though they be sinners. Even if they
have conspired against him for evil, the man who does what is

good overcomes evil. God watches over him, and he loves the unrighteous as his own life. If anyone is honoured, he is not jealous, if another is enriched, he is not envious. If one be courageous, he praises him, he trusts himself to the prudent, he has pity on the poor and compassion on the weak; God he glorifies. The one who fears God, he takes under his protection, with him who loves God he joins in work; one who ignores the Most High he corrects and converts; one who has the grace of the spirit of goodness he loves according to his own soul.

5. If you preserve a good intention, my sons, even wicked men will be at peace with you; the unholy will be put to shame by you, and turn back towards the good; avaritious men will not only recoil from their vice but will give of their abundance to those in need. If what you do is good, even the unclean spirits will flee from you, and the wild beasts will be afraid of you, for where the light of good works shines in the mind, darkness will fly away. If anyone should insult a holy man, he will come to repentance, for the holy man will be compassionate on the slanderer, and keep silence. If anyone betray the life of a righteous man, that righteous man will pray, and his humiliation will last but a moment; very soon he will be honoured and respected, as happened to Joseph my brother.

6. The plans of a good man are not in the hands of Belial, the spirit of deception, for the angel of peace will guide his soul. He will not look eagerly at transitory things, nor will he accumulate wealth for his own delight. He will not devote himself to pleasure, nor will he grieve his neighbour. He will not fill himself with food, nor be enticed by distracting sights. The Lord is his portion. The man of good intent is not swayed by the praise or the disdain of men; he knows nothing of lies and deceit, quarrels and slander. The Lord dwells within him, and enlightens his soul. At all times he shares the joy of all. A good intention does not have two tongues, for blessing and for cursing, for pride and for honour, for grief and for gladness, placidity and strife, deceit and truth, poverty and wealth,

but it has one disposition, pure and holy, for all circumstances. Such a man does not have a twofold sight or hearing, for whatever he does, or says or sees, he knows that the Lord scrutinises his heart and purifies his mind, that he may not be rebuked either by God or men. It is Belial who performs every work twofold, and is without singleness of purpose.

7. For that reason, my children, I tell you, flee from the wickedness of Belial, for he gives a sword to those who obey him, and that sword is the mother of seven evils. To begin with, the mind conceives by Belial, and her children are, first envy, second perdition, third tribulation, fourth captivity, fifth want, sixth disturbance, seventh desolation. That is why Cain was handed over to sevenfold vengeance by God, for every hundred years the Lord brought upon him one plague. He suffered for two hundred years, and in his nine hundredth year he was overwhelmed in the Deluge, because of Abel his righteous brother. For seven hundred years Cain was condemned, and Lamech for seventy times seven. To the end of time those who are like Cain, jealous and hating their brothers, will be condemned to the same punishment.

8. Oh my children, run far from wickedness, envy and the hatred of your brothers, cling to goodness and charity. He whose intentions are pure and charitable will not look on a woman for fornication, for he has no such stain on his heart, since the spirit of God dwells within him. Just as the sun is not defiled when it shines on filth and refuse, but dries them both up and takes away their odour, in the same way a pure mind, observing the defilement of this world is not defiled but instead improves what it sees.

Benjamin then prophesies to his children about the terrible crimes that will be associated with the tribe of Benjamin. The dreadful story is found at the end of Judges (chapters 19–21), and foreshadowed in the dubious blessing Jacob gives his spoilt youngest son: 'Benjamin is a ravenous wolf, in the morning devouring the prey, and at even dividing the spoil' (Genesis 49:27). Despite that, however, the holy city of Jerusalem is

to be in the tribal area allotted to Benjamin (Joshua 18:28), and the
Testament proceeds to predict the Incarnation and the Lord's entry
into his Temple in explicit terms:

9. I am aware that there will be evil deeds done among you,
as I have read in the book of Enoch the just. You will commit
uncleanness like the uncleanness of Sodom, and you will be
reduced to a remnant, and you will be renewed through wanton
women, and the kingdom of the Lord will not be among you, for
he himself will immediately reclaim it. Nevertheless, the Temple
of God will be in your portion, and its end will be more glorious
than at the beginning. For the twelve tribes will be assembled
there with all the Gentiles, until the Most High send forth his
salvation, visiting us in the Only Begotten one. He shall enter into
the first temple, and there the Lord will be mocked, and derided,
and lifted up upon the wood. And the veil of the temple will be
rent in two, and the Spirit of God will descend upon the Gentiles,
poured out like fire. And he will rise up from among the dead, and
ascend from the earth to heaven. He knows who will be humble
upon the earth, and who will be glorious in heaven.

Because of this, the final bequest of Benjamin to his descendants is
peace and charity, clearly echoing Our Lord's words at the Last Supper
as recorded by St John:

10. When Joseph was in Egypt, he desired to see the Saviour's
shape, and the appearance of his face; and through the prayers
of our father Jacob he saw him, in the daytime, awake, exactly as
his appearance was. And after saying this Benjamin continued,
You should know now, my sons, that I am dying. Each one of you
should behave to his neighbour in accordance with truth and
righteousness, judge according to faithfulness, and observe the
law of the Lord and his commandments. This teaching I leave
you, as my entire bequest to you. Do the same for your children,
leaving them an eternal inheritance. For thus did Abraham, and
Isaac, and Jacob. They gave us all this as an inheritance, saying,

'Observe the commandments of God, until the Lord shall unveil his salvation for all the nations' (Luke 2:31–2). Then you shall see Enoch, Noah and Shem, Abraham, Isaac and Jacob, raised up on his right hand with rejoicing. Then we too shall be raised up, each one of us with our sceptre, to honour the king of heaven, who has been seen on earth in the form of a lowly man. As many as believed in him on earth shall rejoice together with him, for all shall be raised up, some to glory, and some to disgrace. And the Lord will judge Israel first, because of their injustice towards him, for they did not believe in him when God came in the flesh. And then he shall judge all the nations, as many as did not believe in him when he appeared on earth; in those chosen from the Gentiles he will put Israel to shame, as he once put Esau to shame among the Midianites, who seduced him to become their brother through fornication and idolatry, and turned him away from God. You, my children, will find a share among those who fear the Lord, if you walk forward in holiness before the face of the Lord; you shall live once again with me in hope, and all Israel will be gathered together to the Lord.

The document concludes with another detailed prophecy about St Paul, who had been born Shaul, of the tribe of Benjamin (Philippians 3:5). Reversing the words of Jacob, we hear he is no longer a ravening wolf, but a labourer of the Lord. Among other things, we hear that his writings will be included in the holy books, making this Testament one of the earliest witnesses to the inclusion of the Epistles in what was becoming the New Testament.

11. And I shall no longer be called a ravening wolf, because of your plundering, but a labourer of the Lord, who distributes food to those whose works are righteous. And from my descendants there shall rise up in the last days one who is beloved of the Lord. He shall listen to his voice, and do what is right according to his will, he will enlighten all the nations with a new teaching. He shall kindle a light of knowledge for salvation in Israel, snatching men away from them like a wolf, and giving them to the assembly of

the Gentiles. Until the consummation of the age he shall be in the assemblies of the nations, and among their rulers, like music, a song on the lips of all. And he shall be written into the holy books, both his story and his words; he will be the Chosen One of God for all the ages, and it is because of him that my father Jacob instructed me, saying, 'He shall fill up what is lacking from your tribe.'

12. And when he had finished these words, Benjamin said, I command you, my children, carry my bones away from Egypt, and bury me in Hebron near my fathers. And Benjamin died at the age of 125 years, in a good old age, and they placed him in his coffin. And ninety-one years after the children of Israel came into Egypt, they and their brethren took up the bones of their fathers in secret, from a city of Canaan, and they buried them in Hebron, at the feet of their ancestors. And they went back from the land of Canaan and dwelt in Egypt until the time of their exodus from the land of Egypt.

The final blessing promised to Benjamin by Moses foreshadows an end to the sins and woes of this world, enfolding the chosen one in the love of God. 'Of Benjamin he said, The beloved of the LORD, he dwells in safety by him; he encompasses him all the day long, and makes his dwelling between his shoulders' (Deuteronomy 33:12). Here we come back to St John, the beloved disciple who reclined his head upon the Lord's breast. Yet we are entitled to consider ourselves all 'beloved disciples'—in fact I suspect that is one reason why St John chooses this way of referring to himself. We are beloved, and we can recline on the Lord's bosom, entrusting ourselves to his Sacred Heart. We are beloved disciples, and we must stand at the foot of the Cross and share in his suffering. We, his disciples, can claim his mother to be our mother, to join the number of 'his brothers and sisters' who gather around her and the apostles waiting for Pentecost (Acts 1:14). We, the beloved disciples of the Lord, will remain until he comes in glory, for he has promised that the gates of hell will not prevail against his Church, and we, the Church, must still be watchful until the End.

ENVOI

In following St Benedict's twelve steps on the ladder of humility, we found that Cassian occasionally puts them in a different order. There is a different order again in St Paul's list of the twelve fruits of the Holy Spirit, as expanded by St Thomas Aquinas, and this time we start at the top and work downwards. Moreover the Testaments of the Twelve Patriarchs, which certainly gives the impression of being planned as a treatise on the virtues, follows yet another different order. Where they all agree is that the fear of the Lord is the first stage of wisdom, and charity is the summit and perfection of the Christian life. Excellent reasons can be given for each manner of treatment, but this diversity serves again to remind us that different souls approach perfection by different ways.

St Jerome takes us up the ladder of nine fruits of the Spirit, naturally giving primacy to Charity, without which the others are not virtues at all. Charity, he reminds us, covers a multitude of sins (Proverbs 10:12). From charity derives joy, from joy grows peace which is one of the eight Beatitudes. From peace come both longanimity and patience, two translations of one Greek word; after that benignity, 'which is a light, smooth and tranquil virtue'. Goodness differs greatly from benignity, 'for goodness can be grieved and appear stern'. Fidelity has the next place, then meekness, which is opposed to wrath, quarrelling and dissention— Moses was meek. Finally come continence, which applies to moderation in food and drink as well as chastity, and modesty which is found in the perfect man (Jerome, *Comm. in Gal.* ad loc.; Benedictine edn VII, 510).

St Augustine, as might be expected, concentrates more on the vices opposed to these fruits of the Spirit, 'for these spiritual fruits reign in a man in whom sins do not reign'. He pairs virtues and vices, beginning a tradition which was to undergo several modifications, and lead to some impressive works of art, like the fonts we mentioned at the beginning.

It is St Thomas who treats the fruits of the Holy Spirit most systematically. He makes it clear that there must be twelve of them, since it says so in the Apocalypse (Apocalypse 22:2), and shows us how they follow logically one from another. They are called 'fruits' because they develop and grow organically. Firstly a man's heart should be aware of good and evil in himself: the first awareness of good is through love, from which necessarily follows joy, and joy is perfected in peace. Awareness of evil is divided between patience under immanent threat, and longanimity when the good is deferred. Secondly a man should be aware of his neighbour, and have the will to do him good, that is goodness, and to carry out that intention, which is benignity. Thirdly, awareness of things beneath a man leads to meekness, which endures attack, fidelity which counteracts deceit, modesty with regard to external actions, continence in restraint from what is lawful and chastity which is restraint from what is unlawful (*Summa Theologiae* I-II, lxx, iii, *in corp. art.*).

Undoubtedly all the different treatments of these virtues are valuable in drawing our attention to different aspects of the work of the Holy Spirit. The fact that different holy writers give different lists of virtues and vices should alert us to the fact that in reality all virtue is one, namely charity, and all vice is one, namely selfishness. 'The commandments … are summed up in this sentence, "You shall love your neighbour as yourself"' (Romans 13:9). The Holy Spirit leads us both up and down the ladder, like the angels of Jacob's vision. On every step we need to be aware of the other steps, and we can never presume to chart our own progress. Indeed the summit of humility is knowing ourselves to be at the lowest step of all, which is why St Benedict reintroduces the idea of the fear of the Lord at the twelfth step. It is only when we know that we have absolutely no merits or virtues of our own to boast about that the Holy Spirit can really bear fruit in our lives.

To every virtue there is indeed an opposite vice: it is not difficult to examine our consciences and recognise in ourselves the seeds of every vice. Cassian in his treatise on the eight deadly sins refers to them as 'viruses', and the metaphor is exact. The virus is always there, whether or not it develops into a full-blown disease. If sins develop in our lives, it is our fault for not co-operating with grace; when virtues come to ripeness it is because grace has found a welcome in our hearts. The truly humble saint is one who has no vices, and truly believes that his many virtues are entirely the work of grace. The rest of us need to be permitted by God to fall into sin from time to time, or at least to be vividly aware of our tendencies to sin, for otherwise there would be the terrible risk of imagining that we have somehow achieved perfection by our own efforts. If we are deeply scandalised and shocked by our own sins, that is the measure of our hurt pride; if we are too censorious of others, that is enough to challenge God to allow us to slip back down the ladder for a moment into even worse sins. We are commanded not to condemn others, but to say when we see their falls, 'I should have done far worse if I had been left on my own'. We should not condemn ourselves, for 'Christ Jesus came into the world to save sinners, and I am the foremost of sinners' (I Timothy 1:15). If it is precisely for me, a sinner, that Christ was made flesh; that he died and rose again, for me, he is unlikely to abandon me at this stage!

That is why St John concludes (I John 3:19–23):

> By this we shall know that we are of the truth, and reassure our hearts before him whenever our hearts condemn us; for God is greater than our hearts, and he knows everything. Beloved, if our hearts do not condemn us, we have confidence before God; and we receive from him whatever we ask, because we keep his commandments and do what pleases him. And this is his commandment, that we should believe in the name of his Son Jesus Christ, and love one another, just as he has commanded us.

CPSIA information can be obtained
at www.ICGtesting.com
Printed in the USA
LVHW090535200119
604507LV00057B/133/P